The City as an Entertainment Machine

The City as an Entertainment Machine

Edited by Terry Nichols Clark

LEXINGTON BOOKS
A division of
ROWMAN & LITTLEFIELD PUBLISHERS, INC.
Lanham • Boulder • New York • Toronto • Plymouth, UK

Published by Lexington Books
A division of Rowman & Littlefield Publishers, Inc.
A wholly owned subsidiary of The Rowman & Littlefield Publishing Group, Inc.
4501 Forbes Boulevard, Suite 200, Lanham, Maryland 20706
http://www.lexingtonbooks.com

Estover Road, Plymouth PL6 7PY, United Kingdom

British Library Cataloguing in Publication Information Available

Library of Congress Cataloging-in-Publication Data

The city as an entertainment machine / edited by Terry Nichols Clark.
  p. cm.
 Rev. ed. of: The city as an entertainment machine. Amsterdam [Netherlands] : Boston
[Mass.] : Elsevier/JAI, 2004.
 ISBN 978-0-7391-2422-2 (pbk. : alk. paper)
 1. Sociology, Urban. 2. Recreation—Social aspects. 3. Cities and towns—Growth. 1.
Clark, Terry N.
 HT113.C545 2011
 307.76—dc22

                                                    2010051791

Printed in the United States of America

Dedicated to

Andre´ Malraux, who created Maisons de la Culture for cities across France
and
Richard M. Daley, who created the first major cultural center in an
American city, the Chicago Cultural Center

Contents

Chapter One
Introduction:
Taking Entertainment Seriously

Terry Nichols Clark

This paperback edition deletes a few chapters from the hardback edition, and adds a new chapter on Scenes.

This volume analyzes how consumption and entertainment relate to politics and urban development. People both live and work in cities. And where they choose to live shifts where and how they work. This volume, as the last sentence suggests, explores reversing the causal processes normally assumed to drive cities.

Amenities enter here as new public concerns for many cities in the U.S. and much of Northern Europe. Old ways of thinking, old paradigms—such as "land, labor, capital, and management generate economic development"—are too simple. The developers' classic "location, location, location" is similarly incomplete—location near what? This new, barely charted terrain is critical for policy makers. Urban public officials, business, and non-profit leaders are using culture, entertainment, and urban amenities to (seek to) enhance their locations—for present and future residents, tourists, conventioneers, and shoppers. They are making multi-billion dollar investments in amenities, hoping that these are sound investments. New York and Chicago now report that their first or second largest industrial sector is entertainment or culture. The world's largest industry is tourism, by some counts (reports differ with assumptions about what comprises tourism) (Molotch, in press).

What do we know about these issues, to help codify such policies? What is the current knowledge base and how can we extend it? This book joins work on these concerns from creative thinking in economics, sociology, political science, public policy, geography, and related fields. Many ideas below challenge the

1

established urban wisdom. The most important single challenge is the emphasis in each chapter on consumption, amenities, and culture as drivers of urban policy. There is considerable evidence below about how these drive people to move to or from different cities and regions, and how they are especially critical in attracting innovative persons—the creative class people that Florida (2002) stresses as catalysts in making the modern economy and high tech hum.

Too much past work treated entertainment as trivia or fluff, not real business. Further, among many moralistic observers, entertainment is immoral. Among many leftist observers, it is also counter revolutionary, an opium for the people that should be fought. This is now all changing, gradually, but we still have precious little serious analysis of culture, entertainment, and amenity-related phenomena. Researchers far more often study work, the disadvantaged, or socially deviant. Can these fields learn from what is below? We think so.

What is our focus? Entertainment, consumption, and amenities as they relate to politics and urban development. These distinct concepts are explored below. But the book's bigger message is that all these contrast with the more common assumption: work and production drive life and give it meaning. This common assumption informs the materialist view that "money talks," or the Marxist emphasis on relations to the means of production, or the psychological view (of Maslow or Inglehart) that basic wants are hierarchically ordered, with the physical/material at the bottom. Did the end of the Dot-Com boom or terrorist attacks of September 11th, 2001 bring the end of consumption? Even among those committed to a totally materialist world view, a time of economic turbulence and cutbacks means disruptive changes for people's consumption patterns, implying possible jealousy and invidious comparisons with others who are seen as engaging in overly conspicuous consumption, plus resentment toward bankers or global forces or political leaders that may have brought on such change. The core propositions of Chapter 2 explore how and why such reactions are channeled in different ways by different subcultures.

To counter these simple materialist/production views, it is helpful to note that ethnographers have shown that some preliterate societies contribute their most treasured objects to religious worship, including art and dance. It does not follow, universally, that "only the affluent can afford culture and entertainment." They interpenetrate all of our lives, if we look. How and why specific cultural patterns and priorities are defined, and how they shift, are pursued below.

Much of the excitement in this book came from discovering our independent convergence on amenities, consumption, and entertainment. But once Edward Glaeser, Richard Florida, Gary Gates, Bill Bishop, and I found each other and others with overlapping interests, we have actively exchanged papers, met at conferences, and helped arrange discussions on these issues. Some of the most dramatic sessions have been with groups who previously ignored or even opposed amenities in considering urban development and public policy.

Economists are often considered natural advocates of a materialist or economic interpretation, such as using capital and land to explain why cities grow or decline. But if this may fit many economists—as well as business magazine writers and the general public—a handful of economists have been leaders in analyzing amenities seriously. For some twenty years, a few economists have studied clean air, moderate temperatures, and other amenities, often gauging their impacts on land value, by comparing locations with more or fewer amenities. This method of "hedonic pricing" thus assigns a dollar value to such ostensibly nebulous things as clean air. Why economists? If these were art critics, few might be persuaded. But if even economists have come to stress amenities—as economists in general have not been professionally focused on beaches, clean air, and opera—then we may be onto factors that demand more attention, even by non-economists.

Consider two examples illustrating the recent but important recognition of the importance of entertainment and amenities. In the mid-1990s, the Chicago Federal Reserve Bank provided urban economic analyses of Midwestern cities. It reported twenty or so basic indicators, virtually all concerned with production and population change. I approached William Testa, Senior Economist at the Chicago Fed, and asked, how about consumption and amenities, like restaurants, shopping, tourists, or conventions? He came to one of our meetings, and the next year organized a conference at the Chicago Fed specifically on amenities. Some sixty persons attended, mainly economists. Edward Glaeser and I made presentations featuring amenities. A few speakers countered with strong "amenities are spurious" arguments, but as we saw examples mount, discussion shifted to support amenities. By the end of the day, roughly a third of the participants visibly accepted the importance of amenities, another third were opposed, and a third wavered. Not bad for a day's work.

The second example is the Urban and Community Section of the American Sociological Association, some four hundred persons who communicate nearly daily on a listserve, a quasi-permanent email conference involving everyone who chooses to participate. I would guesstimate that until recently the majority view was that amenities were largely driven by economic factors, rather than vice versa, although many participants had probably not explored the matter. In the Fall of 2002, I circulated a draft of the chapter on Urban Amenities (Chapter 3). Several persons immediately criticized, even lampooned, it. Ray Hutchinson wrote: "Should cities offer Starbucks urban homesteading credits to locate in depressed neighborhoods so that these and other urban amenities can encourage yuppies to move into the area?" Debate ensued. By the second week the entire tone shifted, with even the most outspoken critics reversing themselves. The discussion mounted over the Fall, generating some one hundred pages of email, as people advanced all sorts of evidence, arguments, and counter arguments (Urban and Community Section of the American Sociological Association, Listserve, 2002). After three months, even self-declared Marxists accepted the visible importance of amenities for urban growth. Such shifts in this direction by notoriously skeptical and independent persons provide strong testimony to the importance of studying entertainment (see Chapter 8).

Several of us have been writing and discussing these themes in lectures and conferences around the country, but after Richard Florida's book *The Rise of The Creative Class* came out in 2002, there was a huge increase in attention to related concerns. The book became a blockbuster, one of the best-selling non-fiction books in the U.S., and was discussed in lively sessions with mayors and civic leaders across the U.S., Canada, and various other countries. Themes from the book have helped focus innumerable conferences and professional association discussions, from the U.S. Conference of Mayors to high tech forums to the American Association for the Arts. The book advances arguments shared in several papers below, although there are enough controversial differences to spark debate. A core idea is that past theories of urban development stressed capital, then human capital, but did not ask what attracted human capital (i.e. talented people) to some cities more than others. Florida suggested that amenities mattered, as did tolerance—as registered by numerous gays residing in the area. But just what is tolerance?

MORALITY PLAYS: THE POLITICS OF IMAGINING PEOPLE AND GROUPS

We all do it. We label persons or groups as chic, funky, chauvinist, cool, Uncle Tom, nerdy, liberated, Baby Boomers, and more. Political and religious leaders similarly make moral statements, for instance by applying Biblical characters' names to contemporaries like Bill Clinton or Saddam Hussein—as Satanical or a Good Samaritan. Muslims analogously invoke the Koran.

Social scientists debate social trends by inventing images and labels like bowling alone, racist, inner directed, or Third Way.

To explore the impact of controversial individuals like Bill Clinton or Monica Lewinsky, many use labels that join them to deeper cultural divisions and conflicts. Consumption, long considered an area where brands and labels drive decisions, is becoming a critical focus of politics, nationally and in cities, complementing more traditional issues of production, work, and even taxes. Why is this so important? It signals a deeper transformation of politics away from the classic issues and resources exchanged in class politics and clientelism toward a New Political Culture—a major thesis developed elsewhere (e.g. Clark & Hoffmann-Martinot, 1998). Citizens and the media rise to replace unions and parties, as new leaders succeed by redefining the rules of the game by which politics is played. Populist leaders invoke the legitimacy of the average citizen, and denigrate party leaders and traditional social and religious elites. The consumer/citizen is celebrated, along with aspects of the lives of average citizens like "human interest" stories in the press, TV "news," and personal anecdotes unveiled in talk shows—which were previously beyond the pale of public focus or politics. Simultaneously, however, some persons counter these tendencies by attacking the excesses of individualist egalitarianism, and calling for a new moralism. The so-called "religious right" is the most visible example, and surveys suggest that some 20 percent of the U.S. public support a stricter code of public morality.

The chapters in this volume explore these issues in multiple contexts, using a variety of methods, evidence, and analyses. Rather than justifying our views by invoking grand theorists from the past, or assembling quotations from average persons, we often compare political systems that differ in how they operate, especially local governments. Why? Cities are ideal fruit flies to interpret bigger developments, as cities like Beverly Hills or Jerusalem change faster and illuminate extremes more completely than do national societies. These outlier cities, in addition to the Middletowns, can help chart and interpret complex processes—via case studies as well as statistical methods.

Others act politically in different consumption modes, for instance endorsing ecological concerns by not using plastic cups or not owning a car, but instead by recycling paper and using public transportation.

Still others participate in consumer boycotts, refusing to buy products like those made in South Africa under Apartheid or Nike shoes made in sweatshops. In 2002, the largest purchaser of beef and chicken in the world, the McDonalds Corporation, agreed with animal rights activists and required humane animal husbandry practices for all its suppliers—at costs estimated in the billions.

These are all examples of politics interpenetrating consumption in ways that broadcast a strong moral and political message. Often these are carefully chosen or staged to leverage the act, usually via mass media, far more visibly than "normal" politics. Activists often start with what may seem to be a trivial issue, but by labeling it as a critical marker (e.g. a "non-negotiable demand"), it is powerfully elevated. It becomes a moral issue. This is particularly striking in locations like Southern Italy or much of Latin America, for instance, where traditionally morality and politics were considered totally separate. When President Jimmy Carter spoke about "human rights" in the 1970s, the European press and political leaders largely lampooned the issues as those of an American country bumpkin, unschooled in the cosmopolitan manners of world diplomacy—that is, power politics in the traditional sense. Indeed the entire sub-discipline of political science called IR, International Relations, even in the U.S., is only starting after the year 2000 to break with its long past—the "realism" doctrine of Hans Morgenthau and Henry Kissinger—to introduce non-military, non-economic, and non-geographic considerations. That is, to start to incorporate moral issues like human rights in "serious" analysis and policy advising.

Bowling Alone (Putnam, 2000) has sparked political debate globally. Why? Is not bowling a trivial consumption act? Precisely, Putnam replies, but adds that more Americans bowl than join the Democratic or Republican parties. Yet why should a political scientist like Putnam care? A first answer is that not only are bowling leagues declining, so are unions and civic and organized groups, and voting in most countries. Much debate has focused on the type and magnitude of decline. But the second, deeper issue bowling alone raises is moral: does bowling alone, rather than supporting community bowling groups, signal moral decay? Debate here has focused on the decline of organizations as training grounds for civic leadership. As Tocqueville suggested, this was a key trait of popular democracy. "Social capital," Putnam holds, declines as groups shrink. (This led some critics like Skocpol et al., 2000, to counter that Putnam confused the dynamics of organizational membership; they instead stressed national processes like war and welfare state building as driving membership. Yet this criticism says almost nothing of culture and values.)

The deeper concern, the moral bite, the broader echos from Bowling Alone, I suggest, are not documenting declines in voting turnout or group membership. It is rather the moral degeneracy which they imply which is so provocative. Does their decline indicate that we are growing into more selfish individualists, driven by greed and markets rather than civic responsiveness to people around us? Is there less concern for the poor, since many civic groups have at least partially charitable concerns?

Bill Clinton, Tony Blair, and Gerhard Schroeder are similarly attacked as craven, nasty people, first since they abandoned the left programs of their parties and the poor, second since they were so politically successful in doing so, and third because they were inauthentic, morally uprooted, and blew wherever the wind took them.

Yet even in Clinton's darkest political hour, when the U.S. Congress held hearings to impeach him for his relations with aide Monica Lewinsky, Clinton's support with the U.S. public rose, at least as recorded in the standard public approval ratings (Clark, 2002). The visible public concern about hedonism and personal morality—as quintessentially illustrated by the Clinton impeachment effort—documents the deep divisions characterizing American society. Political battles in France and Turkey over whether Muslim women must or must not cover their heads, or concern with genetically engineered foods (mainly in Western Europe), illustrate the extent to which personal consumption issues have become openly and widely, if not globally, politicized. Debates flare precisely because "personal consumption," especially in entertainment, is a morally loaded act for some, yet for others is not at all. This signals the need for a deeper cultural analysis to interpret these differences in meaning of ostensibly similar behaviors.

The deeper point: bowling alone, McDonalds, animal rights, and recycling should be considered not as isolated and disparate issues. Rather they flow from deeper and more comprehensive cultural conflicts explored below. These issues are contemporary, but are also extensions of older patterns; it helps to dig back to unravel the present. The moral impact of these issues is broad because they flag concerns shared by many persons, increasingly around the globe.

They are part of a populist politics, which is bringing more issues increasingly to the average citizen for arbitration, at least symbolically. Ronald Reagan would regularly say "we have our people working on that issue" whereas Bill Clinton, Tony Blair, and others sought to explain and interpret major policies to the average citizen, heavily using the media.

Details of wartime military campaigns are aired on television even while in process. Generals complain that they can no longer command or expect solders to give their lives; that is leaders and their policies are increasingly held to the same standards of morality as average citizens. If the U.S. may seem to have led in such media-driven populism, many European and other countries have quickly followed, and gone further in areas like women's rights in Scandinavia and green politics in Germany. Global human rights, movements for women, and international tribunals cut far deeper and cross borders in ways unthinkable just a decade or so earlier. The atrocities of Bosnia and Kosovo, with detailed media coverage, spread such messages of concern and outrage further and faster than ever before.

Politicized consumption acts have media repercussions because they raise moral concerns that are shared by some citizens, yet actively opposed by others, like picketing abortion clinics, parades for gay rights, same-sex marriage, or sinking whaling boats in Japan or Norway. Who supports, who opposes these movements and why? Our answer below is that they serve as fault lines for major cultural divisions that have seldom been explored, certainly not by the mass media and scarcely more by social scientists, as these are ostensibly new issues seldom debated by past political leaders. They push the political envelope further and further. Indeed, specific issues are often strategically chosen by their advocates to achieve precisely these cumulatively revolutionary goals.

Entertainment to one person can be sin to another. And the "trivial" issues like bowling assume larger political meaning primarily because politics has grown more populist and egalitarian; such issues can appeal directly to the average person. Precisely because everyone relates immediately to drinking or hairstyles, these personal consumption issues take on heightened political power, and often displace the more traditional economic, financial, and military issues. Or to be more precise, those issues more openly and directly discussed in economic and financial terms—since there are clearly fiscal and economic aspects of consumption.

Why the label Entertainment Machine? Because entertainment is not just an individualized or private sector process, but centrally involves government and collective decisions. Public decisions about cultural policy shift options for nightlife, restaurants, theatre, and music, as well as schools and museums. Even if individuals hold very different conceptions of what constitutes entertainment, their choices are not random, but structured by culture and politics, as Chap. 2 explores. The Machine may be empowering, or flattening, in contrasting perspectives pursued in different chapters. The Entertainment Machine label also stresses a major shift, recent for cities in Northern Europe and North America, to include not just production and growth, but also consumption and entertainment. It suggests that to grow and compete with cities globally, mayors and public officials must add entertainment to their recipes. This constitutes a paradigmatic shift for analysts and policy makers, redefining what government and cities are all about, what rules to follow, and what policies work or fail—themes explored throughout the book, especially Chapter 9.

In sum, to interpret many contemporary political processes, we need to dig deeper into consumption behavior and interpret its moral, cultural, and political meanings.

COMMENTS ON THEMES IN
THE CHAPTERS BELOW

Chapter 2 by Terry Clark outlines an analytical framework for studying consumption and politics. It explores how consumption and political processes interpenetrate each other and have distinct coherence and meaning, if we look closely. For instance women shopping together may discuss clothing styles and personal scandals, which in turn link them to broader moral assessments, which may shift their support for political parties and leaders. Upper status American women voted Republican in the 1950s, but shifted to Democrats by the 1990s. Individual women gradually changed party allegiance over this period, as they made linkages between political candidates' positions and many consumption and lifestyle issues, like women's rights and abortion. This case illustrates a drastic shift in conceiving of politics. Europeans long saw strong parties and their official programs as the heart of political dynamics; citizens were expected to follow party lines. This often happened. But in recent years, parties and unions have declined as individual citizens, the media, and consumer issues have risen, initially in the U.S., later in Europe and much of the globe. Left and right are harder to define, and more often turn on consumption and lifestyle, rather than production and work issues. Women and households are more central public issues, as are issues like children's and animal rights, women's roles, abortion, gay marriage, proper labeling of food for its content, genetically modified food, and all aspects of the environment. These issues are less often party-driven, and more often considered by individuals or their "opinion leaders," and are more "issue specific," varying from one concern to another rather than consistently matching a Left or Right party program. Civic group leaders are less often immediate neighbors and more often linked via the telephone or internet or fax or email.

These changes in political culture do not appear everywhere evenly, but vary across subcultures and subregions. Three are stressed: the New England moralist tradition with its Calvinist Protestant roots, second, the individualist, from John Locke and Adam Smith, and third, traditional Southern and rural culture. The three provide contexts for general propositions about the effects of income, age, education, and the like—as stressed in most past work. Data are used from citizens surveyed in 3,111 U.S. counties merged with several other data sources to test selected propositions. Mini case studies that link to these broader issues are featured in boxes in several subsequent chapters.

Chapter 3, also by Terry Clark, focuses on urban amenities as driving urban development. Past studies stress human capital, plus the traditional factors of land, labor, capital, and management to explain urban development. This chapter reformulates these models by incorporating amenities and cultural concerns, to include explicit specification of where and how human capital locates itself. The chapter analyzes empirically how amenities differ for distinct population subgroups. Amenities include such *natural amenities* as climate, land topography, and access to water, while *constructed amenities* include opera, research libraries, used and rare bookstores, *Starbucks* coffee shops, juice bars, and bicycle events. Such amenities differentially attract distinct subgroups. For instance, the elderly move toward natural amenities, college graduates move toward constructed amenities, but creative persons (those who take out patents) move toward both. The main data are for 3,111 U.S. counties.

Edward Glaeser is a leading urban economist, and far more. Chapter 4 takes a fresh look at what cities do, by asking seriously how cities enhance consumption. Glaeser, Kolko and Saiz stress density as facilitating many urban amenities, such as increasing the speed with which one can access restaurants, museums, theaters and films, as well as marriage markets. And speed matters more as people grow more affluent and busy. They find that cities with such amenities have grown more quickly over the past twenty years both in the U.S. and in France. In cities with more educated populations, rents have gone up more quickly than wages since 1970—suggesting that quality of life has risen faster than productivity in places with more educated workers.

Throughout the book many chapters stress the shift in political culture toward amenities and consumption in recent years. How to capture and analyze such changes remains challenging. Anne Bartlett developed a new approach: analyzing website information. A particularly controversial case of shift in culture and policy was British government under Prime Minister Tony Blair. He came to power by redefining the Labour Party program into New Labour. He broke with the unions and the older party issues of labor/management conflict. Instead he appealed to a broader set of citizens, emphasizing amenities and lifestyle. But just where individual local governments stood on these issues was not clear. At outset he did not have clear control of the entire party, especially among local elected officials. Many local elections were staggered, so although he won in Parliament, many local officials had been elected in earlier years. Local autonomy thus heightened the implications of where each locality fell on these old versus new issues. While the British case is sharp, similar transitions have been underway worldwide which we have theorized about in this volume. How to capture them?

Anne Bartlett had the creative idea of reading reports posted on the websites of different British local governments. She downloaded reports from sixty-eight localities, and coded them in terms of the number of lines which emphasized old versus new types of themes. Then she analyzed how the emergence of these new themes meshed with changes in socio-economic makeup of the localities. Here she converged with earlier analysts of these issues who had used our FAUI surveys (see last section of chapter), and joined these with several projects generating fiscal and socio-economic data. The results show indeed that the locations declining in jobs and population, older industrial locations, have more of the old Labor themes, while the New Political Culture emerges more clearly in growing, more affluent locations, with more highly educated residents. The results are generally consistent with the theory in this area—an unusual occurrence for hopeful researchers. This pioneering study opens the way to using globally accessible website materials for thematic analyses of culture and politics. The relatively inexpensive method encourages careful comparative analysis.

Richard Florida and Gary Gates present controversial ideas and results in Chapter 6, on "Technology and Tolerance," which provocatively joins these two concepts. Past work on urban economic development stressed corporate location and job growth. The policy implication was that local governments should offer tax abatements, cheap land, and similar incentives to attract firms and jobs. Florida and Gates illustrate how this has changed by quoting Hewlett Packard CEO Carly Fiorina, who told a conference of governors: "Keep your tax incentives and highway interchanges, we will go where the highly skilled people are." Her words are codified by economists who stress that "human capital" increasingly drives development. Florida and Gates take this a step further to ask what brings human capital to a city? Their main answer in this paper is tolerance. How measure tolerance? Here is their most controversial argument: gays flag tolerance. They use the Census to obtain the percent gay households in the fifty largest metro areas which they then correlate with levels and change in high tech jobs (such as the Milken index, one of the standard high tech measures of the proportion of jobs in high tech). They compute correlations and regressions which show that locations with more gays have more high tech growth, even controlling several other standard measures like population size. These findings are among those which have been the most challenging and heatedly discussed since Richard Florida published his book The Rise of the Creative Class in 2002. Public officials in locations like Detroit and its suburbs told the press that they were adopting policies to attract gays so as to help foster high tech growth.

Terry Clark explores this gay factor in Chapter 7, and finds, surprisingly, that it may be spurious. Reanalyzing the identical data that Gates and Florida used for the fifty largest U.S. metro areas, Clark finds that gays correlate very highly ($r = 0.7$) with percent college graduates, and it may be that the college graduates are more critical than gays. These results shift when the analysis is repeated for three hundred metro areas and then 3,111 counties; Results show minimal impacts of gays. Next individual citizen survey data are analyzed separately for the 3,111 counties to see if gays are associated with many value and attitudinal traits of locations as hypothesized. But we find that percent gay households are minimally related to tolerance, risk-taking, Asian immigrants, college faculty and students, or percent college graduates (unlike the fifty metro areas). Gays are slightly associated with amenities. Still, all these results about gays and growth are so new and preliminary that it is important for us and others to continue exploring just how they operate.

Chapter 9, Amenities Drive Urban Growth: Leadership and Policy Linkages by Terry Nichols Clark with Richard Lloyd, Kenneth K. Wong, and Pushpam Jain, first locates the shift toward amenities in the urban literature, and suggests how past thinking about urban development demands revision, given the salience of amenities and globalization. It next shows how leadership in U.S. cities has been transformed in the last decade or so, as new mayors have come to office, committed to the New Political Culture of consumption, citizen responsiveness, and efficient management. These patterns are summarized from surveys of all U.S. cities over twenty-five thousand (some 1,400), sketched for the seven largest cities, and explored in a case study of Chicago.

The Chicago case shows how committed political leadership and a firm management style dramatically transformed the schools and parks to make them more responsive to average and low-income citizens, despite battles with unions and contractors. Chicago is distinctly interesting in this regard precisely because it was not a Paris or Venice, but a blue-collar industrial city that drastically transformed itself in just a decade or so. There are many kinds of cities. Each requires polices matched to its circumstances. But Chicago has many lessons worth considering by other locations. The past traditions of open clientelism, initial public skepticism about amenities, and blue-collar political style make it resemble many other cities worldwide. Indeed Tokyo, Naples, and London are just among the most visible examples of cities pursuing many similar policies. The success of the policies we explore for Chicago makes them important for others to consider. Numerous policy specifics are thus detailed in the last sections of the chapter.

Since publishing the hardback edition of this volume, we have elaborated the idea of "scenes" as cluster of individual amenities. The scene, we suggest, emerges as distinctly salient in post-industrial societies where consumption specifics merge into production. For instance, restaurants attract more customers if they are embedded in a neighborhood filled with other appealing, related activities—as in a Chinatown or bohemian area like Greenwich Village. With the decline of primordial characteristics like race, class, gender, and national origin (they now explain only some 15 percent of items like civic activities), scenes rise. Which scenes? This depends on the preferences of the participants. How to map them? Thoughtful economists started working on amenities a few decades back, but they treated them atomistically for the most part: adding one or a few into their models, not seeking to match these to concepts like niche markets. Our innovation is to assemble hundreds of individual amenities and assign scores to them on fifteen more general dimensions: neighborliness, transgression, glamour, and more. These general dimensions are deep structures of scenes that can be recombined to create more specific types such as bohemia or Bobo.

Scenes analyses are currently in progress in the US, Canada, France, Korea, Japan, and China. The concluding chapter, by Clark, Daniel Silver and Clemente Navarro, provides an overview.

This volume thus suggests an agenda for future work in many areas of our social and political lives. We recommend more serious incorporation of amenities, lifestyle, and entertainment to capture key dynamics. Most past models in the social sciences have built on older processes, that often continue but are interpenetrated and complemented by culture, amenities, and entertainment. These new concerns can most obviously enter when persons choose where to live. People, especially talented persons who are key drivers of our modern societies, increasingly look for a location with the package of amenities they prefer—as well as a job. Jobs and leisure are more highly interpenetrated than in the past, making consumption more salient economically and politically. If we only analyze jobs and work, we misunderstand many key social and economic dynamics affecting our complex post-industrial, knowledge-driven societies. But selecting, implementing, and managing amenities is no simple task. It requires expensive and risky decisions. These can generate many conflicts, and they can fail—as can all policies. But like it or not, we are entering a new era where urban policy makers and policy analysts must incorporate amenity concerns into their choices if they are to keep abreast of our ever more global world.

ORIGINAL DATA, MUCH NOW INTERNET ACCESSIBLE

A recent stimulus for more general theorizing derives from the synergy of recently combining multiple new data sources. These permit analyzing individual citizens in their cultural and social contexts more powerfully than ever before. For persons in the future to reassess or improve on hypotheses throughout this volume, it is critical to access some of these sorts of data. The data have been assembled over several decades by investing many millions of dollars. Most are now available free of charge over the internet.
Sources:

- The Fiscal Austerity and Urban Innovation Project, which now has original survey data from local officials plus official data from some ten thousand localities in twenty-five countries. Some six hundred variables come from original surveys, such as mayor and council spending preferences, and organized group activities and impact. The DDB Life Style Survey, a national survey of some eighty-eight thousand U.S. citizens from 1975 to the late 1990s, collected for marketing and long kept private. It has recently become publicly available and includes county identifiers, thus permitting local contextual analysis by merging with other local-area data. It has some seven hundred variables like how much do you volunteer time, eat out, and go to church, as well as "The car I drive is a reflection of who I am . . .

(agree/disagree)." This is the first study we know of that analyzes DDB local variations.

- The PEW Tracking surveys of U.S. citizens are distinctly attuned to new political and civic developments. They address concerns like the Internet and its use, political contacts, sources of media information, and more.
- The World Values Surveys which from 1980 to present have grown to include over 100,000 citizens in over fifty countries.
- New variables and data, like the percent gays and unmarried households in a U.S. locality, amenity measures like museums and juice bars, a Bohemian index of distinct occupations, patents, and high tech growth (as considered in chapters by Gates and Florida, Glaeser and Clark). These help capture issues emerging with post-industrial society, where citizens and consumption are increasingly central.
- The quantitative sources above are complemented by an ethnography and oral history of Chicago in the last half of the twentieth century, which explores the same themes which we link to past ethnographies and case studies. Chapter 8 draws on a longer work (book manuscript and original interviews are available).Title: *Trees and Real Violins: Building Post-Industrial Chicago. An Oral History from Mayors Daley I to Daley II.*

Most data are being made publicly available over the internet (esp. via http://www.src.uchicago.edu/depts/faui/archive.html or tnclark@uchicago.edu).

BIBLIOGRAPHY

Bell, D. (1978, 1996). *The Cultural Contradictions of Capitalism.* New York: Basic Books.

Clark, T. N. (2002). The Presidency and the New Political Culture. *American Behavioral Scientist,* 46 (4),535–552.

Clark, T. N., and Hoffmann-Martinot, V. (Eds) (1998). *The New Political Culture.* Boulder: Westview.

Florida, R. (2002). *The Rise of the Creative Class.* New York: Basic Books/Perseus.

Molotch, Harvey (in press). *Where Stuff Comes From.* New York: Routledge.

Parsons, T., and Platt, G.M.(1973). *The American University.* Cambridge, MA: Harvard University Press.

Putnam, R. (2000). *Bowling Alone.* New York: Simon and Schuster.

Skocpol, T., Marshall, G., & Ziad, M. (2000). A Nation of Organizers. *American Political Science Review,* 94 , 527–561.

Urban and Community Section of the American Sociological Association, Listserve (2002). Starbucks, Bicycle Paths, and Urban Growth Machines: Emails Among Members. October–November, Compiled by Terry Nichols Clark, tnclark@uchicago.edu

Chapter Two
A Political Theory of Consumption

Terry Nichols Clark

> The crowd is the veil through which the familiar city beckons to the flaneur as phantasmagoria—now a landscape, now a room. Both become elements of the department store, which makes use of flanerie itself to sell goods. The department store is the last promenade for the flaneur.
> From *The Arcades Project* by Walter Benjamin (1999, p. 10).

We lack a coherent theory of consumption. This is surprising given the critical importance of consumers. The consumer drives the modern economy. Governments strive toward citizen responsiveness. Sociologists and anthropologists chronicle social status in home decor and personal lifestyle. But most conceptualization is limited.

Considerable social criticism invokes consumption, especially by contemporary Europeans; Americans focus more on production. The European sensitivity derives from aristocratic traditions saved in castles and museums, the fashion centers of Milan and Paris—and resistance to American mass marketing. Such resistance grew politically active in the early twenty–first century, with demonstrations and laws limiting fast food shops in Paris and Rome. Resistance mounted after World War II when American cars, soaps, dishwashers, and refrigerators took Europe by storm (De Grazia, 2001; Ross, 1995). The debate was less about hamburger than the destruction of European civilization. Americans have been less sensitive to broader implications of consumption, in part since they interpret consumption with three distinctive prisms, or subcultures, explored below. Outside the U.S., the similarity of these cultural prisms to others worldwide is often not recognized; instead the consumer objects themselves are stripped of culture to become, for some, imperialist shock troops of global capitalism.

It can help especially non-U.S. readers to re-examine consumption using some explicit moral guides, and to consider how similar the cultural counterparts are which operate elsewhere. What role does local culture play in, say, Bangkok, as Thais see foreigners in their streets hawking products as distinct as women's rights and Mormon religion, as well as DVDs? Thais, like Americans, interpret all of these through their "cultural bias," which we seek to make more explicit (Thompson, Ellis & Wildavsky, 1990, explore many limits and strengths of cultural analysis).

The ideological significance of consumption rose in the early twenty-first century as globalization grew more rapid and visible. With the end of the Soviet Union in 1989, the one clear alternative to the West disappeared. How to interpret the emerging global society is thus in contention. For some it is "capitalism." But this label is too narrow. Just as critical as who invests is how responsive are the polity and economy to individual consumer/citizens. Our emerging global world is more than production and finance and jobs; it is increasingly about consumption, culture, lifestyle, politics, and religion—which are not deterministically linked to investment or capital. Analysis of these interpenetrating activities is thus essential to clarify the role of consumption along with the other globalizing processes. It is illuminating that few radical/critical commentators today, including environmentalists, elevate a clear alternative to the mass consumption society—as Marxists did before 1989. There may be deep and probing criticism of specifics, but no clear alternative, like the Soviet system, is present.

Consumption thus takes on heightened political significance, as many of its aspects are globally shared. Some interpret consumption forces as driving toward global domination by key firms and styles like Disney or McDonalds, as competitors seek new markets. Yet national political and economic leaders are in decline as there is increasing "decentralization," pressure to focus locally, to remain ever more sensitive to individual consumers and consumption issues in all aspects of citizens' lives, wherever the line is drawn between private and public sector. The citizen-responsive Bill Clinton and Tony Blair are a world apart from Jack Kennedy and Winston Churchill, whose popularity rose even as they demanded personal sacrifice by citizens. Political campaigns and ongoing citizen surveys are often conducted by consulting and marketing firms that work for political candidates as well as corporations, especially so in the U.S., but increasingly worldwide. Perhaps the demand for better theory has grown as fewer accept as theoretically comprehensive or adequate the social criticisms of consumption common in the past. This is especially for those theories dismissing consumption as determined by production and late capitalism, that would be transformed in a future of world socialism.

Theorists and social critics have nevertheless articulated increasing concern about the content of an emerging global culture, that some see as pressing toward "one size fits all," manufactured in Hollywood and at McDonald's Hamburger University (it does exist, in suburban Chicago!). George Ritzer, author of several books on global McDonaldization, and editor of the new *Journal of Consumer Culture*, writes: "Thus, we have the paradox of a virtual absence of a sociology of consumption in a nation which is without doubt the world leader in consumption and is aggressively exporting its consumer goods and its means of consumption to much of the rest of the world" (Ritzer et al., n.d.).

The time is ripe to extend and enrich our thinking about consumption and to explore its political assumptions and implications. This is illustrated for instance by the launching in 2001 of the *Journal of Consumer Culture* and the Section on Consumers, Commodities, and Consumption of the American Sociological Association (see Langlois, 2002; Ritzer et al., n.d. for recent syntheses of past theory and current work).

Hence this essay. It codifies some current thinking about consumption and stresses how socio-political contexts shift many common patterns, widely considered "universal." It thus brings social context to individualistic thinking. Most of this essay consists of propositions that together constitute a middle-range theory, a codification of multiple overlapping subfields that concern consumption politics. The broader theories and bigger changes which underlie much of our contemporary world are being continually recast, in some respects faster than ever. It would take us too far afield to consider these theories and processes systematically, but to frame our perspective we sketch how some major elements join with what follows.

THEORETICAL BACKGROUND

The framework below extends theorizing from three theoretical traditions. First is the individualistic emphasis from John Locke, John Stuart Mill, Jeremy Bentham, and Adam Smith that stressed how contracts among free individuals and free trade would transform the world toward individualistic, egalitarian democracy, and market capitalism. The philosophy of Bentham's utilitarianism shaped contemporary economics and psychology. The subjective aspects of individualism were explored by Stendhal, Neitzsche, and then modern psychology. This legacy is active today in some policy statements of world trade organizations and U.S. officials under Presidents Clinton and Bush, especially in trade and foreign policy. Many political leaders in East Europe and Latin America in the 1990s came to power articulating concerns that some described as "neo-liberalism," especially in their advocacy of global markets. One part of this tradition is what economists term "consumer sovereignty"—the view that the individual consumer/citizen knows his interests and preferences best, and seeks to pursue (and sometimes maximize) them. Thus, advertising may provide information but does not shift basic preferences. If consumers want new stuff, firms in the market should provide it—at least in this first tradition.

Second is the Marxist tradition stressing class conflict as driving history from feudal to capitalist to socialist stages. A strong collective/class identity was invoked to counter the individualism of the above predominantly Anglo-Saxon theorists. The Frankfurt School of T. W. Adorno and Max Horkheimer joined Marx with Freud to create a powerful criticism of contemporary society. In works by Eric Fromm, Leo Lowenthal, Herbert Marcuse, Juergen Habermas, and others, these ideas helped shape core ideas from student leaders of the late 1960s to critical sociologists and many post-modern cultural theorists. Some analysts have sought to extend broadly Marxist themes of conflict and exploitation via cultural domination, such as A. Gramsci, Michel Foucault, Pierre Bourdieu, and David Harvey (cf. Harvey, 1990).

Many stress how capitalism needs ever growing markets and thus capitalists advertise to create new needs among consumers. The capitalist profit and production logics are thus seen as generally driving the consumption of individuals, rather than vice versa. The individual consumer is not sovereign, but is inside a neon cage, entertained with songs and dances from Walt Disney and other Hollywood fare (Langman, 2002). This cage of mass consumerism is driven by hegemonic corporations that promote false consciousness and define new "needs." Walter Benjamin was an astute analyst in this general tradition in the 1930s, yet he differed by invoking the consumer as a potentially independent actor. He focused on Paris, stressing the fashion-conscious flaneur/shopper who seeks individualization and thus drives fashion, and the rise of department stores offering dreams for sale. Benjamin paved the way toward a conclusion that others articulated: Marx may have had things backward in arguing that classes are defined by their means of production. Yet classes define themselves increasingly by their means of consumption.

Third is the tradition from Max Weber, Emile Durkheim, Talcott Parsons, and much mainstream sociology today that rejects both the strong utilitarian individualism and the rigidity of Marxist classes. Weber's Protestant ethic and Durkheim's collective consciousness joined in later analyses of values and norms, varying across subgroups like Protestants or African-Americans or the counter culture. This tradition stresses the multi-causality of complex societies, where no single class of variables—economic or religious, individual or collective—consistently drives others.

While sociologists, anthropologists, and political scientists today build more on this third tradition than the two earlier ones, most theorizing is less grand. As societies have grown more complex and differentiated, so has the division of labor among social scientists led to narrower specialties, like the decline of voter turnout or changing women's roles. Much theorizing thus consists of middle-range propositions that link to general theories as well as empirical research. This chapter is organized around such propositions.

We also build on a specific extension of the third tradition: theorizing about what Daniel Bell termed Post-Industrial Society (deliberately invoking a Marxist label). Lipset, Inglehart, and I elaborated this approach by adding concepts listed in Table 2.1. This approach contrasts with those of individualist theorists and

Table 2.1. A Core List of Elements Contrasting Post-Industrial Society with Neo-Marxist and Individualistic Concepts

Post-Industrial Society Concept	Neo-Marxist Concept	Individualistic Concept
Consumption	Production	Utility, preferences (more abstract)
Leisure	Jobs	Work and Amenities
Consumers	Workers	Subsets of utilities, clusters of attitudes
Home	Workplace	Individual
Women and their Families	Men and their Work	Less attention to context
Personal influence, social Interaction	Social Structural Characteristics (Class, etc.)	Interaction
Citizen-focused	System-focused, e.g. capitalism, aristocracy	Individual / preferences / personality focused
Buying consumer products	Investing capital	Maximizing utility
Talking with friends to form opinions	Organizing Class Consciousness	
Informal organization; unanticipated consequences	Class Conflict	
Organizational/Management Structure	Ownership of the Means of Production	
Goal displacement; cooptation; subcultures	Classe An Sich to Classe Fuer Sich	
Issue-Politics; Issue Specificity	Coherent Party Program	Cognitive consistency
More Social Liberalism, e.g. new women's roles	Fiscal/Economic Policy Positions	Attitude structure
Voluntary Associations	Vanguard Party Focus	
Cross-Pressures; Role Conflict	False consciousness	Cognitive dissonance
Pluralism	Power Elites	
Autonomous mass media	Class-controlled Propaganda	
Autonomous Scientific Community	Science Subordinated to Hierarchy	
Students as Political Vanguard	Proletariat moving toward revolution	
New Class	Fordism/Regulation Theory	
Knowledge/R & D, High Tech	Manufacturing products	
Rising professional autonomy of workers	Rising global monopolies, regulated by states	
Weak unions& parties, strong Individualism	Strong Unions and class-based parties	
Consumer based indvid'l aesthetics	Historical Materialism	
Democratic Processes	Class Responsiveness	
Intellectuals/cultural creation	Class domination, surplus value	

Sources: This is adapted from a summary of post-industrial society theories, sources for which are in Table 2.2. Individualistic theories tend not to address some more social structural items. Hence they are left blank.

Table 2.2. Contrasting Emphases in Alternative Versions of Post-Industrial Theories

Columbia/Post-Industrial Society Concept	Bell, TCPIS	Bell, CCC	Inglehart	Lipset	Clark, NPC
Consumption		x	x		x
Leisure		x	x		x
Consumers		x	x		x
Home		x			x
Women and their Families		x			x
Personal influence, social interaction					
Citizen-focused			x		x
Buying consumer products		x			
Talking with friends to form opinions					
Informal organization;					
unanticipated consequences					
Organizational/Management Structure					
Goal displacement; cooptation; subcultures					
Issue-Politics; Issue Specificity			x		x
More Social Liberalism,		x	x		x
e.g. new women's roles					
Voluntary Associations			x		x
Cross-Pressures; Role Conflict				x	
Pluralism			x	x	x
Autonomous mass media					
Autonomous Scientific Community	x				
Students as Political vanguard		x		x	
New Class	x	x		x	
Knowledge/R & D, High Tech	x		x	x	x
Rising professional autonomy of workers	x		x		x
Weak unions & parties, strong individualism				x	x
Consumer based indvid'l aesthetics		x			x
Democratic Processes				x	x
Intellectuals/cultural creation	x	x		x	

Notes: The point of this table is merely to highlight, quite roughly, major differences in emphasis among alternative formulations of post-industrial society. The main references are Bell, *The Coming of Post-Industrial Society* (1973), Bell, *The Cultural Contradictions of Capitalism* (1978, 1996), Lipset various works cited, esp. *Political Man* (1981) and *American Exceptionalism* (1996), Inglehart, *Modernism and Postmodernism* (1997) and earlier works, Clark and Hoffmann-Martinot, *The New Political Culture* (1998).

neo-Marxists in its core concepts, strategic research sites, and analyses suggested, as summarized in Table 2.2. Note the concern for consumption and average citizens, rather than elites or classes, especially by Bell, Inglehart, and Clark. Specifics from these tables are pursued below.

How to resolve conflicts among these three theoretical traditions? Our solution is to apply to the theories themselves a contextual and cultural relativism. Stated simply, it seems clear that there were and are many strong individualists as well as many class-oriented people in the world. The three theoretical traditions were initially fueled by descriptions of real people, and some average persons as well as political leaders and parties carry on these traditions today. Rather than posit that one theory or approach explains most things, or that people act in one consistent manner, we elaborate three cultures that capture some major fault lines of political and cultural conflict across the world today.

We concur with the postmodern description of the breakdown of single, coherent value orientations and rising ironic distance heightened by global media. But we do not conclude, as do some postmodernists, that the result is cultural fragmentation, sometimes bordering on atomistic individualism—even while recognizing clear tensions in this direction. If we dig deeper, we may identify foundational elements for individuals seeking to construct new identities. This tension between atomistic individualism versus culturally constrained meaning is a theme explored through the chapter, and is featured in several boxed cases. The null hypothesis is that individual atomism dominates; the challenge to find more, and interpret it.

Particularly useful here is the work of Daniel Elazar, who wrote of three political cultures: moralistic, individualistic, and traditional. In global context, the New Political Culture is a contemporary elaboration of Elazar's moralistic and individualistic cultures. From the moralistic comes egalitarianism, stressing the right of each citizen to participate equally and for leaders to respond to them. As egalitarian criteria are extended to new areas, like women, children, animals, and nature, these define "new social issues" for politics. Such democratic responsiveness emerged in the past from communal concerns that were religiously, often Protestant, based, in which local parish members would help each other, and control deviants. Political parties of the left added class in defining community, often seeking more support for workers and a stronger welfare state. By contrast, individualists traditionally stressed markets, rights, civic volunteerism, and small government—right party issues. What is new in the New Political Culture (NPC) is the combination of issues and tactics from the past left and right: market individualism is joined with social responsiveness, left politicians use the mass media and consumer marketing tactics to appeal to individual citizens, and so forth. Leaders like Bill Clinton and Tony Blair illustrate this NPC. They and similar leaders stress consumption in politics: old issues of jobs and work conditions have been complemented if not replaced by the environment, amenities, tourism, stadiums, public culture, lifestyle, human rights, and other new themes that avoid the right and left positions staked out by major parties in Europe and the U.S. over the twentieth century (e.g. Clark & Hoffmann-Martinot, 1998, Chapters 2 and 5). The citizen is elevated from a "cog" in a political machine or a union or ethnic group member to an independent driving force—a critical part of the NPC transformation. Social progressivism and individualism are combined by stressing new multi-issue politics and government productivity. The NPC is itself spreading to all regions of the U.S. as well as globally, via the Internet, Hollywood movies, CNN and BBC, NGOs, and global trade and migration (Clark & Elazar, in draft; Hoggart & Clark, 2000). Sometimes the changes are welcomed, other times fought. And of course the NPC is substantially adapted to local specifics even if general themes like human rights and environmental improvement are visible globally. Yet despite some apparent convergences, proponents of the NPC often do battle with others advocating class politics or traditional hierarchy and clientelism, which still dominate most of the world. In the U.S. and Western Europe, some 60–80 percent of citizens support NPC views. In less developed countries this can fall to ten percent or less (Clark & Elazar, in draft; Clark & Rempel, 1997).

In many propositions below, three cultural contexts are used, mainly explored for the U.S., although they also operate globally. They were first identified by Daniel Elazar (1998). We extend his ideas to focus on consumption politics.

- Moralistic culture comes from Calvinist Protestantism, in Switzerland and Northwest Europe. Self-abnegation and Calvinist precepts of doing good works define distinct approaches to consumption and politics—and to capitalism, per Max Weber, who focused on Calvinists as core carriers of his Protestant Ethic. Plain clothes, frugality, and social sensitivity continue even if their theological basis has weakened. The Calvinist roots were shared with many Northwest European Protestants, who in the U.S. migrated west from New England across the northern part of the country to areas like Minneapolis and Seattle. More critical, many elements of this world view are now spreading nationally and globally, via nonprofits, talk shows, and lawsuits.
- Individualist culture comes from the tradition of Adam Smith and John Locke, stressing individual rights and markets. From Scotland and England, it too has spread globally; inside the U.S., it was historically strongest in the Middle Atlantic states. It legitimates individual ambition and reward, even if these conflict with the broader public—as Moralists point out. Individualists denigrate tradition, family, and lineage compared to individual achievement. Individualism is widely identified with Western civilization, especially by non-Westerners, but this threefold distinction of cultures stresses that it is only one element of three, and conflicts with the two others.
- Traditional culture, strongest in the American South, idealized the aristocratic hierarchy as a model of consumption, and leadership based on family and lineage, legitimately inherited. Material display here becomes aesthetic ritual: following Louis XIV, Neiman Marcus in Dallas continues the tradition of *le superflu, chose très necessaire*, by marketing airplanes and other necessities for Christmas stockings via mail order and the Internet. This conspicuous consumption has long generated strong populist and anti-elitist reactions which continue today. Most visible are African-Americans whose links to the South were grounded in slavery and whose (moralistic) resentment of the closed elitism fueled civic and political activism, like that of Martin Luther King. This kindled a powerful egalitarianism and search for

respect in battles with symbols of the hierarchical past. In electronic preachers and evangelical missions, the religious fervor of this anti-hierarchical and egalitarian version of Southern culture is spreading globally today. It adapts elements of Moralistic culture to fight the Traditional legacy.

Many conflicts and ambiguities in contemporary politics and consumption are clarified if we look at them as cases of these three subcultures bumping up against each other, transforming themselves and people who try to continue them, in multifarious ways. Several boxes below explore such themes—some are tragic, some are humorous, some are both.

A Porn Virgin No Longer

Okay, so I'm 28 years old, and yet I had a first this week. Monday was the first time I'd ever bought porn. Well, okay, kind-of. I bought a copy of this month's Playboy, but I can assure you, it was just for the articles, or, to be specific, one article. It turns out that my friend Eve's site, In Passing, was mentioned in the "living online" section (page 28, at the bottom), and naturally, I had to see for myself. When I went to the news-stand to get my copy and the cashier put it in a black plastic bag I thought that was strange, then remembered that you don't usually see people walking down the street, flipping through Playboy. I now find myself with the mildly unusual task of having to find a place for my "porn stash."

Source: A dotcom veteran, Kevin Fox is currently an interaction designer at Yahoo! http://fury.com/article/1241.php

---

What of class? In some locations and time periods, class trumps everything, and may constitute a distinct culture. But in the U.S. in recent decades, race, especially African-American, has been the most important surrogate for class. Why? Due to the linkage of African-Americans to slavery and continuing racial segregation. Some dynamics are included here as part of Traditional culture. Given the main empirical focus of this book on the U.S., we do not seek to elaborate class as a distinct culture, but have explored these issues in considerable detail elsewhere.[1] Several ideas from the Post-Industrial Society and New Political Culture areas (Tables 2.1 and 2.2) have clear class linkages. These are extended below by incorporating class into propositions and empirical analysis via occupation, income, education, and other components of class.[2]

While these three cultures had clear historical/geographic roots, they have since partially dispersed, making the individual citizen/consumer distinctly appropriate for studying their current operation. We illustrate this below using surveys of individuals. Still, individuals live in contexts that variously encourage or discourage distinct styles of consumption and politics. Hence the value of specifying the individual in his/her social context, as illustrated in propositions about contexts.

Are Individualists Spread "Too Thinly" Across America?
A Proposed Solution: Recruiting by Internet

The Free State Project is a plan in which 20,000 or more liberty-oriented people will move to a single state of the U.S., where they may work within the political system to reduce the size and scope of government. The success of the Free State Project would likely entail reductions in burdensome taxation and regulation, reforms in state and local law, an end to federal mandates, and a restoration of constitutional federalism, demonstrating the benefits of liberty to the rest of the nation and the world. . . .

We don't require your money, just your signature—and when the time comes, your willingness to carry through on your word of honor.

From: www.freestateproject.org/

Most of the Scandinavian countries implemented Free City projects, dropping many national taxes and regulations for a few cities, on an experimental basis after the 1980s. See Baldersheim and Ståhlberg (1999).

For instance Veblen's conspicuous consumption, Bourdieu's distinction, and Inglehart's post-materialism are often discussed as universal. Propositions below show how and why such patterns are not universal, but substantially shift in different cultures.

The propositions build up cumulatively from five areas where past work has identified consumption drivers. We start with these five to link with past traditions, and clarify how we extend each toward a new synthesis, which emerges as we proceed. The five areas are:

- individual preferences about specific aspects of consumption and politics.
- deeper individual values, including religion and moral/ethical outlooks.
- personal influence via social processes in making decisions, networks including both strong bonding ties and weak ties that bridge across different types of persons.
- status concerns, like those who feel "clothes make the man" or social sensitivity and acting in groups—versus others who act more individualistically, and may bowl and vote alone.
- the social context within which individuals make decisions, which can suppress or facilitate distinct individual preferences and group activities. The main contexts are the three political cultures adapted from Elazar, and the

local geographic area (county or municipality). We measure the three both geographically and via the culture that individuals carry as they move.

There are far more ideas here than a single book can test. Rather than narrow the ideas to the data, we suggest many hypotheses that may interest others. We "test" just a few. The most detailed testing of propositions is in the two chapters below on urban amenities and gays. Data and results come from the several newly combined data sources discussed in the Introduction. The results both ground the propositions and illustrate some of the rich potential of these new data.

Consumption has been a central topic of novelists and social commentators for centuries. As social scientists build theories, we should incorporate some of the subtlety and insights of observers like Proust or Faulkner. What's "in" among teenagers is similarly relevant. Much of the power of a Proust or Faulkner comes from pinpointing the conflicts among competing values and processes. Proust charted the values of the aristocracy as they were being vanquished by competing worldviews. Faulkner's Old South was similarly disappearing. Yet by probing the conflicting values and visions of three brothers –the idiot/biologically driven, the romantic/idealistic, and the materialist/individualist—as they anguish over their sister Candace, Faulkner in The Sound and the Fury show how the most powerful conflicts can even be within a single head. When Quentin crushes his watch crystal and grinds his thumb into the watch hands, it symbolizes using the flesh of his Southern thumb to seek to repress the rationality of New England time. Goffman (1986) labeled interpreting such conflicts "frame analysis." Many boxes we feature in this chapter similarly illustrate conflicting frames and visions, and the dramas of resolving them. Or not resolving them: Quentin chose suicide.

While we flag such subtleties at outset, if we are to advance our understanding and analysis, we nevertheless must chart basic processes in more precise and explicit ways if we and others are to dissect, test, or extend them. The core ideas in the theory below are thus stated as propositions of the X causes Y variety. These are posited as probabilistic statements of moderate relations where other things are considered equal. Context is added to X causes Y type statements by later propositions that posit "interactive" relations, for instance as Z rises, it increases the impact of X on Y. An example: if Z is cultural diversity among city residents, then as cultural diversity rises, education (X) may have more impact on political participation (Y). By contrast, in "boring locations" where "everyone" has more similar cultural views, fewer persons may participate in local civic groups since they seldom disagree. Brief references are included to supporting findings, as well some new results from the data sources in Chap. 1. The propositions start with the individual and simpler patterns, then add social relations, context, and more complex interrelationships.

INDIVIDUAL PREFERENCES

These have been conceived of in two basic ways. In the first, they are "atomized." For economists, consumers may "demand" almost any combination of new products and activities—from Nike shoes to merengue dance steps to Bill Clinton's politics—as new goods and tastes emerge. Any such preference element can be simply added to a demand or utility function following this approach. There are no contextual shifts or interaction effects. How do these preferences join in clusters, emerge, or change? Economists normally avoid these questions; for them specific preferences are classically termed "exogenous" to economic theory. They thus relegate preferences to persons in other disciplines to define or codify. Analogously, survey attitude analysts often lump many individual items together under categories like "social liberalism" or "the family," like Converse (1992) and Davis (1992). Indeed Converse's interpretation, which dominated for decades, was that most items posed to the general population (like support for gun control or abortion) were relatively "unconstrained." That is, they were largely unrelated to other attitudes or political party membership or a general left-right continuum. The exception: less than ten percent of the population that was highly interested, active, and ideologically coherent (see details and references in Alvarez & Brehm, 2002; Clark & Rempel, 1997, esp. 9–56).

An alternative perspective seeks to build a small number of deductive, general propositions. Thus, Maslow and Inglehart (1990) posited hierarchies of needs, which people move up after they satisfy lower needs (from food and shelter to aesthetics and so forth). Stigler and Becker (1977) also suggest that tastes are not atomistic and unsystematic. They posit some core general preferences that are fairly constant, yet shift with the context and availability of products to the consumer. Still, Stigler and Becker eschew detail about the specific content of consumer preferences, and the mechanisms (like shopping in a group, or discussing politics with workplace members) that may explain their operation. Rather they suggest extending the core tools of neo-classical economics—supply, demand, price, etc.—to clarify our thinking, which they do with panache. Market researchers and sociologists by contrast have been relatively descriptive, generating vast quantities of data and tables about who reads or buys or thinks what, yet with far less coherence in theorizing why (Ritzer et al., n.d. illustrate exceptions). Market researchers use such concepts as "niche markets" which are often operationalized in simple, specific ways, such as "people who buy Coca-Cola." Findings are correspondingly narrow: Coke buyers are more likely to eat hamburgers than are other persons. Or in Gallup polls, Democrats favor abortion rights more than Republicans.

Social scientists have generated such major surveys as the General Social Survey at the National Opinion Research Center, University of Chicago and the National Election Study at the University of Michigan. These long-term projects foster cumulative collection of vast quantities of data over time. They permit analysts to adapt them to many uses, as we do here.

But the more data we have, the more critical theory becomes—to make sense of the seas of data. The rise of the Internet illustrates the same point: it brings so much that the user needs sharper tools to focus.

Core propositions:

(1) *Individuals develop many basic preferences in socialization during childhood and early adolescence. This has classically led to invoking parents,ethnicity, religion, and social class to interpret individual preferences.*

We could spend much time elaborating these ideas, and surely they still are empirically important. But it is more interesting to stress how and why Proposition No. 1 is changing.

(2) *The socio-economic context and historical time period are critical environments for the young; social patterns dominant around persons in their late teens and twenties are especially critical in influencing their outlooks that continue through life; data on attitudes over time document dramatic differences by age cohort.*

Three kinds of effects on individual attitudes thus demand separate analysis and interpretation: the time or historical period of a survey (all respondents may shift their answers in a recession), cohort effects common to all respondents of the same age group (such as persons growing up in the 1960s may remain more socially liberal for life), and age effects (old persons see things differently from young persons). Standard methods for distinguishing these are available (e.g. Firebaugh, 1997).

(3) *As resources and products rise in number and diversity, individuals can explore and consume a broader range of products and activities. The most drastic changes are shifts from highly parochial villages to global markets. This change came rapidly to many locations around the world–with the end of the Cold War, cheap air travel, the Internet, television news, etc. These cosmopolitanization/globalization factors undermine many social background, individual, and cohort effects isolated in past research. Why?*

(4) *As resources and information increase, individual's social background characteristics decline in explanatory power. For instance African-Americans in the U.S. traditionally consumed less housing (due in part to past housing discrimination and low income). But with more income, education, travel, and exposure to national media, being African-American (or Polish or Jewish) has less power in explaining such consumer or political decisions. Still these weakened social background effects clearly vary by is-*

sue area, shifting first with small decisions and last with the deeper values
(e.g. earlier impact on shoe buying than on self-esteem).

(5) As social background characteristics, especially those concerning class,
     ethnic, and religious groups, decline in explanatory power, more general
     values and attitudes rise in explanatory power, including subcultural
     identification, niche markets and lifestyle politics.

These propositions draw from several related works that also report many
empirical findings, such as Inglehart (1990), Clark and Rempel (1997), Clark
and Lipset (2001), Manza and Brooks (1999), Lipset (1997), Alvarez and Brehm
(2002).

Propositions No. 1 to No. 5 could be explored with many DDB items
concerning consumption and politics (see Introduction on the DDB). We list
here just a few items to sample the richness of the data. They show modest
relations between social background characteristics and many DDB items (Table
2.3).

A few surprises, perhaps: bowling is positively related with income. So is
gambling in a casino. Although many public discussions suggest that gambling
is an affliction of the poor, about half of DDB respondents claiming the highest
incomes ($90 or $100,000) said they gambled at least once in the last twelve
months. This is surprising enough to report in detail (Fig. 2.1).

BASIC VALUES AND MORAL OUTLOOKS

More general than individual preferences are broad outlooks like "the protestant
ethic" distinguishing persons and societies. These were core concerns of classic
social theorists like Durkheim or Max Weber. More recently Samuel Huntington
(1993) suggested that a "clash of civilizations" is a new axis of world conflict,
replacing the Cold War with religiously-derived cleavages. What are some
salient basic values of advanced Western societies, to simplify our purview?
The three cultures invoked at the start of this paper have parallel socio-political
cleavages inside Europe. These classically divide Northern vs. Southern Europe,
individualist vs. collectivist, Protestant vs. Catholic, egalitarian vs. hierarchical.
In the Northern European model, candidates for office classically compete over
policies, whether from party programs or on separate issues, which candidates
articulate in appeals for votes. By contrast the (traditional) Southern European
model of politics is clientelism and patronage, where personal relations
dominate ideas: the candidate offers followers private goods, such as a favor, job
or contract. In the Northern European model, such private exchanges are
immoral or corrupt; only public goods, more general policies, are legitimate.
Moralism was largely absent from traditional clientelist politics, as elaborated
below.

Table 2.3. Social Background Characteristics are Modestly Related to Most DDB Items

	Pearson Correlations				
	Into which one of the following categories does your annual household income fall?	Level of Education Completed	Respondent's age	Occupation of respondent (High score is Low Status Occupation)	African American All Yrs, DDB
I am in favor of legalized abortions	.16**	.16**	0.00	-.09**	.02**
The government should restrict imported products	-.13**	-.22**	.10**	.13**	-.03**
Rode a bicycle (freq last 12 months)	.07**	.10**	-.19**	-.03**	-.04**
Went bowling (freq last 12 months)	.05**	-.02**	-.16**	.01**	-.03**
Went camping (freq last 12 months)	.03**	-.01**	-.14**	.05**	-.08**
Gambled in a casino (freq last 12 months)	.13**	.01*	.06**	-.02**	0.01
Attended church or other place of worship (freq last 12 months)	0.00	.07**	.13**	-.09**	.02**
Went to a classical concert (freq last 12 months)	.13**	.23**	.13**	-.16**	-.01**
Went clothes shopping (freq last 12 months)	.17**	.11**	-.12**	-.14**	.02**
Dressing well is an important part of my life	0	.02**	.02**	-.10**	.08**
Went to a club meeting (freq last 12 months)	.07**	.13**	.15**	-.11**	-.03**
The car I drive is a reflection of who I am	.08**	.04**	.02**	-.03**	-.03**
Worked on a community project (freq last 12 months)	.09**	.16**	.09**	-.11**	0.00
Contributed to an environmental or conservation organization (freq last 12 months)	.11**	.08**	.06**	-.07**	-.03*
Went to an exercise class (freq last 12 months)	.09**	.12**	-.11**	-.09**	.02**
Did exercises at home (not at a class) (freq last 12 months)	.09**	.15**	-.05**	-.10**	-.02**
Went fishing (freq last 12 months)	-.02**	-.10**	-.13**	.11**	-.05**
Went hunting (freq last 12 months)	-.06*	-.13**	-.11**	.08**	-.07**
Jogged (freq last 12 months)	.10**	.15**	-.18**	-.04**	.01**
Went to a library (freq last 12 months)	.09**	.30**	-.08**	-.20**	.01**

Table 2.3. (Continued)

	Into which one of the following categories does your annual household income fall?	Level of Education Completed	Respondent's age	Occupation of respondent (High score is Low Status Occupation)	African American All Yrs, DDB
			Pearson Correlations		
Watched a professional men's sporting event on TV (freq last 12 months)	.16**	.10**	-.04*	-.04*	-0.03
Went to a pop or rock concert (freq last 12 months)	.09**	.10**	-.21**	-.04**	.03**
Went to an auto race (NASCAR, Formula 1, etc.) (freq last 12 months)	0.01	-0.01	-.07**	.03*	0.02
When snow skiing or snowboarding (freq last 12 months)	.06**	.10**	-.08**	-0.02	0.00
Went skiing (freq last 12 months)	.11**	.11**	-.13**	-.05**	-.03**
Went snow skiing (freq last 12 months)	.12**	.09**	-.10**	-.05*	-.04**
Visited an art gallery or museum (freq last 12 months)	.20**	.29**	.01*	-.18**	-.03**
Rented an x-rated movie (freq last 12 months)	-.03*	-.04**	-.20**	.09**	.10**
I am a homebody	-.12**	-.13**	.17**	.05**	-.01**
Television is my primary form of entertainment	-.17**	-.18**	.03**	.12**	.02**

Notes: Occupation includes nine standard categories from 1 Professionals to 8 Farm, Forestry, Fishing and 9 Service

Sources: DDB Lifestyle Survey

* Correlation is significant at the 0.05 level (one-tailed).

** Correlation is significant at the 0.01 level (one-tailed).

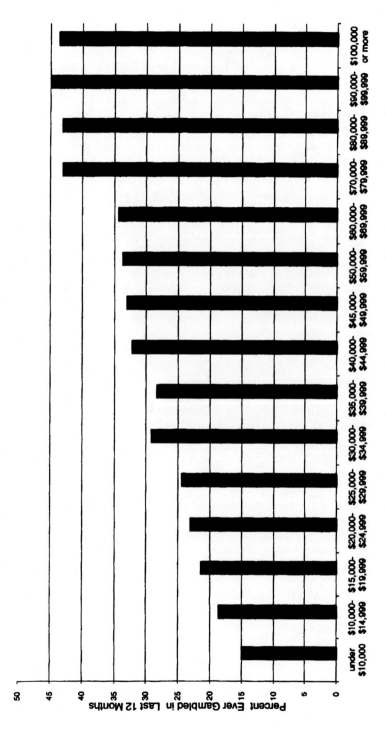

Figure 2.1. Upper-Income Persons Say They Gambled at a Casino More Than Twice as Often as Lower-Income Persons in the Last twelve Months.
Sources: DDB Lifestyle Survey and DDB survey of US citizens, 1975 to late 1990

Much of this Northern vs. Southern conflict repeats itself globally. But change is rapid. By the end of the twentieth century, the Northern European values were diffusing south and globally: the top political issues in the early twenty-first century in even Rio or Taipei concern eliminating clientelism and making politics more open, transparent, and citizen responsive. This transformation also implies, usually, imposing a moralistic evaluation of political issues and policies, far more than under classic clientelist politics, which was often "non-ideological," not explicitly moralistic (Clark, 1975; Roniger & Gunes-Ayata, 1994). Communist China was an important exception, combining clientelism with Marxist ideology (Walder, 1991).

What drives, or once drove, these Northern vs. Southern differences remains in dispute. Yet considerable evidence suggests that they comprise an empirically powerfully axis on which we can locate primary value orientations of world socio-political systems. The World Values Survey and related analyses by its initiator, Ronald Inglehart, supply strong evidence for this general conclusion (e.g. Clark & Rempel, 1997; Inglehart, 1997). So do other analyses (Clark & Elazar, in draft; Goldsmith & Page, 1987).

The classic socio-political cleavages were traditionally two. First cleavages over land in agricultural societies often generated clientelist politics and dependency relations, centered on a Padrone. Second with industry came class politics, dividing rich and poor, or bourgeois and manual laborers. But with post-industrialism rising since the 1960s, the percentage of manual workers (agricultural and industrial) has dropped by about half in most countries of the world. Many political parties have correspondingly shifted to new issues, abandoning the production politics of class and a more comprehensive welfare state. Instead, new issues like the environment have been embraced by even many left parties and citizens. Old issues are then combined in new ways. Result: many social and political distinctions like class belong increasingly to the past (Clark & Lipset, 2001).

Many Americans Say Environmental Concerns Drive Their Consumption Decisions

The 1990s have been heralded as the Earth Decade, with environmentalism becoming a movement of massive worldwide force. Eight in ten Americans already regard themselves as environmentalists (Gutfield, 1990). In surveys, 75 percent of consumers have said their purchasing decisions are influenced by a company's reputation with respect to the environment, and eight in ten have said they would pay more for products that are environmentally friendly (Klein, 1990). One survey notes that 85 percent have said they believe that U.S. companies should be doing more to become environmentally responsible (Chase & Smith, 1992). Even a casual review of the business press suggests that a majority of organizations already consider themselves to be environmentally sensitive (Goldman, 1991; Winski, 1991). News and feature stories on green products, green packaging, and even green factories abound as more organizations become players in the burgeoning environmental movement (e.g. Bird, 1990; Eisenhart, 1990; Woodruff, 1991). From 1985 to 1990, green product introductions increased at an average annual rate of more than 100 percent (Klein, 1990), and sales of green products are estimated to total $8.8 billion by 1995 (Winski, 1991).

From: Minette E. Drumwright "Socially responsible organizational buying: Environmental concern as a non-economic buying criterion," Journal of Marketing, 58(3), July 1994, pp. 1ff.

Among the most powerful new social movements with strong consumption and political messages were environmental and women's movements. After the 1970s, both sought to "raise the consciousness" of the general public by applying moral precepts and adding symbolic meaning where it was previously absent, such as "despoiling nature" or "sexual harassment." These new concepts directly invoke a Protestant, ascetic concern to restrict access and "exploitation" of nature or womankind. Yet these views are by no means universally embraced, which leads to a proposition:

(6) *The stronger the commitment to moral asceticism, particularly as it emerged with Calvinist Protestantism, the more that personal consumption and public behavior by the individual and his society are defined or constrained by moral precepts and beliefs. By contrast, secular persons or "non-believers" should be constrained less by more general values; their personal consumption and political concerns should be driven more by other factors.*

(7) *For some persons these moral principles are driven in a direct, literal manner by organized religious norms and institutions: devout Muslims do not drink alcohol, etc.*

Joining a specific religious group has increased in salience globally in the last decade, with massive conversion to fundamentalist Islam and Protestantism in world regions that were long bastions of Buddhism (like China) or Roman Catholicism (like Brazil which now claims more practicing Protestants than Catholics). Similarly, Hispanic-Americans have converted to Protestantism in huge numbers, indicating the potential for serious shifts in value commitments in this time of global turbulence (Martin, 1990). Globalization—with its secular multiculturalism, consumerisms, and postmodern hyperpluralism—brings moral turbulence to traditional world areas. These largely Western global views are spread by mass media, and embraced by some young elites in traditional areas, who can thus articulate these new global-linked views to every country and rural county of the world—as bankers, engineers, doctors, or NGO social workers. But the cultural shock they generate in turn encourages the rise of fundamentalism, as an active religious effort to affirm moral roots in a world where traditional moorings seem weakened or lost. In locations like the American South, as well as Southern and Eastern Europe, Latin America, and parts of the Islamic world, elites were traditionally linked to the church, and dispensed patronage and clientelism to lower status persons. With globalization, clientelism as a classic foundation of traditional political culture is losing political support globally, and being branded as morally corrupt. A popular counter is fundamentalism as a movement of common persons seeking a new identity and moral commitment unsullied by traditional clientelist relations and elite associations. Fundamentalism is politically and morally critical of traditional elites. Fundamentalism is the strong global counterpart of our Moralistic political culture. Both refuse to separate politics from morality. Terrorism is the most extreme political outcome, but its roots go far deeper.

(8) *For many other persons, more important than organized religious specifics are the deep, basic value orientations which religion may foster—like egalitarianism, asceticism, thrift, or honesty—which can lead to more specific attitudes like support for political transparency.*

Thus, the analyst may use religious background as a marker flagging the potential for a distinct value orientation, but the value orientation (like "honesty in politics") exists distinct from organized religious belief and practice. In consumption matters, for instance, asceticism is important in its own right (irrespective of Calvinist, Buddhist or other roots) if it leads the modern ascetic citizen to support statements like "clothes do not define who I am."

The Protestant ethic for Max Weber reinforced the spirit of capitalism, more powerfully because it was unintended and unselfconscious. Gorski's recent work (unpublished) shows the comprehensive impact of Calvinism in many domains that Weber did not—from low crime in the Netherlands, to labeling the poor as deserving or undeserving, to raising trust in public debt for Northern European nations, etc. The critical point today is that the Calvinist ethic in the broad sense of fundamentalist Protestantism is spreading globally at the dawn of the twenty-first century with rapidity and force. Implications of this spread are drastic.

Pietism was not stressed by Weber, but recent research suggests that it was more supportive of hedonistic consumption than Calvinism. To explore such competing value orientations for their impacts on consumption patterns is precisely the sort of approach that we encourage here. Examples follow.

Still, basic values are too general to predict many specific consumption and political decisions, which leaves room for other processes.

Table 2.4. Religion Correlates with Several Attitudes and Activities

	Pearson Correlations		
	Religion is an Important Part of My Life	Religious Fundamentalism is the Greatest Peril in the Country Today	Attended Church or Other Place of Worship (Freq Last 12 months)
I am in favor of legalized abortions	-.39**	.18**	-.38**
The government should restrict imported products	.08**	.06**	.03**
Dressing well is an important part of my life	.17**	.05**	.12**
The car I drive is a reflection of who I am	-.02**	.04**	-0.01
Went to a club meeting (freq last 12 months)	.14**	-0.02	.23**
Told a lie (freq last 12 months)	-.09**	0	-.05**
If a cashier accidentally gives you too much change, I say it's OK to keep it	-.27**	.10**	-.23**
It's okay to cheat on your income taxes	-.15**	.09**	-.12**
I am in favor of very strict enforcement of all laws	.17**	.(a)	.13**

Sources: DDB Lifestyle Survey
.(a) Cannot be computed because at least one of the variables is constant.
** Correlation is significant at the 0.01 level (2-tailed).

We can thus ask, using basic DDB measures, how they vary by religiosity or general moral commitment of the respondent. For example more religious respondents to the DDB are more opposed to abortion, more favorable to restricting imports, more concerned not to lie, cheat, or violate laws (Table 2.4). While more religious persons are more concerned with dress than the *less* religious, the more religious feel their cars are less a reflection of who they are.

Southern Baptists Take Their Message to Strip Clubs
By Julia Lieblich Tribune religion reporter, *Chicago Tribune*, June 10th, 2002

ST. LOUIS—Valerie Vorpi heard that some of her fellow Southern Baptists were going to evangelize dancers in southern Illinois strip clubs, but she had no interest in being among church ladies telling naked women they are headed for hell.

After learning that planners had rejected a judgmental approach, she joined more than fifty women Saturday in their two-day mission to meet dancers with names like "Kitty Kat" and "Wonder" in clubs such as Dream Girls and Doll House.

"We were just going to let the girls know that people out there care about them," said Vorpi, 42. "We've all made poor choices. We've all been victimized. We're not all that far apart."

Their mission was part of the evangelizing blitz that takes place in cities hosting the Southern Baptist Convention's two-day annual meeting, which begins Tuesday in St. Louis. Throughout the city, Southern Baptists hosted block parties and walked through neighborhoods praying . . . .

Over the years the Southern Baptists have tried a wide array of approaches to outsiders. In a highly controversial campaign, the denomination asked members to pray for the conversion of Jews, Muslims and Hindus. More recently Southern Baptists drew criticism from religious leaders for a plan, never fully realized, to bring 100,000 missionaries to Chicago.

Now some Southern Baptist groups are turning to smaller efforts, targeting people they feel are ignored, adopting a less confrontational style and staying in touch over time.

Vorpi and her group were determined to reach women who would skip the church block parties. After the annual meeting, the Baptist women hoped to guide the dancers they met toward both spiritual and practical assistance such as transitional housing.

"Go out without judgment or condemnation and let the women know they have value," Lura Sheppard, a mission organizer, told teams of volunteers in a Fairview Heights church. At 1 p.m. Saturday, six women set out for Roxy's: Just a Kiss Away, a sprawling shedlike building in Brooklyn, Ill., near East St. Louis.

A male parishioner preceded them into the club, where he gave the manager a fruit basket and talked him into letting in more Baptists bearing gifts. Three women followed carrying more than a dozen canvas bags filled with toilet articles, jewelry and New Testaments, and sat down in leather chairs in the back of the darkened club.

Three more women stayed in the van and prayed.

The Baptists tried not to look at a naked woman dancing for a male patron on a table in front of them, seeking instead the attention of dancers and waitresses walking the floor.

Linda Gonzales, who organized the mission, handed a gift bag to a dancer in a black-negligee and invited her to talk. The dancer said she was a single mother who sent her 10-year-old son to a Baptist school. Another dancer put on a cutoff T-shirt that read "Cheerleader" and walked over to see the gifts. "I'm going back to school in Chicago in two weeks," she told the women.

Tracy Basham, 30, of Galatia, Ill., handed the dancer a tote bag and a gold coin, saying it was to remind her that God knows her true value.

"God values me after this?" the dancer asked, pointing to the stage. Then she hugged Basham and left with a bag that read, "Trust in the Lord."

A tall woman in a glow-in-the-dark T-shirt that read "Heartbreak" sat down next. "What's your motive?" she demanded. "Do you have a problem with what we do?"

The Baptists were silent for a moment. Then they each told her that God cared about her no matter what she did . . . .

"Do you know for sure that if you died tonight you would go to heaven?" she said. When the dancer hesitated, Lewis urged her to read the New Testament in her bag. Then the women exchanged phone numbers on napkins.

Addendum by Erica Coslor: so if churches had strippers, would it increase attendance?

Three Foundational Cultures

It is useful to build on the ideas of Daniel Elazar (See the website http://www.jcpa.org/djeindex.htm or his four volume series, e.g. Elazar, 1998). As sketched above, he distinguished three main approaches to culture and politics. The three cultures were carried via three distinct migration streams from Europe to the Eastern U.S. and then to the U.S. West coast. They continue to spread globally, lending them heightened international interest. First is the Calvinist, or Communal-Moralist culture expressing its politics in New England puritan churches and town meetings. Politics here is an openly moralist expression of basic values, with clear religious roots, infusing all aspects of life. It was carried from the Netherlands and England to Boston and Minneapolis to Seattle and Northern California. It continues to spread globally in updated form via the investigatory journalism of BBC and CNN, ecological activism, non-profits advocating many strains of human rights, inter alia. Second the Individualist culture stresses the market in economics and individual solutions to political issues, such as the "deal" of a politician with an interest group. Politics is not moralistic, but often dirty. It is not the moral duty of all to participate, as in New England; rather politics is delegated to politicians and lawyers so that gentlemen and ladies need not sully themselves. Individualism was carried from the European context to the U.S. mid-Atlantic states like New York and Pennsylvania to Chicago to San Francisco. Third is the Southern culture of tradition, honor, lineage, and hierarchy, incarnated by the slave-based plantation where authority lines were clear. This third culture was modeled on the English gentry house and European aristocratic courts, stressing conspicuous consumption, military prowess, and elegant taste. African Americans are distinct today due in part to their continuing to fight against elitist elements of this Southern tradition, which also generated Huey Long, evangelical preachers, and William Faulkner. Indeed Faulkner's novels are among the most graphic accounts of the subtleties of conflict and change in Southern traditional culture. A continuing theme is the conflict between Faulkner's upper status Copsons and lower status Snopes. V.O. Key, in his classic Southern Politics, points out that every Southern state had both a delta, with plantations and hierarchy, and a highlands, peopled with heavily Scotch-Irish residents (like the country singers in Nashville). The egalitarian highlanders fought the planter elite, usually defeating them with a radical populist politics, championed initially by whites like Huey Long and continued by black civil rights leaders like Jesse Jackson. Aspects of this Southern culture were carried west through Texas to Southern California, where electronic preachers, evangelists and Hollywood actors beam aspects of it nationally and internationally. In the 1920s, the Anaheim City Council elected a majority of Ku Klux Klan members; today Anaheim is home to Disneyland.

From: Michèle Lamont and Virág Molnár "How Blacks Use Consumption to Shape their Collective Identity: Evidence from Marketing Specialists." *Journal of Consumer Culture*, June 2000, *1*(1):

Ethnic or multicultural marketing became the marketing mantra of the 1980s in the United States. This new marketing paradigm views the market as divided into segments and aims at gathering information regarding the customs, traditions, rituals, relationships, and identities of these segments of potential consumers. The three predominant segments are "blacks" "Hispanics," and the "general market." The black segment is pursued by top advertising agencies and by (often black-owned) black advertising agencies, which have been around since the 1960s . . .

The shift to segmented ethnic marketing has entailed a broadening of the technical tools used by marketing specialists, including the incorporation of interpretive approaches such as ethnographies and personal interviews, to better capture ethnic cultural worlds. These new developments make specialists in black marketing a particularly suitable source of information on black consumers.

The marketing specialists we interviewed discussed at length the centrality of consumption as a way for blacks to affirm and gain recognition of their full membership in American society.

Marketers interpret the buying habits of blacks as strongly guided by a desire to be recognized as equal and full participating members of society and to disprove the stereotype of blacks as belonging to an underclass deprived of buying power. This desire is manifested in distinct consumption patterns: in comparison to whites, blacks spend disproportionately more on items that they view as affirming their equal standing . . .

In this context, it is interesting to note that data on consumption behavior confirms that "dressing up" or "getting clean" is more crucial to blacks than to whites. Indeed, black women spend 41 percent more on personal-care services than white women. Also, on average, black households spend four times as much on boy's suits and sport coats as their white counterparts. They also spend 46 percent more than white households on girls' skirts, 67 percent more on girls' accessories and 86 percent more on boys' footwear (Schmeltzer, 1998) (Sales and Marketing Management, 1991) . . . are twice as likely as whites, when they purchase a car, to opt for an expensive foreign model such as an Audi, BMW or Mercedes (Reid, 1995).

A black top executive working for one of the largest black advertising agenc(ies) in the United States believes that consumption is a more important means of signaling and acquiring status for blacks than education or membership in the black church. In his view, branded consumer goods, often referred to as "portable status symbols" are obtained more easily than employment, housing or membership in certain groups and organizations. Also, when asked what images of blacks they try to convey, this and other marketing specialists often described black people shopping at Saks Fifth Avenue and engaging in consumption patterns that are characteristic, not of the average American, but of the top 5-10 percent of the American population, black or white. Although some referred to marketing campaigns aimed at K-mart consumers, implicitly or explicitly, all stressed that consuming luxury items, and not ordinary items ("Remy Martin, not Coors beer" as one of them puts it), provides social membership.

Good For The Soul—And The Bottom Line

Firms Promote Spirituality In Workplace And Find It Pays

By Bill Broadway, Washington Post Staff Writer, Washington Post, Sunday, August 19th, 2001; Page A01.

Talk of soul and spirituality is flowing freely in the workplace these days. Many chief executives are unabashedly defining their companies' business missions in moral terms.

Some are adding a dimension of social responsibility through environmentally friendly practices. Some pay employees to mentor students or work at shelters for the homeless. Others have infused their employee handbooks with ethics-based philosophy or altered workday routines to allow time for meditation, yoga or napping. (Napping is said to encourage spiritual development and mental and physical renewal.)

Alternately called spiritual economics, soul in the workplace and values-driven leadership, this is a quasi-religious movement, one without a god or theological foundation but filled with moral attitudes and guidelines common to all religions.

The trend has drawn criticism from some ethicists and theologians, who warn that management efforts to promote work as spiritually fulfilling can lure employees into working longer hours away from family and friends.

What seems beyond debate is that emphasizing morality over profitability has turned out to be good for the bottom line. Executives who have embraced the approach are the first to acknowledge that it has helped them build loyalty among employees and customers.

"We were raised to think we had to screw around with other people to be successful. But taking the opposite approach of J. R. Ewing is probably going to be more successful," said Kip Tindell, chief executive of the Container Store.

Tindell's Dallas-based retail chain, which tells workers they are morally obligated to help customers solve problems and not just sell them products, has posted average annual sales increases of 20–25 percent since opening its first store in 1978 and has been No. 1 for the past two years on *Fortune* magazine's list of 100 Best Companies to Work For.

And scores of publications on the subject—including the books "Bringing Your Soul to Work" and "God Is My CEO" and the journals *Business Spirit* and *Spirit at Work*—have increased discussions of workplace spirituality. Elizabeth A. Denton, an executive consultant who has worked with dozens of companies and is co-author of the book "A Spiritual Audit of Corporate America."

She and co-author Ian I. Mitroff interviewed more than one hundred CEOs and upper-level managers. They found that about one-fourth of them were trying to make their businesses more spiritual and that most of the others wanted to move in that direction but were not sure how to go about it.

Gone With the Wind dramatizes the conflict of Scarlet O'Hara by featuring her individualism in fighting tradition; it is the most popular film across the globe ever, surpassing all Ingmar Bergman's films even in his native Sweden.

The American South is not just history; its deep social and economic contrasts, ethnic conflict, bitterness from losing, and a fading but glorious past are themes that resonate with many people globally. They are important themes to counter Horatio Alger's strident individualism. The Southern legacy has grown into a TV-driven spectre that haunts many Americans, especially those with moralistic leanings. Corollary: the three cultures are strengthened by attacking one another's excesses—in neighbors and high school non-friends and political candidates.[3]

Here are selections from a very contemporary website, blending moralism and environmentalism with austere consumption, called:

The Dollar Stretcher: Living Better for Less

http://www.stretcher.com/stories/00/000814n.cfm

Confusing Simplicity With Frugality
by Nita Jackson

I shop at Salvation Army for clothes (very time consuming), but if it gets ripped or stained no big deal! Often clothing might need a button or mending (not simplicity at its best).

Natural Bug Control
by Mira Dessy
mdessy@together.net

Dear Mira,

This makes a good bug spray for plants.
One cup of each of the following in two gallon pressure sprayer:
- Dawn dish washing detergent
- No name window spray
- Tobacco juice (make this by putting a generous clump of chewing tobacco in a pint jar of water, let remain overnight—strain prior to putting in with remaining ingredients)
- Fill remaining space in sprayer with water

Spray generously on plants . . .

—Stan

Solar Ovens: Let God Pay Your Utility Bills

Dave writes:

You can also construct your own solar oven for under $10.

Home Power Magazine's

Heaven's Flame

a new book by Joseph Radabaugh

http://www.homepower.com/hflame.htm

To order Call 800-707-6585 or 530-475-0830 outside the U.S., or order on-line.
$15

I don't receive any kickbacks from the sale of the above products, but as a citizen of planet Earth I do receive the satisfaction of a little cleaner air every time a solar oven gets used!

– Dave

Building Your Own Log Cabin

Do-It-Yourself to the Max!

by Paul and Mary Paxton

pmpaxton@aol.com

Before I begin, I'd like to say that we are just regular, middle-aged, people. We don't have any special talents. If anything qualified us to build our own home, it was the desire to have a home without going in debt.

In 1995, we had been on the road for over two years, looking for "The Promised Land." We managed an RV Park in the Southern Rocky Mountains in New Mexico. We realized we'd found the place we wanted to be, when the season ended and we didn't want to leave!

That winter we brought the trees down, skinned them, cataloged them and drew our plans. We could hardly wait for Spring to come! As soon as the

> weather allowed, we poured concrete piers and began the cabin. We had no
> help, so had to devise a way to position the logs. We used our trusty old
> "come-along" and a pick-up to pull them into place . . .
>
> When we started the project, we had a total of $20,000 to buy land and con-
> struct the cabin. At the end of the project we had money left! (We already had
> the solar set up, so that is not included in what we spent.) We were living in
> the cabin nine months after the construction started and had no help at all.

Paradox? More income may not lead to conspicuous consumption if it is
channeled by preferences for austerity and self-disciplined moralism. This is a
classic New England value strain, even if seldom featured in the national media.
Affluent Boston sea captains in 1800 had the same concern as Silicon Valley
executives today: how not to spoil their children. Is the moralistic pattern in decline? How does it "interact" with the Inglehart/Maslow logic that rising income
should shift priorities from material concerns to more symbolic and "post-
modernist" issues? One might expect that:

(9) *Differences in income or material well-being should vary within the three
cultural types. The core Inglehart proposition (income changes values and
behavior) should be largest within Individualist culture, since Individualists
start from a more materialist position resembling Inglehart's materialist
individuals. By contrast, among Moralistic/Communalist persons, and in
locations where they are more numerous, more income should permit more
assiduous pursuit of political reform (anti-clientelism, etc.) Income should
bring smaller value changes in personal lifestyle than for individualists. The
simple frugality of affluent New Englanders is legendary. Spending on
conspicuous consumption for yourself is "sinfully indulgent." By contrast a
Traditionalist from the American South, living in a culturally consistent
small town, should be similarly resistant to the value transition of Inglehart.
More income, rather than changing values away from "materialism" a` la
Inglehart, may facilitate more "royalist" indulgence—as was long
considered normal in Southern culture by persons high or low in income,
and in much of the world, especially its Southern areas.*

Strong political moralism is generated less by money than exposure to traditional New England culture. Just as Cambridge and Boston Abolitionists in 1800
used personal funds to spread their cause to the West and South of the U.S., so
did "strong ecologists" in 2000 use funds to spread their cause globally.

(10) *Still, the prime change among the three types is the movement of the
national culture toward elements of New England Moralism—not in its
traditional local and puritanical form, but in "cosmopolitan moralism"-a*

broad concern to apply morality to politics, reforming leadership patterns to more fully implement ideals of democracy, due process, equal citizen rights, fighting clientelism and corruption, advocating transparency in administrative procedures, and the like.

Similar transformations are under way worldwide, but are seriously adapted to different local traditions, especially via such critical figures as Gandhi or Mao or Nelson Mandela who reformulated ideas from the West to fit their home cultures.

(11)*Values are less coherent and less stable among persons who have been exposed to multiple conflicting value orientations, especially in their early years. Such loose value orientations can also lead to greater innovation and social tolerance. The interpenetration of disparate cultural elements leads people toward a greater aesthetic sense of irony and cosmopolitanism.*

This proposition extends the aesthetic of what Susan Sontag called camp (like finding humor in going to a retro, 1950s style diner/restaurant). It recurs when musical and artistic elements from disparate cultural areas are combined, and felt, in this cosmopolitan aesthetic, to blend together positively. An ironic or alienated aesthetic outlook implies a greater cosmopolitanism: individuals are less totally submerged in one culture, but take pleasure in exploring diversity and have enough psychological distance and detachment from their own roots to resonate positively to such eclecticism.

This proposition could be explored in content analyses of themes in such sources as music, books, theater, movies, television, comedy clubs, humor magazines, video games, radio talk shows and other cultural products—ideally scoring them in cultural distance. While the proposition points to a rise in parody and irony, all citizens of the globe do not shift equally; huge diversity persists and many if not most citizens of the world still live in relatively homogeneous cultures, even if penetrated by global media. The ironic distance of camp recurs in many boxes through this chapter.

Sensitivity to such consistent or disparate cultural elements has been central to social-psychological research for decades, around concepts like social tolerance, ethnocentrism, and the famous F-scale of the Frankfurt sociologists. The proposition suggests that as citizens' cognitive maps change and grow more eclectic, so do their consumption preferences move toward more irony and distance. These tendencies are likely to be most pronounced by new immigrants, who thus develop cosmopolitan personal identities joining their past(s) and present location. Still, who goes "too far," and what constitutes pornography or bad taste varies dramatically. In the 1930s, when Brett Hart said "I don't give a damn" to Scarlet O'Hara in Gone With the Wind, it raised a furor. French films of interracial couples were similarly banned from the U.S. in that decade as violating racial separateness. Yet by 2000, videos and many U.S. films are practically uncensored, artists strive to "push the envelope," generating ever more extreme acts and contrasts from the culturally eclectic to the sexually perverse. How to "control" pornography and political extremism on the Internet are continuations of this theme. One solution for many persons is to move to a town where the balance of new and old fits one's personal temperament. We explore examples in the next two chapters.

(12) *Extending Proposition No. 11, these changes should lead audiences for cultural events to grow more diverse, since more cosmopolitan citizens are culturally interested in disparate styles and contrasting forms of entertainment. Aesthetically this implies the interpenetration of "high" and "mass culture" and generally weakening linkages between social background characteristics and cultural products. Countless other cultural variations should grow as citizens become both more cosmopolitan, and for the more culturally demanding, hungry for distinctly original cultural fare.*

Historical comparisons suggest that "high" culture emerged in the late 19th century in the U.S. as part of an effort to create distance among social groups (DiMaggio, 1982). Such differences seem to have flattened since the 1960s, but where and how remains controversial (Blau, 1989; Strom, 2002). How much have symphony concert audiences grown more diverse from the past and how do they compare to audiences at other events, like opera, Broadway musicals, or buyers of CDs of various forms of music? These same trends help interpret why one similarly finds great controversy over "authenticity," sparked by the suspicion that the actor is a mere cultural "impersonator." For African-Americans, rap music is an extreme case, in that it often is used as a marker for black identity, or is often intended as such. In some rap performances, whites in the audience are thus openly insulted or unwelcomed. Conversely, other rap performers who "water down" their lyrics in hopes of reaching a broader (white) audience are branded as selling out to commercial capitalism and the white establishment. See Jones (2002) in the box below.

Rap and Black Identity

"Consumption is a mode of being, a way of gaining identity, meaning, and prestige in contemporary society" (Sarup, 1996, p. 105). While consumers do not gain a Black identity by buying CDs and going to concerts, by consuming images of blackness they gain access to a community that they would not be part of otherwise. Rap artist Ice Cube is cynical in his assessment of social integration: "It's kind of like being at the zoo. You can look into that world, but you don't have to touch it. It's safe" (Farley, 1999). Sarup refers to consumption as "the primary mode of social integration" (Sarup, 1996, p. 107), and in the widespread proliferation of hip hop culture, people can participate in hip hop culture vicariously by attending concerts, purchasing CD's, and so forth.

From: Jane Jones, The Search for Identity and a Diminishing Dialogue:
Racial Identity Formation in Rap Music, BA thesis, Dept of Sociology,
University of Chicago, 2002.

Still, the above proposition suggests that these rap dynamics may be more
of an exception, even a direct reaction against the main trend toward tolerance
and diversity. It is one poignant case illustrating the broader reaction against
"global Hollywood," or Disnification (which some Californians pronounce as
Disfornication) of culture. That is, many artists and culturally sensitive persons
strive to preserve local cultural specifics by: (1) preserving traditions (Grazian);
or (2) developing new and distinct cultural forms, such as poetry jams, where-
poets recite their own works, sometimes competing against other local poets (see
Lloyd, 2002 on related examples).
Inside the U.S. and perhaps other countries, migration, rapid communication,
national media, and a stronger national government weakened regional subcultures over the twentieth century, thus fostering hybrids. The more that individuals are exposed to different cultures, via broken families, travel, attending
schools or college in culturally-distant locations, and in other ways, the more
these should disrupt the consistency of the three cultures. (Unfortunately most
sample surveys, including the DDB, do not ask about migration and where the
respondent lived over time, which would facilitate sharper linking of culture to
geographic places.) One might thus expect that more travel, education, and contact with national values would lead individuals in a nation to become more similar to one another, but also that these would lead to a relative increase in the
(cosmopolitan) moralistic value patterns Similarly, migrations have been so extensive that the specific regional cultures have been transformed within the three
U.S. regions. This fits our general proposition above about the declining impact
on values from social characteristics like class, region, and ethnic background
which is driven by the media, migration, and general cosmopolitanism. These
changes imply the importance of focusing on interrelations among several value
patterns and actions, rather than invoking social background characteristics to
interpret differences. We thus measure the three types with attitudes and values
of individual citizens and see that they are (only) moderately related to current
region of residence.[4]
We created measures of each of the three cultural types using items from
the DDB survey of 84,989 U.S. citizens from 1975 through 1998 (detailed in
Appendix 1). Many DDB items correlate in interesting ways with the three
political cultures. Most are generally consistent with the sketches above. For
instance, Traditionalists are lower in education, income, more often men, chur-
chgoers, living in the South, and who describe themselves as "old fashioned,"
oppose unmarried couples and same sex marriages, favor guns in every home,

Table 2.5. Citizens Political Cultures Are Associated with Many Lifestyle Differences: Correlations of DDB Responses.

	Pearson Correlations		
	Individualistic	Traditional	Moralistic
Level of education completed	.16**	-.13**	.22**
Into which one of the following categories does your annual household income fall?	.13**	-.09**	.14**
Five years from now our family income will probably be a lot higher than it is now	.21**	-.03**	.06**
Marital status	.03**	-.09**	.11**
Attended church or other place of worship (freq last 12 months).	.04**	.31**	-.18**
Sex of respondent	-.06**	-.12**	.06**
MIDATL	.07**	-.03**	-.02**
SOUTH	-.02**	.14**	-.11**
I am a homebody	-.13**	-.01*	-.08**
I have somewhat old fashioned tastes and habits	-.04**	.23**	-.14**
My opinions on things don't count very much	-.21**	.09**	-.10**
Do you really enjoy your job?	-.09**	-.02**	-.03*
On a job, security is more important than money	.00	.10*	-.02**
I am in favor of legalizing same sex marriages	.08**	-.38**	.(a)
Went to an exercise class (freq last 12 months)	.09**	-.02**	.11**
Our whole family usually eats dinner together	.03**	.10**	-.04**
Went fishing (freq last 12 months)	.06**	.07**	-.01*
I would do better than average in a fist fight	.25**	.08**	-.03**
I often wish for the good old days	-.03**	.19**	-.12**
Sent a greeting card (freq last 12 months)	.05**	-.03**	.13**
There should be a gun in every home	.07**	.18**	-.12**
Went hiking (freq last 12 months)	.11**	.01	.12**
Visited an art gallery or museum (freq last 12 months)	.15**	-.08**	.21**
An honest man cannot get elected to high office	-.02**	.09**	-.05**
I CLUBMEE	.16**	.27**	.35**
I am the kind of person who would try anything once	.21**	.01*	.10**
I frequently get indigestion	-.02**	.09**	-.07**
Stayed late at work (freq last 12 months)	.16**	-.07**	.10**
I work very hard most of the time	.18**	.04**	-.02**
I would rather live in the city than in the suburbs.	.06**	-.03**	.05**
We will probably move at least once in the next five years	.09**	-.06**	.05**
Couples should live together before getting married	.11**	-.27**	.27**
Made long-distance call from home (freq last 12 months)	.15**	-.03	.09**
The use of marijuana should be legalized	.08**	-.20**	.19**
The United States spends too much money on national defense	.04**	-.07**	.(a)
I don't have a clue what the internet is and what it can do for me	-.13**	.15**	.(a)
How many issues of the news section of the newspaper do you yourself read?	.08**	0	.09**
I very seldom make detailed plans	-.13**	.05**	-.08**
Police should use whatever force is necessary to maintain law and order	.01*	.20**	-.11**

Table 2.5. (Continued)

	Pearson Correlations		
	Individualistic	Traditional	Moralistic
Went to a public library (freq last 12 months)	.05**	-.08**	.16**
Religion is an important part of my life	.03**	.32**	-.22**
I would be content to live in the same town the rest of my life	-.07**	.13**	-.07**
I am not very good at saving money	-.04**	.02**	-.03**

Notes: The three political culture indexes (Individualistic, etc.) were constructed using items listed in the Appendix.
.(a) Cannot be computed because at least one of the variables is constant
* Correlation is significant at the 0.05 level (one-tailed).
** Correlation is significant at the 0.01 level (one-tailed).

seldom use the Internet, and go fishing—more than Moralists or Individualists. Moralists oppose Traditionalists most on these items, while Individualists are in between, albeit often closer to Moralists. Individualists are nevertheless distinct from the two others in their willingness to "try anything once" and in disagreeing with items like "my opinions don't count very much," or "I am a homebody." Individualists also claim that they would "do better than average in a fist fight" (Table 2.5 shows details).

Can we find then a spread of Moralism and decline of Traditionalism, as we hypothesize from global trends, as in Propositions No. 3 and 10 concerning the spread of electronic media, education and decline of clientelism? Even over the relatively short historical period of the DDB surveys, we find a strong increase in the percent of Moralists, and smaller decline in Traditionalists (Table 2.6).We find analogous changes internationally in analyzing changes in items about democratic participation and conceptions of politics, using the World Values Surveys (Table 2.7).

We tested Proposition No. 9 about income effects varying across political cultures, using the DDB items combined with census and other data. For instance in contrasting the three types of cultures, moralistic persons engage more often in consumption and political behaviors with more moralistic implications, as discussed further in the Appendix.

Table 2.6. Persons Reporting Moralistic Political Culture Have Increased Over the 1975 to 1998 Period

YEAR	Type of Political Culture		
	Moralistic	Individualist	Traditional
1975	2.52	19.46	17.67
1976	2.64	19.00	17.73
1977	2.61	19.24	17.16
1978	2.69	18.64	16.75
1979	2.71	18.64	16.58
1980	2.62	18.40	17.05
1981	3.21	18.79	16.93
1982	3.25	18.73	16.56
1983	3.32	18.52	16.10
1984	3.40	18.77	16.14
1985	3.53	19.07	15.83
1986	3.60	18.89	15.68
1987	3.74	18.82	15.42
1988	3.64	19.04	15.55
1989	3.42	18.82	15.37
1990	3.49	18.64	15.30
1991	3.45	18.51	15.27
1992	3.88	18.72	15.02
1993	4.07	18.64	14.73
1994	4.02	18.57	14.82
1995	3.94	18.59	14.53
1996	4.14	18.79	14.24
1997	4.28	18.56	13.90
1998	4.14	18.82	13.95

Notes: These are averages for each of the indexes in each year. They are calculated for all respondents to items used in three indexes. All changes from the early to later years are statistically significant if we consider change over the full period.
Sources: DDB Indexes, components for which are reported in the Appendix

Table 2.7. NPC Responses Increased Globally, 1981–1997.

	Number of Waves	N. Europe	S. Europe	Latin America	South Asia	East Asia	Africa	E.C. Europe	USA	Total
How active are you in each of the following groups: (1) Active member (2) Inactive member (3) Don't belong—Non political organizations, such as social welfare, religious, education and culture, trade unions, professional, youth, sports, women's, animal rights or health	3	+	+	+	+	+	+	+	+	+
Generally speaking, can most people be trusted or that you can't be too careful in who you are dealing with? (1) Most people can be trusted (2) Can't be too careful (3) Don't know	2	+	+	+	+	+	+	+	+	+
Please use the scale where 1 means "none at all" and 10 means "a great deal" to indicate how much freedom of choice and control you feel you have over the way your life turns out. (recoded 1 thru 3 = 1; 4 thru 7 = 2; 8 thru 10 = 3)	3	+	+	+	+	+	+	+	+	+
Tell me for each of the following statements whether you think it can always be justified, never be justified, something in between—abortion	3	+	+	+	+	+	-	+	+	+
How interested would you say you are in politics?	3	-	-	+	+	+	+	+	-	-

These are different forms of political action people can take; tell me whether you have actually done any of these things = 1, whether you might do it = 2, or would never, under any circumstances = 3; don't know = 9

	Number of Waves	N. Europe	S. Europe	Latin America	South Asia	East Asia	Africa	E.C. Europe	USA	Total
Sign petition	3	-	-	+	+	+		+	-	+
Join boycott	3	-	-	+	+	+		+	-	+
Attend demonstration	3	+	-	+	+	+		+	-	+
Join strike	3	+	+	+	+	+		+		+
Occupy building	2	+	+	+	-	+	-	+		+
Total actions	3	+	+	+	-	-	-	-		+

Table 2.7. (Continued)

How would you place your views on this scale? 1 = you agree completely with the first statement listed; 10 = you agree completely with the second statement; if your views fall in between, you can choose a number in between

	Number of Waves	N. Europe	S. Europe	Latin America	South Asia	East Asia	Africa	E.C. Europe	USA	Total
First: Incomes should be more equal Second: We need larger income differences as incentives for individual effort.	2	+	+	+	+	-	-	+	-	+
First: Private ownership of business and industry should be increased. Second: Government ownership of business and industry should be increased.	2	-	-	+	+	-	+	+		+
First: The government should take more responsibility to ensure that everyone is provided for. Second: People should take more responsibility to provide for themselves.	2	+	+	+	+		-	+	-	+
First: Competition is good. It stimulates people to work hard and develop new ideas. Second: Competition is harmful. It brings out t the worst in people (recoded 1 thru 3 = 1; 4 thru 7 = 2; 8 thru 10 = 3).	2	+	+	+	+	+		+		+
First: In the long run, hard work usually brings a better life. Second: Hard work doesn't generally bring success— it's more a matter of luck and connections (recoded 1 thru 3 = 1; 4 thru 7 = 2; 8 thru 10 = 3).	2	+	+	+	+	-		+		+

Table 2.7. (Continued)

Tell me how much confidence you have in each organization: is it a great deal of confidence = 1, quite a lot of confidence = 2, not very much confidence = 3, none at all = 4; don't know = 9

	Number of Waves	N. Europe	S. Europe	Latin America	South Asia	East Asia	Africa	E.C. Europe	USA	Total
Church	2	+	+	-	+	-	+	+	-	+
Armed forces	3	+	+	-	+	-	+	+	+	+
Legal system	3	+	+	+	+	-	+	+	+	+
Press	2	+	+	+	+	-	+	+	+	+
Unions	3	+	+	+	+	+	+	+	+	+
Police	3	+	+	+	+	-	+	+	+	+
Parliament	3	+	+	+	+	-	+	+	+	+
Civil service	3	+	+	+	+	-	+	+	+	+
Companies	3	+	+	-	+	-	+	+	+	+

Tell me for each of the following statements whether you think it can always be justified, never be justified, something in between (scale 1–10, don't know = 99) (recoded 1 thru 3 = 1; 4 thru 7 = 2; 8 thru 10 = 3)

	Number of Waves	N. Europe	S. Europe	Latin America	South Asia	East Asia	Africa	E.C. Europe	USA	Total
Claim benefits	3	+	+	+	+	+	-	+	-	+
Avoid transport fare	3	+	+	+	+	+		+	-	+
Cheat on tax	3	+	+	+	+	+	-	+	-	+
Buy stolen goods	3	+	+	+	+	+	-	+	-	+
Accept bribe	3	+	+	+	+	+		+	-	+
Homosexuality	3	+	+	+	+	+	+	+	+	+
Prostitution	3	+	+	+	+	+	-	+		+
Divorce	3	+	+	+	+	+	-	+	+	+
Euthanasia	3	+	+	+	+	-	-	+	+	+
Suicide	3	+	+	+	+	-	-	+	+	+

Notes: From the World Values Survey (WVS), we selected items related to the New Political Culture (democratization, citizen participation, etc. see Clark & Hoffmann-Martinot, 1998). We then compared citizen responses across the two or three waves of surveys, from 1981 to 1997. Change in the NPC direction appears as a plus in the table. Minus is change in the non-hypothesized direction. Blank indicates no statistically significant change.

(Note continued): The striking result is that most changes were plus and blanks were few. Results are shown for the total World in the far right column. In results by region, the main blanks or minuses were for Africa and East Asia, where we would theoretically expect the least change. One-tail t-tests were used to compare mean changes over time between waves. Some items were repeated in just two waves, indicated in the first column. Indices were created as follows:

Non-political organizations included church or religious, sport or recreation, education or art/music, labor union, environmental, professional, charitable, voluntary (v28–31, 33–36).
No organization was created from "don't belong" responses for these same organizations.
Total actions was created from signing a petition, joining in boycotts, attending a lawful demonstration, joining unofficial strikes, occupying buildings or factories.

World regions were defined as:

Northern Europe: France, Great Britain, West Germany, Netherlands, Denmark, Belgium, Ireland, Northern Ireland, Norway, Sweden, Iceland, Finland, Switzerland, East Germany, Austria
Southern Europe: Italy, Spain, Slovenia, Portugal, Basque Country, Andalusia, Galicia, Valencia
Latin America: Mexico, Argentina, Brazil, Chile, Peru, Venezuela, Uruguay, Dominican Republic, Colombia
South Asia: India, Pakistan, Bangladesh East Asia: Japan, China, Philippines Africa: Nigeria, Ghana
East-Central Europe: Hungary, Poland, Belarus, Czech Republic, Bulgaria, Romania, Moscow, Lithuania, Latvia, Estonia, Ukraine, Russia, Moldova, Georgia, Serbia, Montenegro, Macedonia, Croatia, Slovakia, Bosnia-Herzegovina

Wave 1: 1981; Wave 2: 1990; Wave 3: 1995–1997. More information about the World Values Survey is at http://wvs.isr.umich.edu.

PERSONAL INFLUENCE VIA SOCIAL PROCESSES IN MAKING DECISIONS

Where does personal influence via social relations matter? Many theories stress the quasi-atomistic individual, acting alone: as in the two last sections. Propositions in the first section were driven by individual preferences or interests, while those in the second were driven by deeper values. An alternative perspective stresses that individuals are socially-embedded. While no man is an island, the Northern European theorists from Locke, Hobbes, and Adam Smith long privileged an individual focus for moralists and social analysts. The normal antithesis has been the collectivity that envelops the individual so totally that no individual characteristics remain: the proletariat, the bourgeoisie, Yuppies, Boomers, and others.

Paul Lazarsfeld and Robert Merton developed an alternative view at Columbia University in the 1950s and 1960s, in concepts like "contextual analysis" and "structural effects." Here individuals are "cross-pressured" by their multiple group memberships toward decisions that are neither just individual nor group-driven. Rather, the distinct combinations of cross-cutting pressures and networks of social relations are critical to explain decisions.

It is thus useful to relativize the above two main lines of theorizing in some contextual propositions:

(13) *Social contexts may shift individual preferences, encouraging certain behaviors, while quelling others. One person may be particularly knowledgeable, and exercise more "personal influence" on consumption decisions or political choices than the others, who are influenced via this personalized contact.*

The classic example: shopping. Women (as it is often a gendered cultural pattern) who "go shopping" may have lunch, take a walk, and "stop by a few stores" to explore what is new or on sale—together. Being sociable means in part participating in conversations about these interrelated activities.

This proposition summarizes the widely accepted finding from Columbia in Katz and Lazarsfeld (1955). They had the further insight that consumption and political choices work in parallel: opinion leaders encourage followers to vote for political candidates in a manner similar to buying red or black shoes. This was a small revolution in using consumption behavior, often by women, as a model for politics, rather than men on the job or in the factory, as with Marx, Weber, and many others (Clark, 2000). And it potentially reverses the causal direction, suggesting that consumption patterns drive political and economic decisions. Others have extended this linkage, like Lipovetsky, who even suggests that the frivolity of fashion prepared people for modern democratic government. The more that fashion dominates the personal realm, "the more stable, profoundly unified, and reconciled with their pluralist principles the democracies become" (Lipovetsky, 1987/1994, p. 7, cited in Ritzer, n.d.). A central legacy of modernism in the last two centuries has been destroying tradition, including the monopoly of an aristocracy or a social class to dress in a particular manner or hunt over wide swaths of land. Thus, hunting today, even violating laws limiting its time and place, is seen as an assertion of democratic rights by French common persons (Sainteny, 2000). Others wear wild hats and bright-colored hair to épater les bourgeois. Are we more democratic, or socially tolerant, from seeing such diversity advertised around us? Perhaps.

DDB items that capture such personal influence are in Table 2.8. It suggests that persons are more often (self-reported) Influentials if they are higher in income, education, and occupation, older, and African-American.[5]

While classic shoppers may be women in groups, romantic couples also shop. As Miller (1998, p. 148, cited in Ritzer) observes, the primary "purpose behind shopping is not so much to buy the things that people want, but to strive to be in a relationship with subjects that want these things." The celebration of love and devotion can thus intermingle with discussions of consumption, such that the process of shopping, ideally, interacts with central human relations. Shops in small towns were often centers of village conversation, posting messages, shopkeepers extending credit, and more (Satterwaite, 2001). Yet this social integration came at the cost of excluding some who did not fit in, classically newcomers and ethnic minorities. Cohen (1992, 2003) analyzes how poor blacks in the New Deal era felt unwelcome in white Catholic neighborhoods, and sided with affluent white Protestants and Jews in patronizing and staffing chain stores where they could avoid personalistic/clientelist ties. National chains like Sears and Walgreens thus spread out across Chicago and America after World War I. They helped destroy the neighborhood shops and in turn, eventually, the neighborhood-based social groups and politics.

The theorist extending this idea was Walter Benjamin, considered by some the leading intellectual of Weimar Germany. His major work was on the rise of Paris as world capital of consumption. He explored the arcades of small adjacent shops that grew into department stores and later malls. He located these in a grand theoretical perspective combining Marx with Surrealism, Freud, and Baudelaire. The "flaneur" wandering through shops, looking for the perfect cravat or umbrella, thus became the new driving force of capitalism. Benjamin wrote of consumption sites as "monuments of the bourgeoisie" which were "ruins even before they have crumbled." He stressed how shopping was informed by wild flights of the imagination, dreams, which department stores and advertising would fuel to their utmost. The (bourgeois) shopper could thus buy and transform the home into a fantasy living space, built on dreams plus consumption, creating a "phantasmagoria of the interior" (Benjamin, 1999, p. 10ff.).[6] Benjamin worked in parallel with Adorno and Horkheimer in Frankfurt, who like Benjamin sought to theorize consumption by joining Marx and Freud. But they conceived of production and capitalist concerns as manipulating consumers by advertising, such that consumers did not play the dynamic role which Benjamin or, later, Lazarsfeld and Merton assigned to them.

Not all respond equally to personal influence. Tensions erupt in life and in theories, between doing things alone or in groups. One interpretation was David Riesman's (1950) *The Lonely Crowd*, which held that the large corporation dominated post 1945 America and fostered an "other-directedness." It was good corporate politics, he held, for people to get along easily, and not be "rugged individualists." This social sensitivity was widely discussed in these years, in phrases like "keeping up with the Joneses." Films explored ambiguities, like The *Man in the Grey Flannel Suit* or Jacques Tati who played the traditional Frenchman with raincoat, hat, and pipe, riding his old bicycle, ever shocking the yuppie-like suburbanites with fancy new homes and cars. Riesman the moralist

Table 2.8. Personal Influence Varies by Social Background, DDB Items

	Age Over 40—DDB		College Graduate or More Education		Respondent's Occupation (High Score is Low Status Occupation)		Blacks, All Years, DDB		All Respondents: DDB
	Yes	No	Yes	No	Yes	No	Yes	No	
My friends and neighbors often come to me for advice about products and brands	3.16	3.1	3.04	3.22	3.15	2.89	3.12	3.29	3.13
I am influential in my neighborhood	2.91	3.05	2.86	3.1	2.99	2.89	2.97	3.22	2.98
I like to be considered a leader	4.05	3.82	3.64	4.21	3.93	3.81	3.91	4.16	3.92

Notes: that some items are scored non-intuitively, as shown in the headings and below:

Response Categories:

(1) Definitely Disagree
(2) Generally Disagree
(3) Moderately Disagree
(4) Moderately Agree
(5) Generally Agree
(6) Definitely Agree

Sources: DDB Lifestyle surveys

held that other-directedness conflicted with and also represented a watering down of core values of strong, morally-driven persons. But the entrepreneurial individualism which encouraged New England sea captains to explore the five continents, attack large whales in small boats, or advance the Frontier westward, did not die. Indeed demand for these resurfaced as large industrial corporations declined in the late twentieth century. Some analysts like David Birch (1979) see the driving force for the new economy in entrepreneurial individuals and small firms, which grow and merge. Surveys of business school students show that many prefer small over large firms (see the controversies on these points in Clark & Hoffmann-Martinot, 1998, p. 67). The small is more visible in the U.S. than the Europe of the EU, but some argue that pressures from world markets extend these patterns globally. The danger of many aggregate or census-based studies is that they omit preferences and values of individuals about these things. How to capture values?

One DDB item that captures some elements is labeled PLEASE. "Trying to please people is a waste of time." Correlations with our culture indexes show that both Moralists and Individualists disagree with the statement, but Individualists do so less ($r = -0.04$ with Individualism versus -0.064 with Moralism Index, both significant at 0.000 level). This demands elaboration.

The Crowd and its Social Influence

Most matches pit good against evil and as a rule justice does not triumph. But it will. Rematches go on until the routine becomes jaded; then right prevails. The most entertaining match to the sensitive fan is the first contest between two wrestlers who hitherto have borne the true-blue stamp. Action will be very fast, ostentatiously clean, and may continue so to the end. This is rare. More likely, one man displays a character flaw.

The spectator's participation is not unlike the chorus in Greek drama, explaining and warning. In combat there are a number of conventions which theoretically must be upheld: when action comes to the ring border where either wrestler touches the ropes, they must break openly, as boxers from a clinch, and begin anew; strangle-holds, eye-gouging, punching, or the use of abrasive materials such as adhesive tape or peanuts, are technically forbidden. However, the referees as a group are typically ineffectual, a failing which the villain does not hesitate to exploit shamelessly. Thus, the responsibility devolves upon the crowd, to call the arbiter to his duty, to warn the hero and to shame the villain. There is a quality, not unlike the responses in a prayer-meeting, appealing but dignified, which inhere in the cries of "Rope!," "Peanut!," etc., that rise from the crowd.

Less than half the actual fighting time is spent at grips. A goodly bit passes in appeals to the referee and the crowd, and much to pacing and circling with gestures and grimaces of pain, wrath, or steely determination. The latter is the perquisite of the hero, and the villain's counter is the skulk or leer of menace. Naturally, there is a great range in ability of expression but a similarity in technique. For example, all good fellows must simulate blindness since, sooner or later, the villain rubs a peanut or a thumb into his eyes . . . The crowd knows better; sympathy and love for justice weld in a mighty current of feeling.

From: D.M. Fisher, "Circuses And Kings," Canadian Forum, August, 1950; From The WAWLI (Wrestling As We Liked It), Papers, 1(14), August 28th, 1996 Edited by J Michael Kenyon, Issue No. 595, Sunday, October 3rd, 1999, oldfallguy@aol.com

---

Who Is The (Wrestling) Crowd?

Some fifty fans, carrying lunches, waited five and a half hours under a blazing sun to be admitted to the studio. Most of them were women, many wearing their stockings rolled below their knees. They scrambled into the studio, pouncing on the front-row seats, and when they saw Cowboy Bill pass through the studio they greeted him profanely and obscenely with the sort of language used during race riots.

From: Myron Cope, "The Rich, Full Life Of A Bad Guy," Look Magazine, circa 1965, in The WAWLI (Wrestling As We Liked It), Papers, 1(14), August 28th,1996, Edited by J Michael Kenyon, Issue No. 595, Sunday, October 3rd, 1999, oldfallguy@aol.com

---

One basic social arrangement is the decline of class as an entity defining lifestyle and dress. In parts of feudal Europe, clothes were legally defined as proper or improper for certain persons to wear, based on lineage and occupation. By the nineteenth century, "class" was the main category linked to lifestyle and dress by many analysts. Maurice Halbwachs (1912) studied family budgets to quantify class outlooks in consumption. But by the 1960s, rich and poor grew often indistinguishable in dress and many aspects of lifestyle. Or more precisely, consumption grew increasingly divorced from production and work, such that individuality and self-expression were seen as so powerful that multiple social and political identities could explain more about consumption than one's job. How far have we come from the world of Marcel Proust, who composed his major works explicitly to capture the disappearing lifestyle of the aristocracy. Proust considered himself "nude" if he left the house sans hat, gloves, and cane (Langlois, 2002). The classic "explanation" of income or status permitting one to dress elegantly (as in Bourdieu, 1984) falls flat in considering many "lower status" groups like African-Americans, or even more powerfully the poorest residents of Rio, who save all year for their Mardi Gras costumes—not in most cases for tourism or work, but for the pleasure of personal consumption—which Langman (2002) elaborates. Countless similar religious festivals across Europe go back for centuries.

Most economies of the world have reached a point where income minimally determines dress and basic lifestyle activities; subcultural variations have more impact. We see this in views toward lifestyle issues differing in the three political cultures. Some of the most clear findings in the DDB lifestyle items concern African-Americans, who are among the most visible carriers of Traditional culture in the U.S., updating a (formerly aristocratic) aesthetic of elegance and sensuality to the point of shocking persons of Moralistic background. They are more visible than traditional southern whites since African-Americans have migrated across the U.S., are heavily featured in the national media and sports, and yet remain more segregated in housing, jobs, and many aspects of life than other ethnic groups (as documented in decades of research, such as O'Connor, Tilly & Bobo, 2001). Surely there is much ambivalence and subtlety about how, why, or why not specific cultural elements are passed on, even to one child but not another in the same family—this was a central theme motivating William Faulkner's four great novels (and his life, Blotner, 1974) exploring reverberations across generations of the aristocratic code of honor among blacks in intimate relations to whites. We are usually not conscious of such issues. Certainly few African-Americans today openly discuss historical origins of current cultural practices, like the street term "dis" to refer to a dishonoring action. Most members of any ethnic group are unclear about their pasts; but lack of self-consciousness need not diminish ethnic differences—as Greeley (1974) showed for such practices as Italian-Americans hugging their children, but not seeing it as Italian. That these issues remain so emotionally controversial for African-Americans some 140 years after the Civil War, and despite "Disnification," is powerful evidence for persistent cultural conflicts. The blending of such themes between current middle class and lower class blacks is subtly explored by Mary Pattillo-McCoy (1999). Lamont (2000) even argues that white American workers today derive much of their social identity by distinguishing themselves from "indulgent" and "risque" blacks.

The DDB shows substantial differences in consumption preferences and behaviors by African-Americans in comparison to other respondents. Differences are clearer if we separate black men and women, since black women are closer to white lifestyle patterns. Gender differences among African-Americans run deeper than for many other ethnic groups, for reasons historians and sociologists are still unraveling (e.g. Patterson, 1999). Some gender patterns recur in Africa and the Caribbean. Under slavery in the U.S. South, black men usually worked in the fields while some women worked in the master's house and were thus closer to white elite models. But unlike the Southern white highlanders, almost all blacks lived nearby whites. Even at the end of the nineteenth century, Max Weber noted that whites in Northern cities seemed threatened by blacks nearby, and thus moved to racially segregated neighborhoods—yet not in the South where black and white children played together in the streets. White supremacy was so unquestioned that personal relations did not threaten it in the South, but they did in the more egalitarian, individualistic, and socially insecure North.

Aspects of the traditional South are alive today in racial lifestyle differences. For instance, Black men and women, compared to other DDB respondents, are statistically more likely to favor legalizing marijuana, agree that "there should be a gun in every home," favor distributing condoms to high school students, and to say saving is a luxury they cannot afford. Black men and women report that they "went bowling" less than other Americans. Black men report that they rented X-rated movies and "went to a bar or tavern" in the last twelve months more often than other Americans, and less often "worked on a community project." However black women report less frequent visits to bars and were the same as Americans in general in working on community projects; they also report more frequent shopping for clothes, while black men shop less for clothes than other Americans. Are these results explained by current income as well as by race and cultural background, of which income is an obvious component? Surprisingly refuting the common materialist interpretation, in partial correlations of all these same variables, controlling for income, not one of the eighteen correlations mentioned above changes significantly. Are such lifestyle differences reactions against other aspects of racial discrimination or positive continuations of a deeper past? Surely both.

The "decline of hierarchy" is one of the deepest changes driving the New Political Culture. The same basic dynamics recur in transforming race relations as inside modern firms. New labels like flexible production, contracting out, the new public management, and new economy, have entered the economic lexicon to deal with more complex inter-organizational relations (cf. Florida, 2002). The term "governance," analogously, designates multiple public officials who negotiate among themselves to reach decisions—in direct contrast to the command and control model of large hierarchical organizations (government or corporate)—cf. Judge, Stoker and Wolman (1995). This mention of economic and governmental change reminds us of the diversity available in modern (or postmodern) societies, such that one is likely to find individuals following each of these competing outlooks in different locations.

A fundamental shift over the twentieth century was slimming of the family. Individuals became less family-integrated as migration increased for work, welfare state support rose for education, health and retirement, and married women increasingly worked outside the home. Indeed Miller (1995) suggests the family is in such decline that anthropologists should shift from kinship to consumption styles for the core of their discipline. Ritzer et al. (n.d.) maintain that the family has even lost sex: "its social functions—for example, binding together the nuclear family—have waned. Furthermore, the symbolic meaning of sex, upon which the entire Freudian edifice is based, seems to be in flux. Sex has entered fashion as part of the system of consumer objects. Everything is sexualized even as sex no longer really means anything in particular. Sex in the system of consumption promises meaning, just as advertised meanings promise sex, but both function merely as lures whose effect is to entice more objects into the fashion system."

(14) *As the family slims, individuals are left more to other sources of information and cultural orientation, including mass media, educational institutions, and age group peers. Similarly, social tolerance may rise, especially for new gender roles, children's rights, and autonomy of the elderly.*

(15) *Individuals from "slimmer families" will have weaker "family values" in the broad sense of sharing their concerns with family and others nearby, and are more likely to change both general orientations and specific preferences and behavior—since they have been exposed to more diversity outside a nuclear family from a younger age.*

Contrast here the popular image of the "homebody," the person who enjoys the values and activities in the confines of his or her home. These home/family lifestyle differences are likely to rechannel social processes. How?

(16) *Persons who spend more time at home are more socially integrated with values shared with others in the home, and less exposed to and less likely to respond to or engage in new forms of politics and culture. Home bodies should thus act less individualistically than those outside the home, not only because of differences in exposure, but since their stronger values of home and family should suppress impacts of other influences.*

(17) *As the main carriers of value change qua "home makers" or "family slimmers," women and their distinct roles take on large weight. While they may respond to broader national and religious group influences, as mothers and wives in their home contexts, they exert distinct impact on others around them, especially on new consumption and politics questions.*

Many family changes are captured in DDB survey items, such as how much time is spent outside the home, what are the authority figures for children (how much are they replaced by persons not in the family), time spent with the family, time at home, meals at home, women working outside the home—to describe one's life and how people evaluate them.

The "homebodies," as expected, generally support more "traditional" values and are less concerned with dressing well, according to our DDB results. But they do feel their cars reflect who they are more than those who support Women's Lib (Table 2.9).

Faulkner's older women in such novels as Absalom, Absalom are Ur-homebodies, living for decades in their homes without leaving the grounds. What should not be ignored, pace our propositions, is that such an outwardly local and parochial lifestyle can combine with deep and subtle understanding of human relations and the broader world. Indeed, this is one of Faulkner's larger

Table 2.9. The Moral Foundations of Women's Liberation and Couch Potatoes

	Pearson Correlation		
	I Think the Women's Liberation Movement is a Good Thing	A Woman's Place is in the Home	I Guess I'm what You would Call a "Couch Potato"
I am in favor of legalized abortions	.30**	-.24**	.03**
The government should restrict imported products	-.06**	.10**	.06**
Dressing well is an important part of my life	.05**	-.01**	-.11**
The car I drive is a reflection of who I am	.02**	.05**	.02*
Went to a club meeting (freq last 12 months)	-.01*	.01*	-.10**
Told a lie (freq last 12 months)	.04*	-.07**	.09**
If a cashier accidentally gives you too much change, I say it's OK to keep it	.13**	-.02	.13**
It's okay to cheat on your income taxes	.04*	-.02	.09**
I am in favor of very strict enforcement of all laws	-.14**	.19**	.a

Sources: DDB Lifestyle survey

.a Cannot be computed because at least one of the variables is constant.

* Correlation is significant at the 0.05 level (2-tailed).

** Correlation is significant at the 0.01 level (2-tailed).

messages, whose residents of rural Yoknapawpha County, Mississippi pursue Biblical adventures, exploring the entire human landscape in book after book. Introspection can drive the imagination of some like Jeremy Bentham, who reputedly stayed in his London home for years, or the older Marcel Proust, who wrote confined inside his cork-lined study, only occasionally touring late night Paris by coach.

(18) *The more the individual works in organizations that favor socially sensitive behavior (large firms, government agencies, strong unions, dense personal relations, etc.) the more that he or she will report the salience of personal influence relations in a wide range of non-work related matters, such as personal consumption and civic and political decisions.*

(19) *Causality can run from personal lifestyle and values to work and vice versa; there is much self-selection and turnover especially in U.S. work-places—many other societies have less, suggesting more congruence between workplace and personal values in the U.S. (or within a country, inside firms and contexts like big cities which foster higher turnover and migration).*

This idea might be tested by seeing if persons in cities with higher net migration rates, or looser social ties, have more heterogeneous attitudes and values, or behaviors as measured with various consumption data.

(20) *Individuals belong to many clubs and informal groups, like neighborhood or sports groups. These multiple membership patterns encourage "issue-*

specificity" and discourage general leadership. That is, individuals turn for advice and technical information to persons who have detailed knowledge in a specific issue area like recycling garbage or car repair. This issue-specificity contrasts with the traditional clientelist Padrone or patriarchal father or political party leader who exercised general leadership. Specialization of leadership in distinct issue areas is encouraged by the Internet, global social movements, non-profits, and a more educated, traveled, and consequently empowered citizenry. Issue-area leaders are typically more attuned to cosmopolitan sources of changing information (fashion magazines, new political ideas, Internet chat). Followers are content to act in a more parochial manner than leaders—in that single issue area. But unlike within the traditional hierarchical model, leaders in one issue area are followers in most others. Leadership is thus seen less as a general personality trait and as more narrowly circumscribed. "Collegiality," participatory management, networking, and governance are watchwords marking such new social patterns—as these often emerge from conflict with the older and more hierarchical patterns.

(21) *Individuals can activate their social contacts to achieve their personal goals more fully if they are connected to appropriate social networks. Social contacts thus become social capital.*

Proposition No. 21 is the core idea of Coleman (1990), Putnam (2000) and others. In Putnam's discussions, however, he strongly privileges the intense face-to-face contacts of traditional small towns, that "bond," and doubts the value of large membership organizations like the Sierra Club that link persons mainly through membership fees, even if these "bridge" socially diverse groups. Putnam's view may apply to citizen trust in leaders, for instance, but we should be cautious about denigrating "weak ties" (that bridge but not bond) as they may be important for work and more.

Everyone has strong and weak social ties. How do they operate to distinct effect? For instance weak ties may be more important for finding a job. For workers or employers, many weak ties provide potential job contacts. The contextual shifting condition here is a willingness to hire persons who you do not know closely or who are not recommended by close personal associates. In a business like retail insurance or home sales, more weak ties and wide contacts imply more potential customers. Or to push the logic even further, if you are highly connected to just one supplier of, say, computers, and that supplier does not upgrade with the rest of the market, you lag in computer power. Mancur Olson (1982) even argued that Japan and Germany developed their economies with great success after World War II because the unions and traditional organizations were weakened—as they had been compromised by association with fascism. By contrast in France and England, unions and political parties were stronger, and held down economic growth.

(22) *Very strong social capital can suppress innovative decisions.*

Think of the small parochial town that limits dissent. Or high school social groups that mandate what students can wear or say, and undermine intellectualization.

Urban Life Organizations In San Francisco, California, Illustrate Diversity And Specialization, And Often Visible Moral Focus, Especially For Environmentalism. More Issue-Specificity is Visible Here Than in Small Towns.

Action Resource Center
Alliance for Golden Gate Park
ArtSpan (San Francisco)
Bay Area Coalition for Urban Agriculture
Berkeley Peace and Justice Ministries Center (Berkeley)
Bike Traffic (San Francisco)
Brownfields Leadership and Community Revitalization
Project (San Francisco)
Center for Young Women's Development (San Francisco)
City CarShare (San Francisco)
Communities for a Better Environment (Oakland)
Craigslist (San Francisco)
Dedicated Urban Bikeways Project
Ecocity Builders (Berkeley)
Friends of the Urban Forest (San Francisco)
Glide Memorial United Methodist Church (San Francisco)
Green City Project (San Francisco)
Greenbelt Alliance (San Francisco)
International Bicycle
Fund Labor/Community Strategy Center
Literacy for Environmental Justice (San Francisco)
Mission Bay Community Church (San Francisco)
Right Of Way
San Francisco Bicycle Coalition (San Francisco)
San Francisco League of Urban Gardeners (San Francisco)
Solar Powered Urban Radio Transmissions
Surface Transportation Policy Project
Transportation Choices Forum (Oakland)
Urban Ecology, Inc. (Oakland)
Urban View (Oakland)
Urban Watershed Project (San Francisco)
Vegetation Management Video Project Committee
YouthBuild San Francisco (San Francisco)
Source: website listings.

But the logic of this argument can reverse itself. For instance, members of engineering professional associations may confer with each other on new products, but not feel compelled to buy from each other, or follow advice literally, since their ties are often weak. Systematizing:

(23) *In a dynamic industry like computer software or hardware, weak ties may be more important than strong ties in facilitating a flow of new ideas, personnel, products, and firms with whom one may work. Strong ties may potentially narrow one's search behavior and constrain options that one subjectively feels are appropriate (like not firing an incompetent lawyer since he is an old friend)*

(24) *In personal, sensitive issues—such as intimate lifestyle judgments, advice on major life course decisions, or handling an inheritance honorably after you are dead—strong ties trump weak ties. Still in most such instances the strength of the tie is a prior, but not the critical causal factor—which may be more deeply shared values and norms.*

An example of this last is the warring family whose members are deeply connected, but disagree over norms and values. In situations where the analyst lacks detailed data on shared norms and values, the strength of the social ties may be used as a (misleading) proxy for shared norms and values.

Gays Seek Adopt-a-Highway Sign and Get Cold Shoulder Policy: S. Dakota denies marker to an 'advocacy' body. Governor may scrap entire program

Los Angeles Times

August 15th, 2001.

By ERIC SLATER, TIMES STAFF WRITER

CHICAGO—The practicing pagans of Salt Lake City keep an eye on 2.9 miles of state highway. The Ashland, Ore., Friends of John Denver chapter has a two-mile stretch of Interstate 5. Nudists in Florida, Wiccans in New Jersey and the Ku Klux Klan of Missouri all have toiled to keep America clean through Adopt-a-Highway programs.

So the Sioux Empire Gay and Lesbian Coalition of Sioux City, S.D., figured they'd sign up for two miles of Highway 38, do their part and get a little state-sanctioned advertising in the process. The state Department of Transportation figured differently, saying the coalition was an "advocacy group" and would therefore not be issued an official roadside sign.

Advocacy seems a dubious rationale for disqualification: The College

Republicans, the Yankton County Democrats and the Animal Rights Advocates of South Dakota already have their names emblazoned along the state's highways. Now, nine months after the coalition filled out its application, rancor over the highway sign has grown to the point that Gov. William Janklow has threatened to scrap the entire program statewide, tearing down about one thousand signs proclaiming the good, trash-hauling deeds of everyone from the South Dakota Wheat Growers Assn. to the Rushmore Lions Club to various Rapid City Boy Scout troops.

Janklow said he would be especially perturbed if the coalition filed suit over such a well-intended program. Late Monday, it did just that, filing a federal complaint alleging equal protection and free speech violations.

"You may call it frivolous if you want to, governor, but, respectfully, let's call this what it is, 1st Amendment protection," said coalition President Barbara Himmel-Roberts.

Janklow, a colorful, conservative Republican dubbed by some critics "Wild Bill, the Indian Fighter," for his frequent head-butting with Native American tribes, was traveling Tuesday and could not be reached. He has said he would announce the program's fate by week's end.

The squabble has created deep divisions in the state over whether the group should be allowed to participate, with the American Civil Liberties Union coming down on the side of the coalition and the head of the religious Family Policy Council in Sioux Falls openly worrying that allowing them a roadway sign might lead to, say, same-sex marriages.

The DDB included several items like "people turn to me for advice." These permit analysis of personal influence impacts on various decisions.

Putnam (2000: for instance 98–105) made heavy use of DDB items to document the decline in social contacts among Americans, from 1975 to 1998, using Attended Church Service, Visited Relatives, Entertained at Home Last Year, and Played Cards. But he theorized minimally about strong versus weak ties; he focused more on overall decline, especially of stronger social ties.

We summed DDB items to generate two indexes, one for weak and one for strong social ties (Appendix 2). How do they relate to these widely debated issues?

We first look at strong and weak ties in relation to political confidence, support for government, and happiness—items closer to those considered by past analysts of social capital, from Coleman (1990) who stressed primary groups to explain voting turnout, Putnam (2000) on civic support, to Glaeser (2000), a brave urban economist who showed that social contacts increased happiness (per standard survey items) more than did jobs or income. Similarly family sociologists Waite and Gallagher (2000) showed that stable couples and marriage increase happiness. We find, no surprise, the same in the DBB items using the strong ties measure to explain similar items. And strong ties as expected have more impact than weak ties on these items—concerning personal

---

New York Times

January 10th, 2001

Ads Now Seek Recruits for "An Army of One"

By JAMES DAO

WASHINGTON, Jan. 9th—In the most sweeping revision of its marketing practices in two decades, the Army this week will scrap its memorable advertising slogan, "Be all you can be," and replace it with one intended to appeal to the individualism and independence of today's youth: "An Army of one."

Based on research showing that young people view military life as dehumanizing, the motto will be the centerpiece of a $150 million campaign that uses slick commercials, a new logo and an interactive Web site, GoArmy.com, to bolster the Army's recruiting programs, which have missed their goals two of the last three years.

It all kicks off when the Army premieres the first of its new commercials not during a Sunday football game, as might have been the case in the past, but during the popular NBC sitcom "Friends" this Thursday night. The Army has been criticized for broadcasting too many advertisements during televised sporting events, and the choice of "Friends" is intended to help broaden its audience and shake off its stodgy, male-only image. The commercial will also appear during "The Simpsons" on Fox and "Buffy the Vampire Slayer" on WB, among other programs, and on MTV, Comedy Central and Channel 1, which is broadcast in high schools.

The 60-second spot, produced by the Army's new advertising agency, Leo Burnett U.S.A. of Chicago, tries to counter what Army officials said was the widespread perception among young men and women that soldiers were faceless, nameless cogs in an impersonal military machine.

The commercial features a lone corporal running across the barren terrain of the Mojave Desert at dawn. At one point, a squad of soldiers runs past in the opposite direction; later, a Blackhawk helicopter flies by overhead. But the corporal never veers from his solitary path, panting under the weight of his 35-pound pack as his polished dog tags glint brilliantly in the rising sun.

"Even though there are 1,045,690 soldiers just like me, I am my own force," the corporal, Richard P. Lovett, says. "With technology, with training, with support, who I am has become better than who I was."

"And I'll be the first to tell you, the might of the U.S. Army doesn't lie in numbers," Corporal Lovett continues. "It lies in me. I am an Army of one."

It might seem incongruous for the Army, which for two centuries has trained its recruits in the art of selflessness and unit cohesion, to promote itself as an incubator of self-actualization. Indeed, in recent decades many military officials have come to view the armed forces as a redoubt against unbridled individualism.

But Louis Caldera, the departing secretary of the Army, who initiated and championed the marketing makeover, said that no one should be worried that the Army is advocating self-centered behavior.

"They are going to get the ethic of selfless service, duty, honor and country in basic training and in every unit they are assigned to," Mr. Caldera said. "But you've got to get them in the door to try selfless service. And you've got to let them know that even though it is about selfless service, they are still individuals . . ."

Under Mr. Caldera, the Army created a four-person marketing office at the Pentagon. It hired McKinsey & Company and RAND to review marketing practices and conduct an extensive survey of potential recruits. And it ended its thirteen-year relationship with Young & Rubicam, hiring Leo Burnett last summer to be its lead advertising agency. Leo Burnett's clients include McDonald's, Walt Disney and Coca-Cola.

relations with other friends and citizens in general. But if we shift to items about honesty of leaders, the story changes: weak and strong ties are equally important in generating the response that leaders and the press are honest. Most of these items were asked in only a few years by the DDB, so the Ns were too low for most regressions that we sought to estimate (Table 2.10).

To test the ideas in Propositions No. 23 about new ideas, we use the number of patents issued by the U.S. Patent Office, classified by the county of residence of the first-named patent holder. We started with all 1.2 million patents issued to U.S. residents from January 1st, 1975 to December 31st, 1999. The patent holders were recorded by zip code, so these were assigned to each of 3,111 U.S. counties. The Patent Office records patents into 434 classes. We broke these into three types: Patents concerned with Entertainment, High Tech and Other. The fifty highest ranked counties for total patents are listed in Table 2.11, which also shows the three types. The three types are highly intercorrelated: $r =$ from 0.77 to 0.82. We also computed patents per capita, which elevates smaller locations, like Rochester and Steuben, NY where Xerox, Kodak and Steuben Glass downsized major facilities, leading former employees to found hundreds of small firms—and win patents for their inventions. These high-ranking counties are often suburban parts of large metro areas. Patents are analyzed in regressions in the next chapter.

STATUS CONCERNS VS. "INHERENT" CHARACTERISTICS

Identifying the status message of clothes or homes is a classic activity of novelists and social scientists like Thorstein Veblen who coined the term "conspi-

Table 2.10. Strong and Weak Ties and their Associations

	Pearson Correlation	
	Index Weak Ties SUM	Index Strong Ties SUM
I worry a lot about myself or a family member becoming a victim of a crime	-.07**	.02**
I'm much happier now than I ever was before	.09**	.15**
Most people are honest	.06**	.13**
An honest man cannot get elected to high office	-.09**	-.07**
You really can't trust the news media to cover events and issues fairly	-.01*	-.02*
I wish I could leave my present life and do something entirely different	-.08**	-.11**
I am very satisfied with the way things are going in my life these days	.14**	.19**

Notes: The Indexes of Weak and Strong ties are detailed in the appendix.
Sources: DDB Lifestyle survey
* Correlation is significant at the 0.05 level (one-tailed).
** Correlation is significant at the 0.01 level (one-tailed).

cuous consumption." Max Weber similarly stressed that status and honor were distinct from economic activities. Analogously, Marcel Mauss famously documented in The Gift how some preliterate tribes were so insistent on demonstrating their status by offering gifts to other tribes, that they could devastate themselves economically. These concepts suggest, if nothing else, the indeterminacy of income. The danger here is overemphasis, reading consumption as primarily or exclusively as "conspicuous," the common tendency in works like Bourdieu's (1984) Distinction. Or Baudrillard (1970) and many post-materialists (Harvey, 1990) who discuss signs and symbols so minutely that they seem to forget that clothes also serve non-status functions, like keeping warm.

Every human is not equally concerned about status. And types of status vary considerably. Persons who "dress to kill" may care little about how to replace a PC hard drive. But hard drive experts may reciprocate by dressing with indifference. There are potentially as many status dimensions or "situses" as there are human activities and dreams. Many writers too facilely assume that status is one clear dimension.

How does status relate to personal influence or atomistic individualism? Atomistic individuals can still have high status consciousness. Thorstein Veblen's conspicuous consumption or clothing subtleties of teenage "crowds" may be pursued by atomistic individuals in market-like contexts. Or, the same actions may come from personal influence by friends. The lack of "status consciousness" by some persons may remain invisible to status-oriented analysts. But it is

Table 2.11. Counties Ranked by Total Patents Registered with US Patent Office, 1975-1998 (Top Fifty Counties Only)

COUNTY	Total Patents	Entertainment Patents	HighTech Patents	Other Patents
Los Angeles, CA	41,369	5,240	4,173	32,007
Santa Clara, CA	40,526	3,168	8,598	29,096
Cook, IL	29,220	3,511	4,096	21,634
Middlesex, MA	22,796	1,831	4,759	16,307
Orange, CA	21,945	2,010	3,398	16,571
Harris, TX	20,327	1,036	3,736	15,646
Monroe, NY	19,186	2,074	1,288	15,837
San Diego, CA	17,615	1,631	3,217	12,795
Oakland, MI	15,286	836	1,048	13,406
Maricopa, AZ	13,478	1,160	1,517	10,902
Fairfield, CT	12,947	1,012	2,386	9,574
DuPage, IL	12,845	1,003	1,836	10,018
Dallas, TX	12,745	1,011	1,188	10,586
Allegheny, PA	12,537	550	2,112	9,878
King, WA	11,643	1,216	2,234	8,250
Hennepin, MN	11,053	1,029	2,206	7,843
Alameda, CA	10,396	889	1,997	7,553
Cuyahoga, OH	10,037	649	1,599	7,794
San Mateo, CA	9,959	942	2,163	6,888
Wayne, MI	9,658	495	1,177	7,988
Westchester, NY	9,535	1,120	1,922	6,524
Morris, NJ	9,396	615	2,326	6,461
Lake, IL	9,279	866	2,109	6,311
New Castle, DE	8,871	348	3,682	4,844
Montgomery, PA	8,691	446	3,238	5,016
Travis, TX	8,430	672	3,185	4,737
Mercer, NJ	8,298	627	2,629	5,047
New York, NY	8,297	1,487	1,848	4,981
Hamilton, OH	8,172	654	1,963	5,555
Bergen, NJ	7,751	831	1,863	5,059
Middlesex, NJ	7,750	667	2,404	4,682
Union, NJ	7,691	389	2,437	4,881
Monmouth, NJ	7,663	886	1,125	5,663
Somerset, NJ	7,651	411	2,875	4,374
Montgomery, MD	7,490	503	1,596	5,414
Hartford, CT	7,209	317	448	6,447
New Haven, CT	6,940	364	1,653	4,931
Nassau, NY	6,757	1,059	628	5,074
Contra Costa, CA	6,613	404	1,505	4,711
St. Louis, MO	6,534	449	1,503	4,587
Norfolk, MA	6,259	487	1,357	4,438
Suffolk, NY	6,245	628	611	5,014
Summit, OH	6,022	229	2,073	3,721
Washington, MN	5,949	280	1,443	4,230
Bucks, PA	5,703	387	3,859	1,459
Macomb, MI	5,571	312	4,962	297
Marion, IN	5,565	607	3,092	1,868

Sources: US Patent Office. The county of the first named holder of the patent on the cover sheet was used to generate the county scores. Data coded and cleaned by Bob Cushing, University of Texas.

captured by social labels like "nerds" and similar colorful terms that (socially sensitive) teenagers and others apply to those

The lack of "status consciousness" by some persons may remain invisible to status-oriented analysts. But it is captured by social labels like "nerds" and similar colorful terms that (socially sensitive) teenagers and others apply to those "killjoys" who snub or ignore status hierarchies.

The DDB survey includes items like "The car I drive is a reflection of who I am," "The clothes I wear reflect who I am as a person," and "Dressing well is an important part of my life." These nicely link status concern to consumption specifics. We can thus test how much such status consciousness drives decisions. For instance status consciousness may be critical for buying a hula hoop or designer shoes, but unimportant for an auto muffler. Lacking a better term, we label as "inherent" those products or actions that are insignificant for status. Novelists have long noted that the same action shifts in meaning as people move socially, like eating by hungry cowboys on a ranch, or eating at an elegant restaurant. These are sharp illustrations of how labeling or framing an action can be "inherent" in one context but "status-conferring" in another, and consequently how each is socially constructed. Goffman (1986) pushes this logic in multiple directions, introducing such concepts as "keying" a "strip of activity" like "dressing" to a status concern, for instance, and then transforming and retransforming "dressing" and contexts in multiple ways to generate satirical or dramatic resonances.

DESIGN DISPATCH: THE CZAR DIDN'T SLEEP HERE
The New York Times

January 9th, 2003

by Sophia Kishkovsky

"It's not respectable to be a bandit," Mr. Kharit said. "Now everyone wants to be an aristocrat . . ."

(Building) country estates, known as usadby, for a new class of Russians who have grown wealthy ... Nastya Yegorova, a Moscow architect who has designed three usadby, said she even created a coat of arms to mount on the facade of one family's usadba. "Everyone is promoting their name," she said. "They want to create origins, an aristocracy. All of that was cut off so suddenly here. Now they want to restore it."

In a modern twist on the usadba concept, Konti, a Moscow developer, has built an usadba condominium complex called Pokrovskoye-Glebovo on the grounds of an old estate, long since fallen into ruin, where Catherine the Great took tea and Tolstoy met his future wife. Not surprisingly, Konti is playing up the history: its promotional booklet calls the complex a "XXI century aristocratic estate" and says that residents can rightly call themselves "new aristocrats."

The complex, which will have a formal garden based on Peter the Great's Peterhof and Bach piped into the parking garage, was the brainchild of Timur Timerbulatov, a developer and former Soviet tank commander who is known for giving building sizes in tank lengths and making sarcastic references to Marx. Ninety percent of the completed apartments have been sold, at up to $1 million, according to Konit.

(25) *Persons and decisions vary in their status-sensitivity, which shifts the import of different causal mechanisms. For persons and decisions where status is important, the prestige of the brand, social visibility of the object, and related social-status characteristics affect their decisions. By contrast, for less status-conscious persons, status-related factors should be weaker or insignificant for their decisions. The same individual may vary in status concern across issue-areas (dressing for a wedding versus dressing to work in a private garden).*

While we commonly speak of persons as concerned or not concerned with status, variations in concern by issue area has been minimally explored. Yet the diversity of responses to the more specific DDB items suggests that the totally "consistent" consumer is no more likely to exist than the totally consistent voter—which Converse suggested was less that 5 percent of the U.S. population.

Status involves evaluation of a person or activity in terms of a deeper value, like occupational achievement. This makes explicit the distinctiveness of multiple status hierarchies in societies with competing values. Rather than assume that "everyone" responds favorably to conspicuous clothes or automobiles—as one might imagine from too much TV viewing—look for signs of diversity, and they are there. For instance, on many campus newsstands, worldwide, one now finds a magazine called *Adbusters*. Its theme is "I want you to curb your consumption," repeated in multiple languages and with strident anti-intuitive photos—such as a masked young man about to throw a bouquet of flowers. The Vancouver-based magazine promotes a Buy Nothing Day, "you have twenty-four hours and nothing on your shopping list," and similar activist suggestions. There is a huge and growing literature and web-based industry of such environment-friendly, anti-traditional consumption suggestions, alternative technologies, of all political and moralistic stripes. Major foundations and corporations have recognized the breadth of support for these matters, and now feature them in marketing, such as Benetton clothes stressing a cosmopolitan austerity, of sorts, or McDonalds' featuring animal-friendly procedures. The MIT Press lists a huge array of books on environmentally-friendly topics, like *Confronting Consumption* and *Greening the Ivory Tower.*

Objects or activities do not convey status; only observers' reactions do. Hula hoops, high-end designer shoes, or exclusive club membership may be status linked. But to show first that that they were chosen for status reasons, and second that they do confer status is complex. The analyst should ideally demonstrate the individual's status-seeking concern by determining its subjective importance to the individual and its significance to others. How to do so properly has fueled huge debates over revealed preferences, strategy, subliminal advertising, and more. Even ascetic exercisers can wear high-end Nike shoes, and rotate with hula hoops at select health clubs. If two adjacent persons dress and act identically, one may be forcefully driven by status, yet the other minimally.[7]

People also invoke different "reference groups" which interpret status differently. One's parents or childhood friends may be critical reference groups for aesthetics and basic values, more than current work associates, for instance, who may have quite different views. This complicates status assessment. But this is also why status can enliven so many novels and style magazines; it is evanescent enough to provide employment for armies of consultants, interpreters, and would-be status-conferrers. Some charge high fees, even if Aunt Suzie does not.

Our approach to such Chinese-box problems is not to pursue cases individually, but to identify broader principles that cover classes of activities—like honor for Traditionalists or status-seeking for Individualists. And to recognize the value of contextualizing or framing concepts like issue area or reference groups. In avoiding the smaller byways, this still provides a general map to the consumer landscape.

THE COMMUNITY CONTEXT

It is hard to ski or hunt in Times Square, or see live opera in Alaska. Contexts shift options. Persons sharing individual preferences consequently shift their actions as they move to different contexts. These obvious technical and physical constraints are paralleled by socio-political and economic constraints: thus Mormons practice polygamy in Utah, but with difficulty outside that state. The Big City has long been the sponge drawing small-town folk by offering Freie Luft, via more impersonality and social distance from neighbors. People act more freely in (many) big cities.

These classic urban observations have nevertheless been largely ignored by even astute observers like Robert Putnam (2000). His *Bowling Alone* analyzed individual respondents mainly sans context. Arguably this omission is often due "simply" to lack of data, but this is too forgiving. That is, the survey research approach launched by Lazarsfeld and others at Columbia was transformed in the 1960s when the University of Michigan led in studies of politics and consumer confidence. In Ann Arbor, the community context was largely lost. The Michigan method was predominantly sample surveys of some 1,500 individuals from across the U.S., chosen as a "representative" sample of citizens. By contrast the Columbia researchers designed studies to see how social and community contexts affected individuals, as in *Union Democracy* (Lipset, Trow & Coleman, 1956) where respondents were surveyed in big and small, hierarchical and participatory branches of a union, etc.

The recent combination of multiple data sets mentioned in the Introduction is doubly attractive: it permits studying community impacts as well as individuals. It combines the best of both traditions: Columbia context and Michigan national representativeness. Since the DDB items are not for 1,500 citizens, but some eighty-thousand, and the PEW survey is over twenty-five thousand, these Ns are large enough to map each citizen by county. The local context can then be joined to the individual by merging data from the Census (population size, income, etc.) and data like patents and opera added from other sources. We can thus directly study contextual effects, as is explored in Chapters 3 and 7.

Some illustrative hypotheses concerning context:

(26) *The more homogenous the local community, the more likely are personal influence and status-concerns to dominate individual decisions. That is, if people see few exceptions, they are less likely to deviate (or report deviation in a survey).*

(27) *The bigger the city's population, the higher the density, and shorter the length of residence, the less salient are personal influence and status concerns. This is a near corollary of No. 26.*

(28) *The more affluent and highly educated are local citizens, and the more professional their employment (which rewards autonomous work habits), the more politically empowered they should feel, and the more they should report individual choice-driven decisions rather than personal influence or status-driven decisions.*

(29) *Locations with more Catholics should suppress effects from individual (atomistic) characteristics. The same should hold more generally for members of religious groups that stress sociability and personal relations over individual action and salvation.*

(30) *Locations with deeper penetration of mass media (newspapers, television, radio, Internet use) should exhibit weaker personal influence and community context effects.*

Two major contextual characteristics are political culture, used repeatedly through the chapter, and urban amenities, explored in Chapters 3 and 7.

CONCLUSION

This chapter has codified a core set of ideas for a theory of political consumption. Drawing on five literatures, we have constructed a body of propositions to encourage more direct assessment, refutation, or extension by others. Propositions start with social characteristics of individuals to explain their preferences, then add deeper values, personal influence relations, status concerns, and contextual characteristics. Throughout we have posited linkages joining atomistic individuals to group constraints and socio-economic contexts. These in turn shift in impact with three types of political cultures—Moralistic, Individualistic, and Traditional, found in different combinations worldwide.

This approach helps specify how and why ideas presented as universal in fact shift substantially within different political cultures. Specifically ideas like Veblen's conspicuous consumption, Bourdieu's distinction, and Inglehart's post-materialist hypothesis vary across political cultures. Some past theories treated citizens as cogs in a political machine, members of social classes, or as manipulated objects of the mass media. We suggest that these views grow less adequate in a Post-Industrial Society where a New Political Culture defines new rules of the game for consumption and politics. Some key new rules are specified along with dynamics for their change.

We tested some critical illustrative propositions using some of the most powerful data ever assembled for political consumption research. The data combine the DDB Lifestyle Survey of 84,989 American citizens with Census data on counties where these citizens reside, plus other data such as patents. We created indexes of the three political cultures and of strong and weak network ties, explained in the Appendix. Central themes from this chapter are explored in later chapters.

ACKNOWLEDGMENTS

Thanks to Liza Weinstein, Alex Chandler, Josh McFeeters, Lauren Langman, Jean-Yves Nevers, George Ritzer, and Jennifer Novak for comments and assistance.

APPENDIX 1: THE THREE CULTURAL INDEXES

Three culture indexes—Moralistic, Individualist, and Traditional—were computed from the following DDB Lifestyle Survey Items.

Moralistic Index: COMPUTE Moral2 = NewEng + ABORTION + RECYCLE + WOMENLIB + POLLUT + CLUBMEET + FAMCHILD − (DRESS + WOMPLACE).

NewEng was a dummy variable for response 1 to GEOGRAPH

331 GEOGRAPH Region of interview
1. New England
2. Mid-Atlantic
3. E. North Central
4. W. North Central
5. S. Atlantic
6. E. South Central
7. W. South Central
8. Mountain
9. Pacific

108 ABORTION I am in favor of legalized abortions
1. Definitely Disagree
2. Generally Disagree
3. Moderately Disagree
4. Moderately Agree
5. Generally Agree
6. Definitely Agree

71 RECYCLE Collected things for recycling (freq last 12 months)
1. None
2. 1–4 times
3. 5–8 times
4. 9–11 times
5. 12–24 times
6. 25–51 times
7. 52+ times

235 WOMENLIB I think the women's Liberation Movement is a good thing
1. Definitely Disagree
2. Generally Disagree
3. Moderately Disagree
4. Moderately Agree
5. Generally Agree
6. Definitely Agree

203 POLLUT I support pollution standards even if it   1. Definitely Disagree

means shutting down some factories

2. Generally Disagree
3. ModeratelyDisagree
4. Moderately Agree
5. Generally Agree
6. Definitely Agree

24 CLUBMEET Went to a club meeting
(freq last 12 months)

1. None
2. 1–4 times
3. 5–8 times
4. 9–11 times
5. 12–24 times
6. 25–51 times
7. 52+ times

145 FAMCHILD When making important family
decisions, consideration of the
children should come first

1. Definitely Disagree
2. Generally Disagree
3. Moderately Disagree
4. Moderately Agree
5. Generally Agree
6. Definitely Agree

139 DRESS Dressing well is an important part
of my life

1. Definitely Disagree
2. Generally Disagree
3. Moderately Disagree
4. Moderately Agree
5. Generally Agree
6. Definitely Agree

236 WOMPLACE A Woman's place is in the home

1. Definitely Disagree
2. Generally Disagree
3. Moderately Disagree
4. Moderately Agree
5. Generally Agree
6. Definitely Agree

Individualistic Index: Compute Indls1 = MidAtl + ADVICE + INFLUENT + LEADER + LOOKDIFF + SELFCON

MidAlt was a dummy variable for response 2 from

331 GEOGRAPH Region of interview

1. New England
2. Mid-Atlantic
3. E. North Central
4. W. North Central

5. S. Atlantic
6. E. South Central
7. W. South Central
8. Mountain
9. Pacific

112 ADVICE My friends and neighbors often
come to me for advice about products and
brands

1. Definitely Disagree
2. Generally Disagree
3. Moderately Disagree
4. Moderately Agree
5. Generally Agree
6. Definitely Agree

171 INFLUENT I am influential in my neighborhood

1. Definitely Disagree
2. Generally Disagree
3. Moderately Disagree
4. Moderately Agree
5. Generally Agree
6. Definitely Agree

176 LEADER I like to be considered a leader

1. Definitely Disagree
2. Generally Disagree
3. Moderately Disagree
4. Moderately Agree
5. Generally Agree
6. Definitely Agree

182 LOOKDIFF I want to look a little different
from others

1. Definitely Disagree
2. Generally Disagree
3. Moderately Disagree
4. Moderately Agree
5. Generally Agree
6. Definitely Agree

217 SELFCON I have more self confidence than
most of my friends

1. Definitely Disagree
2. Generally Disagree
3. Moderately Disagree
4. Moderately Agree
5. Generally Agree
6. Definitely Agree

Traditional Index: Compute Trad1 = South + BOSS + DRESS + MENLEAD + WOMPLACE + BUYAMER + ANYFUN + CARSELF + CLUBMEET − (WOMENLIB + ABORTION).
South was a dummy variable, for responses 5, 6, and 7 of

331 GEOGRAPH Region of interview

1. New England
2. Mid-Atlantic
3. E. North Central
4. W. North Central
5. S. Atlantic
6. E. South Central
7. W. South Central
8. Mountain
9. Pacific

121 BOSS The father should be the boss in the house

1 Definitely Disagree
2. Generally Disagree
3. Moderately Disagree
4. Moderately Agree
5. Generally Agree
6. Definitely Agree

139 DRESS Dressing well is an important part of my life

1. Definitely Disagree
2. Generally Disagree
3. Moderately Disagree
4. Moderately Agree
5. Generally Agree
6. Definitely Agree

185 MENLEAD Men are naturally better leaders than women

1. Definitely Disagree
2. Generally Disagree
3. Moderately Disagree
4. Moderately Agree
5. Generally Agree
6. Definitely Agree

236 WOMPLACE A Woman's place is in the home

1. Definitely Disagree
2. Generally Disagree
3. Moderately Disagree
4. Moderately Agree
5. Generally Agree
6. Definitely Agree

123 BUYAMER Americans should always try to buy American products

1. Definitely Disagree
2. Generally Disagree
3. Moderately Disagree
4. Moderately Agree

5. Generally Agree
6. Definitely Agree

114 ANYFUN I enjoy parties, games, shows
—anything for fun

1. Definitely Disagree
2. Generally Disagree
3. Moderately Disagree
4. Moderately Agree
5. Generally Agree
6. Definitely Agree

124 CARSELF The car I drive is a reflection
of who I am

1. Definitely Disagree
2. Generally Disagree
3. Moderately Disagree
4. Moderately Agree
5. Generally Agree
6. Definitely Agree

1. None
2. 1–4 times
3. 5–8 times
4. 9–11 times
5. 12–24 times
6. 25–51 times
7. 52+ times

24 CLUBMEET Went to a club meeting (freq
last 12 months)

1. Definitely Disagree
2. Generally Disagree
3. Moderately Disagree
4. Moderately Agree
5. Generally Agree
6. Definitely Agree

235 WOMENLIB I think the women's liberation movement is a good thing

1. Definitely Disagree
2. Generally Disagree
3. Moderately Disagree
4. Moderately Agree
5. Generally Agree
6. Definitely Agree

108 ABORTION I am in favor of legalized abortions

1. Definitely Disagree
2. Generally Disagree
3. Moderately Disagree
4. Moderately Agree
5. Generally Agree
6. Definitely Agree

APPENDIX 2: STRONG AND WEAK TIES

No items are in both categories of strong and weak ties. NETWORK variables generally ordered from weak to strong ties. The network variables were chosen (from all DDB variables) using these criteria:

"Network" activities involve other people.
"Network" activities (variables) increase the potential (resources) of meeting (getting to know) other people.
"Network" variables indicate the intensity of (strong) relations.

Weak ties
Lower degree of multiplexity.
Purpose of an activity clearly stated and defined (more formal rules involved) e.g. sport.
Strangers, colleagues, friends, neighbors and family are involved.
Increases one's potential to meet (get to know) strangers.

Strong ties
Higher degree of multiplexity (multiplex ties).
Purpose of activity lies more on being together. More stress on relational roles, positive emotional involvement expected, reciprocal ties. Face-to-face experience involved.
Colleagues, friends, neighbors and family are involved. Strengthens one's already established ties.

Table A2.2.1. ***WEAK TIES*: LIST OF QUESTIONS THAT CAN BE CONSIDERED TO COMPOSE AN INDEX OF WEAK TIES**

DDB Codebook Question	Var Name	Question	Scale
Note: INTERNET—Extremely weak (loose) ties:			
275	CHATROOM	Internet/World Wide Web in the last 12 months to participate in a chat room or online forum.	0 No, 1 Yes
276	CYBRDATE	Have you yourself used the Internet/World Wide Web in the last 12 months to go on a "cyber date?"	0 No, 1 Yes

Table A2.2.1. (Continued)

DDB Codebook Question	Var Name	Question	Scale
Note: INTERNET—Weak (loose) ties:			
278	SNTEMAIL	Have you yourself used the Internet/World Wide Web in the last 12 months to send electronic mail	0 No, 1 Yes
Note: Impersonal Contacts (weak ties)			
33	ENVCONS	Contributed to an environmental or conservation organization	Freq 12: 1–7
51	LETTER	Wrote a letter to an editor of a magazine or newspaper (freq	Freq 12: 1–7
60	OFFICIAL	Contacted a public official (freq last 12 months)	Freq 12: 1–7
Note: ENTERTAINMENT (Activities)—Weak ties (Sports and Entertainment we think one would not do alone)			
223	SPORTFAN	I am an avid sport fan	Agree: 1–6
4	ACATHEVT	Attended amateur or college athletic event (freq last 12 months)	Freq 12: 1–7
7	BEERBAR	Went to a bar or tavern (freq last 12 months)	Freq 12: 1–7
14	CAMPING	Went camping (freq last 12 months)	Freq 12: 1–7
18	CARDS	Played cards (freq last 12 months)	Freq 12: 1–7
22	CLASSIC	Went to a classical concert (freq last 12 months)	Freq 12: 1–7
37	FISHING	Went fishing (freq last 12 months)	Freq 12: 1–7
43	HIKING	Went hiking (freq last 12 months)	Freq 12: 1–7
46	HUNTING	Went hunting (freq last 12 months)	Freq 12: 1–7
50	LECTURE	Attended a lecture (freq last 12 months)	Freq 12: 1–7

Table A2.2.1. (Continued)

DDB Codebook Question	Var Name	Question	Scale
	57	MATHEVNT	Attended a
men's amateur		Freq 12: 1–7 athletic event (freq last 12 months)	
58	MOVIES	Went to the movies (freq last 12 months)	Freq 12: 1–7
62	PATHEVNT	Attended a professional athletic event (freq last 12 months)	Freq 12: 1–7
64	PICNIC	Went on a picnic (freq last 12 months)	Freq 12: 1–7
67	POPROCK	Went to a pop or rock concert (freq last 12 months)	Freq 12: 1–7
70	RACEAUTO	Went to an auto race (NASCAR, Formula 1, etc.) (freq last 12 months)	Freq 12: 1–7
78	SKIBOARD	Went snow skiing or Snowboarding (freq last 12 months)	Freq 12: 1–7
79	SKIING	Went skiing (freq last 12 months)	Freq 12: 1–7
80	SNOWSKI	Went snow skiing (freq last 12 months)	Freq 12: 1–7
83	SPORTING	Attended a sporting event (freq last 12 months)	Freq 12: 1–7
88	VACATION	Went on a vacation (freq last 12 months)	Freq 12: 1–7
89	VACTRP	Took a vacation trip (freq last 12 months)	Freq 12: 1–7
91	VISART	Visited an art gallery or museum (freq last 12 months)	Freq 12: 1–7
97	WATHEVNT	Attended a women's amateur athletic event (women's college game)	Freq 12: 1–7
99	ZOO	Went to a zoo (freq last 12 months	Freq 12: 1–7
104	MOVIE6	Going to the movies (frequency of your activity now compared to this time last year	Comp: 1–5

Table A2.2.1. (Continued)

DDB Codebook Question	Var Name	Question	Scale
Note: ENTERTAINMENT (Activities)—Weak ties (Team Activities)			
34	EXCLASS	Went to an exercise class (freq last 12 months)	Freq 12: 1–7
11	BOWLING	Went bowling (freq last 12 months)	Freq 12: 1–7
74	SCHOOL	Attended school (freq last 12 months)	Freq 12: 1–7
21	CLASS	Attended a class or seminar (freq last 12 months)	Freq 12: 1–7
94	VOLUNT	Did volunteer work (freq last 12 months)	Freq 12: 1–7
27	COMMPROJ	Worked on a community project (freq last 12 months)	Freq 12: 1–7
86	TEAMSPRT	Played a team sport (basketball, softball, volleyball,	Freq 12: 1–7
81	SOFTBALL	Played softball (freq last 12 months)	Freq 12: 1–7
93	VOLLEYB	Played volleyball (freq last 12 months)	Freq 12: 1–7
40	GOLF	Played golf (freq last 12 months)	Freq 12: 1–7
87	TENNIS	Played tennis (freq last 12 months)	Freq 12: 1–7
56	LUNCHRES	Went out to lunch at a restaurant (freq last 12 months)	Freq 12: 1–7
24	CLUBMEET	Went to a club meeting (freq last 12 months)	Freq 12: 1–7
20	CHURCH	Attended church or other place of worship (freq last 12	Freq 12: 1–7

Table A2.2.2. *STRONG TIES*: LIST OF QUESTIONS THAT CAN BE CONSIDERED TO COMPOSE AN INDEX OF STRONG TIES

List of Scales:
Freq 12: 1–7
Agree: 1–6
Comp: 1–5
0 No, 1 Yes
Note: There are four different scales listed below the variables lists (at the end of this Memo).

Table A2.2.2. (Continued)

DDB Codebook Question	Var Name	Question	Scale
Note: FRIENDS/COLLEAGUES WEAK TO STRONG ties:			
112	ADVICE	My friends and neighbors often come to me for advice about products and brands	Agree: 1–6
171	INFLUENT	I am influential in my neighborhood	Agree: 1–6
122	BRANDADC	I often seek out the advice of my friends regarding brands and products	Agree: 1–6
52	LETTFRD	Write a letter to a friend or Relative (freq last 12 months)	Freq 12: 1–7
294	LDPHOCL	How often you yourself make a long distance phone call to friend or family?	Freq 12: 1–7
15	ARDEVNT	Sent a greeting card in honor of an event in someone's life (anniversary, birthday,	Freq 12: 1–7
16	CARDHOLI	Sent a greeting card on a holiday (Christmas, Mother's Day, etc.) (freq last 12 month	Freq 12: 1–7
17	CARDNOSP	Sent a greeting card on no special occasion (just to keep in touch, say hello etc.)	Freq 12: 1–7
41	GREETING	Sent a greeting card (freq last 12 months)	Freq 12: 1–7
65	PLANEPER	Took an airplane trip for personal reasons (freq last 12 months)	Freq 12: 1–7
101	DINNER6	Going out to dinner (frequency of your activity now compared to this time last year)	Comp: 1–5
30	DINPARTY	Gave or attended a dinner party (freq last 12 months)	Freq 12: 1–7
31	DINRES	Went out to dinner at a restaurant (freq last 12 months)	Freq 12: 1–7

Table A2.2.2. (Continued)

DDB Codebook Question	Var Name	Question	Scale
32	ENTHOME	Entertained people in my home (freq last 12 months)	Freq 12: 1–7
102	ENTHOM6	Entertaining in my home (frequency of your activity now compared to this time last year)	Comp: 1–5
5	ADULTPUZ	Bought a toy, game, or puzzle for an adult (freq last 12 months)	Freq 12: 1–7
106	TIMEFAM6	Spending time with friends and family (frequency of your activity now compared to this	Comp: 1–5
231	VISFRD	I spend a lot of time visiting friends	Agree: 1–6

Note: FAMILY STRONG ties: (Weak to strong)

105	STAYHOM6	Staying home (frequency of your activity now compared to this time last year) (–)	Comp: 1–5
164	HOME	I would rather spend a quiet evening at home than go out to a party	Agree: 1–6
224	STAYHOME	I stay home most evenings (–)	Agree: 1–6
114	ANYFUN	I enjoy parties, games, shows— anything for fun	Agree: 1–6
294	LDPHOCL	How often you yourself make a long distance phone call to friend or family?	Freq 12: 1–7
52	LETTFRD	Write a letter to a friend or Relative (freq last 12 months)	Freq 12: 1–7
28	COOKOUT	Cooked outdoors (freq last 12 months)	Freq 12: 1–7
65	PLANEPER	Took an airplane trip for personal reasons (freq last 12 months)	Freq 12: 1–7
92	VISREL	Visited relatives (freq last 12 months)	Freq 12: 1–7
100	DINFAM6	Eating dinner with the whole family (frequency of your activity now compared to this	Comp: 1–5

Table A2.2.2. (Continued)

DDB Codebook Question	Var Name	Question	Scale
101	DINNER6	Going out to dinner (frequency of your activity now compared to this time last year)	Comp: 1–5
106	TIMEFAM6	Spending time with friends and family (frequency of your activity now compared to this	Comp: 1–5
144	FAMBREAK	We usually have a large family breakfast on weekends	Agree: 1–6
149	FAMDIN	Our whole family usually eats dinner together	Agree: 1–6
298	OVRALCAR	Do you currently have major responsibility for the care and well-being of an elderly	0 No, 1 Yes
146	FAMCLOSE	Our family is close-knit (more than most families)	Agree: 1–6

Response Categories (in far right column above)
Freq 12: 1–7
Agree: 1–6
Comp: 1–5
0 No, 1 Yes

Freq 12: 1–7: Frequency last 12 months

1. None
2. 1–4 times
3. 5–8 times
4. 9–11 times
5. 12–24 times
6. 25–51 times
7. 52+ times

Agree: 1–6: Agreement with the statement

1. Definitely Disagree
2. Generally Disagree
3. Moderately Disagree
4. Moderately Agree
5. Generally Agree
6. Definitely Agree

Comp: 1–5: Frequency of your activity now   1. A lot more
     compared to this time last year   2. A little more
                                            3. About the same
                                            4. A little less
                                            5. A lot less

APPENDIX 3: TESTING CONTEXTUAL EFFECTS FOR DIFFERENT TYPES OF CONSUMPTION

The contextual propositions are complex to test, especially Proposition 9 about how income varies by political culture. We tested its core ideas by creating two indexes of consumption behavior using DDB items, one for moralistic consumption and a second for conspicuous consumption:

$$\text{moralcon} = \frac{\text{clubmee1} + \text{lectur1} + \text{letter1} + \text{volunt1} + \text{daily11}}{5}$$

where items are (frequency in last 12 months of): go to club meeting, attend lecture, write letter to a magazine or newspaper, do volunteer work, read a daily

$$\text{conspcon} = \frac{\text{golf1} + \text{stayhom1} + \text{clothe1} + \text{dinpart1} + \text{enthom1}}{5}$$

newspaper where these items are play golf, stay at home, went clothes shopping, attend or give a dinner party, entertained people at my home. These conspicuous consumption items seemed consistent with both the Individualistic and Traditional Political cultures.

We then computed OLS regressions to explain the two types of consumption, including as independent variables income, the political culture indexes, and interaction terms of income multiplied by the political culture indexes—plus several control variables. We did not examine results by subsets of persons, since all respondents received a score on each of the political cultures. Instead we created interaction terms of income times the political culture index. Results indicate:

•persons high on moralistic political culture engage in more moralistic consumption behaviors
•persons high on individualistic culture engage in more conspicuous consumption behaviors
•higher income increases conspicuous consumption and decreases moralistic consumption

The above results are direct effects for all persons in the sample. Next are the interaction effects for income times each of the two political cultures. Here we find in both regressions that the income X individualistic term has a greater impact than the income X moralistic term. This suggests, consistent with our contextualized Inglehart proposition (9), that income effects are larger for persons holding individualistic political cultures. Put differently, moralistic persons with higher and lower income do not differ in their consumption behavior as much as do persons with more individualistic values. Income seems to have a larger impact on persons of individualistic political culture. Main results are in Tables A3.2.1 and A3.2.2.

Still, these results are tentative. They are subject to classic statistical sensitivity: they shift with other variables in the model, with the specific items in the indexes, etc. We offer them not as definitive but as illustrating the richness of these combined data which permit empirical exploration of contextual consumption effects.

NOTES

1. Martin Lipset and I published a paper in 1991 that sparked some 100 papers and six books on these issues. The decade of this (largely international) controversy is synthesized in Clark and Lipset (2001). The central role of race and measures of its overlaps with class (in the U.S.) are presented in detail in Clark (1994). See also the boxes by Jones and Lamont below.

2. Historians draw on social science as they can see concepts which match their evidence. An overview of recent historical research suggests the decline of class and of work and the rise of values linked to immigration, rather like Elazar. "Since 1980, historians of urban social groups have largely abandoned 'modernization' and Marxism for the subcultural theories of sociologist Claude S. Fischer and anthropologist Clifford Geertz. From Italians in the tenements of Elizabeth Street to Jews and Mexicans in the bungalows of Los Angeles, historians emphasize the persistence and adaptability of premigration cultures over time" (Gilfoyle, 1998).

3. As I had parents with New England roots, but grew up in both the North and South, and lived long in Chicago, I am sensitive to the deep differences among the three—even though many Americans, even social scientists, remain surprisingly insensitive to them. I also lived in Paris for five years which encouraged more explicit attention to culture and consumption.

4. The centrality of these three cultural types is reinforced by their independent rediscovery in many other studies. Two of the three values (individualism or achievement and egalitarianism) were defined by Lipset as basic American values, albeit in conflict, in several books on the topic, e.g. Lipset (1997). Lipset like many others paid less attention to the South, and thus traditional values. A classic overview is Lipset and Lowenthal (1961). Alvarez and Brehm (2002) isolate core values of Americans using several

Table A3.2.1. Political Cultures Shift Effects on Consumption, 1

Model	Unstandardized Coefficients		Standardized Coefficients	t	Significance Level
	B	Std. Error	Beta		
1 (Constant)	-0.196	0.09		-2.31	0.02
Blacks, All Yrs., DDB	-0.145	0.03	-0.04	-4.22	0
Respondent's age	9.688 E-03	0.00	0.18	18.15	0
Size of city of residence	-2.55E-02	0.00	-0.07	-7.76	0
Level of education completed	0.152	0.01	0.21	21.69	0
Employment status of R (merged)	2.92E-02	0.01	0.04	4.54	0
Which one of the following best describes your marital status?	-7.23E-03	0.01	-0.01	-1.06	0.29
How many people in your household, including yourself, your spouse, any children at home and any others	2.472E-02	0.01	0.04	4.21	0
Occupation of respondent	-5.94E-03	0.00	-0.02	-1.87	0.06
Occupation of respondent's spouse	-2.99E-03	0.00	-0.01	-1.20	0.23
Sex of respondent	0.115	0.02	0.07	7.54	0
Owns residence?	5.047E-02	0.02	0.02	2.67	0.01
Into which one of the following categories does your annual household income fall?	-5.35E-02	0.01	-0.24	-5.78	0
Individualistic Pol Culture, INDLS1	2.22E-02	0.00	0.11	7.37	0
Moralistic Pol Culture, MORAL2	3.22E-02	0.00	0.20	12.78	0
Interaction term - income*indcult	2.08E-03	0	0.19	4.96	0
Interaction term - income*morcult	1.44E-03	0	0.10	3.70	0

Notes: these data include variables merged from multiple sources for all US counties, mainly the DDB for survey items and and the Census for demographic items. Multiple regressions (OLS) were computed as discussed in Appendix 3.
Dependent Variable: moralistic consumption index 2

Table A3.2.2. Political Cultures Shift Effects on Consumption, 2

Model	Unstandardized Coefficients		Standardized Coefficients	t	Significance Level
	B	Std. Error	Beta		
1 (Constant)	1.024	0.09		11.91	0
Blacks, All Yrs, DDB	-0.252	0.04	-0.06	-7.25	0
Respondent's age	-4.25E-04	0.00	-0.01	-0.79	0.43
Size of city of residence	3.40E-03	0.00	0.01	1.02	0.31
Level of education completed	3.24E-02	0.01	0.05	4.58	0
Employment status of R (merged)	4.47E-03	0.01	0.07	6.87	0
Which one of the following describes your marital status?	-2.55E-02	0.01	-0.04	-3.70	0
How many people in your household, including yourself, your spouse, any children living at home, and any others	-4.58E-02	0.01	-0.08	-7.72	0
Occupation of respondent	-1.39E-02	0.00	-0.04	-4.33	0
Occupation of respondent's spouse	-8.86E-03	0.00	-0.03	-3.50	0
Sex of respondent	0.295	0.02	0.17	19.16	0
Owns residence?	1.74E-02	0.02	0.01	0.91	0.36
Into which of the categories does your annual household income fall?	7.75E-02	0.01	0.35	8.28	0
Individualistic Pol Culture, INDLS1	4.48E-02	0.00	0.23	14.69	0
Moralistic Pol Culture, MORAL2	1.36E-02	0.00	0.09	5.35	0
Interaction Term - income*indcult	-1.06E-03	0	-0.10	-2.50	0.01
Interaction Term - income*morcult	-5.34E-04	0	-0.04	-1.36	0.17

Notes: these data include variables merged from multiple sources for all US counties, mainly the DDB for survey items and the Census for demographic items. Multiple regressions (OLS) were computed as discussed in Appendix 3.
Dependent Variable: conspicuous consumption index 2

complex methods. Three core values that they find recur across many surveys and analyses are egalitarianism, individualism, and authoritarian-traditionalism.

5. Note that the DDB mainly surveys households, so the African-Americans surveyed are probably more established than the total African-American population, which includes many persons living alone. Hence it may not be an exaggeration by these DDB black respondents to report that they are often leaders.

6. A more contemporary consumer theorist echoes Benjamin: "Modern individuals inhabit not just an 'iron cage' of economic necessity, but a castle of romantic dreams, striving through their conduct to turn the one into the other" Campbell (1987, p. 227) quoted in Ritzer (n.d.).

7. Douglas and Isherwood (1978) and Ritzer et al. (n.d.) reach similar conclusions: "Sociologists can no longer build a theory of consumption by assuming either rational or identity-shopping or status-driven consumers" (Ritzer et al. n.d.).

BIBLIOGRAPHY

Alvarez, R. M., & Brehm, J. (2002). *Hard Choices, Easy Answers*. Princeton, NJ: Princeton University Press.

Baldersheim, H., & Ståhlberg, K. (Eds) (1999). *Nordic Region-Building in a European Perspective*. Aldershot: Ashgate.

Baudrillard, J. (1970). *La Société de Consommation*. Paris: Gallimard.

Bell, D. (1973). *The Coming of Post-Industrial Society*. New York: Basic Books.

———(1976). *The Cultural Contradictions of Capitalism*. New York: Basic Books.

Benjamin, W. (1999). *The Arcades Project*. Cambridge, MA: Harvard University Press.

Birch, D. L. (1979). *The Job Generation Process*. Cambridge: The Massachusetts Institute of Technology Program on Neighborhood Change.

Blau, J. (1989). *The Shape of Culture*. Cambridge: Cambridge University Press.

Blotner, J. (1974). *Faulkner: A Biography*. New York: Random House.

Bourdieu, P. (1984). *Distinction*. Cambridge, MA: Harvard University Press.

Campbell, C. (1987). *The Romantic Ethic and the Spirit of Modern Consumerism*. Oxford: Blackwell.

Clark, T. N. (1975). *The Irish Ethic and the Spirit of Patronage*. Ethnicity, 2, 305–359.

———(Ed.) (1994). *Urban Innovation*. Thousand Oaks and London: Sage.

———(2000). *Old and New Paradigms for Urban Research: Globalization and the Fiscal Austerity and Urban Innovation Project*, Featured essay in *Urban Affairs Review*, 36(1) (September), 3–45.

Clark, T. N., & Elazar, D. (in draft). *Political Cultures of the World*. Draft MS.

Clark, T. N., & Hoffmann-Martinot, V. (Eds) (1998). *The New Political Culture*. Boulder: Westview Press.

Clark, T. N., & Lipset, S. M. (Eds) (2001). *The Breakdown of Class Politics: A Debate on Post-Industrial Stratification*. Baltimore: Johns Hopkins University Press.

Clark, T. N., & Rempel, M. (Eds) (1997). *Citizen Politics in Post-Industrial Societies*. Boulder: Westview Press.

Cohen, L. (1992). *Making a New Deal: Industrial Workers in Chicago, 1919–1939*. New York: Cambridge University Press.

———(2003). *A Consumers' Republic: The Politics of Mass Consumption in Postwar America*. New York: Knopf.

Coleman, J. S. (1990). *Foundations of Social Theory*. Cambridge: Harvard University Press.

Converse, P. (1992). Comment on Davis's Changeable Weather in a Cooling Climate atop the Liberal Plateau. *Public Opinion Quarterly*, 56(3) (Fall), 307–310.

Davis, J. (1992). Changeable Weather in a Cooling Climate atop the Liberal Plateau: Conversion and Replacement in Forty-two General Social Survey Items, 1972–1989. *Public Opinion Quarterly*, 56(3) (Fall), 261–306.

De Grazia, V. (2001). *The White Atlantic*. Book Draft, presented to Modern European Workshop, University of Chicago, October 23rd.

DiMaggio, P. (1982). Cultural Entrepreneurship in Nineteenth-Century Boston. *Media, Culture and Society*, 4, 33–50.

Douglas, M., & Isherwood, B. (1978). *The World of Goods: Toward an Anthropology of Consumption*. New York: Basic Books.

Elazar, D. (1998). *The Great Frontier and the Matrix of Federal Democracies*. Transaction Press.

———(1998). *Covenant and Civil Society: The Constitutional Matrix of Modern Democracy. The Covenant Tradition in Politics* (Vol. 4). New Brunswick: Transaction.

Farley, C. J. (1999). Hip Hop Nation. *Time*, February 8th.

Firebaugh, G. (1997). *Analyzing Repeated Surveys*. Thousand Oaks, CA: Sage. Florida, R. (2002). *The Rise of the Creative Class*. New York: BasicBooks/Perseus.

Gilfoyle, T. J. (1998). White Cities, Linguistic Turns, and Disneylands: The New Paradigms of Urban History. http://homepages.luc.edu/%7Etgilfoy/whitecit.htm, which is summarized in *Reviews in American History*, 26(March), 175–204.

Glaeser, E. L. (2000). Cities and Ethics. *Journal of Urban Affairs*, 22(4), 473–494.

Goffman, E. (1986). *Frame Analysis*. Boston; New York: Northeastern University Press.

Goldsmith, M. J., & Page, E. C. (1987). *Central and Local Government Relations*. London: Sage.

Gorski, P. (in press). *Book on Calvinism*. Chicago: University of Chicago Press.

Grazian, D. I. (2003). *Blue Chicago: The Search for Authenticity in Urban Blues Clubs*. Chicago: University of Chicago Press.

Greeley, A. (1974). *Ethnicity in the United States*. New York: Wiley.

Harvey, D. (1990). *The Condition of Postmodernity*. Oxford: Blackwell.

Hoggart, K., & Clark, T. N. (Eds) (2000). *Citizen Responsive Government, Research in Urban Policy* (Vol. 8). JAI Press/Elsevier.

Huntington, S. P. (1993). The Clash of Civilizations. *Foreign Affairs*, 72(3) (Summer), 22–50.

Inglehart, R. (1990). *Culture Shift in Advanced Industrial Society*. Princeton, NJ: Princeton University Press.

———(1997). *Modernization and Postmodernization*. Princeton, NJ: Princeton University Press.

Judge, D., Stoker, G., & Wolman, H. (Eds) (1995). *Theories of Urban Politics*. Newbury Park, CA: Sage.

Katz, E., & Lazarsfeld, P. F. (1955). *Personal Influence*. Glencoe: Free Press.

Lamont, M. (2000). *The Dignity of Working Men*. Cambridge: Harvard University Press.

Langlois, S. (2002). Sociologie de la Consommation. In: R. Boudon, M. Cherkaoui, S. Ringen & B. Valade (Eds), *Dictionnaire Historique de la Sociologie*. Paris: Presses Universitaires de France.

Langman, L. (2002). *The Neon Cage*. Draft Paper, Loyola University of Chicago.

Lipovetsky, G. (1987, 1994). *The Empire of Fashion*. Princeton, NJ: Princeton University Press.

Lipset, S. M. (1981, 1959). *Political Man* (2nd ed.). Baltimore: Johns Hopkins University Press.

———(1997). *American Exceptionalism*. New York: WW Norton.

Lipset, S. M., & Lowenthal, L. (Eds) (1961). *Culture and Social Character*. New York: Free Press.

Lipset, S. M., Trow, M. A., & Coleman, J. S. (1956, 1962). *Union Democracy*. Garden City: Anchor Books.

Lloyd, R. (2002). Neo-Bohemia. Ph.D. dissertation, Department of Sociology, University of Chicago.

Manza, J., & Brooks, C. (1999). *Social Cleavages and Political Change*. New York: Oxford University Press.

Martin, D. (1990). Tongues of Fire: *The Explosion of Protestantism in Latin America*. Oxford, UK and Cambridge, MA: Blackwell.

Miller, D. (Ed.) (1995). *Acknowledging Consumption: A Review of New Studies*. London: Routledge.

———(1998). *A Theory of Shopping*. Ithaca, NY: Cornell University Press.

O'Connor, A., Tilly, C., & Bobo, L. D. (2001). *Urban Inequality*. New York: Russell Sage.

Olson, M. (1982). *The Rise and Decline of Nations: Economic Growth, Stagflation, and Social Rigidities*. New Haven: Yale University Press.

Patterson, O. (1999). *Rituals of Blood: Consequences of Slavery in Two American Centuries*. Washington, DC: Counterpoint Press.

Pattillo-McCoy, M. (1999). *Black Picket Fences*. Chicago: University of Chicago Press.

Putnam, R. (2000). *Bowling Alone*. NY: Simon and Schuster.

Riesman, D. (1950). *The Lonely Crowd*. New Haven: Yale University Press.

Ritzer, G., Goodman, D., & Wiedenhoft, W. (n.d.). *Theories of Consumption*. Draft Paper, University of Maryland.

Roniger, L., & Günes-Ayata, A. (Eds) (1994). *Democracy, Clientelism, and Civil Society*. Boulder, CO: Lynne Rienner.

Ross, K. (1995). *Fast Cars, Clean Bodies: Decolonization and the Reordering of French Culture*. Cambridge, MA: MIT Press.

Sainteny, G. (2000). *L'Introuvable Écologisme Français?* Paris: Presses Universitaires de France.

Sarup, M. (1996). *Identity, Culture, and the Postmodern World*. Edinburgh: Edinburgh University Press.

Satterwaite, A. (2001). *Going Shopping*. New Haven: Yale University Press.

Stigler, G. J., & Becker, G. S. (1977). De Gustibus Non Est Disputandum. *The American Economic Review*, 62(2) (March), 76–90.

Strom, E. (2002). Converting Pork into Porcelain: Cultural Institutions and Downtown Development. *Urban Affairs Review*, 38(1) (September), 3–21.

Thompson, M., Ellis, R., & Wildavsky, A. (1990). *Cultural Theory*. Boulder: Westview.
Waite, L., & Gallagher, M. (2000). *The Case for Marriage*. New York: Doubleday.
Walder, A. G. (1991). *Communist Neo-Traditionalism*. Berkeley: University of California
    Press.

Chapter Three
Urban Amenities:
Lakes, Opera, and Juice Bars—Do They
Drive Development?

Terry Nichols Clark

INTRODUCTION

This chapter explores how amenities affect urban innovation and population growth. The last chapter explored how moral and political perspectives affect consumption. One main theme there was that subcultures vary in consumption patterns. This chapter explores subcultures further, focusing on how different urban amenities attract or repel different types of residents.

Urban researchers are gradually including amenities like convention centers (Strom, 2002), lofts (Zukin, 1982), and tourist attractions (Judd & Fainstein, 1999). Clark (2000) and Clark and Hoffmann-Martinot (1998) offered a new paradigm combining new politics and new economy themes—stressing consumption over production and individual citizen consumers as rivaling parties, class, race, and other traditional factors. Several contributors to this volume explore related themes, especially Glaeser et al. (2000, 2001), Florida (2000, 2002), and the Florida/Gates paper linking gays to tech growth. These stirrings encourage a paradigm change emphasizing consumption and amenities as new drivers of urban dynamics. But more evidence is needed, which this chapter provides.

Urban amenities have been with us since the Olympics and Forums of ancient cities, but despite exceptions like Benjamin (1999) they have mainly been omitted from urban growth analyses. This is especially true in Northern Europe and North America, where the omission is encouraged by an ascetic Protestant-ism, labeling "non-work" as quasi-sinful. Alcohol for instance has long been closely restricted and licensed by time and place, and served surreptitiously—in darkened bars—while southern Europeans or Asians drink in cafes and restau-rants, or with their families. Many socialists condemned entertainment along with religion as an opiate of the people, dismissing both as politically sinful. Despite such resistance, the undeniable rise of amenities in many Northern Eu-ropean and U.S. cities in recent years has led even Marxists and Post-Modernists to grudgingly recognize and start to interpret them, for instance as Disneyfica-tion (e.g. Harvey, 1990).

Some amenities affect everyone in an urban area, like clean air. Pure public goods are jointly shared, potentially consumed by all, and exclusion from them is costly.[1] Yet there are precious few "pure" public goods, or pure private goods; most things are in between. Some write of amenities as "non-market transac-tions" (Glaeser, 2000a); I would broaden this slightly. Amenities like museums or restaurants are semi-private goods, since persons may be excluded, and user fees charged. Some analysts who think individualistically neglect amenity as-pects of restaurants, since they are conceived as providing a purely private good—food—to discrete individuals. But for persons pondering where to live and work, restaurants are more than food on their plate. The presence of distinct restaurants redefines the local context, even for persons who do not eat in them. They are part of the local market baskets of amenities that vary from place to place. I thus include such publicly-noted spillovers from market transactions as amenities, since their cumulative effects can shift individuals' and firms' loca-tion decisions, and hence drive population growth or decline.

This reasoning may seem simple, but it reverses the "traditional economic determinism" which suggests that as individuals (and cities) grow more affluent, they consume more luxury goods, like meals in fine restaurants. In this tradi-tional view, individuals with more income cause restaurants to emerge. But if this is broadly applicable over an individual's life course, to apply the same log-ic to a city is mistaken, powerfully illustrating overextended "methodological individualism." Why? Because discrete individuals move in and out of cities all the time, yet urban amenities like opera or lakefronts change more slowly, and drive location decisions of individuals. This is especially true for talented and younger persons who change jobs frequently—and even the average American changed jobs about every four years in the 1990s. Cities are rich and poor in different amenities in subtle ways that the young and mobile especially stress. Some places are "cool," while others are "out of it," square, and stodgy. Many coolness components are more subtle than Census measures in past urban re-search. Entrepreneurs, local public officials, news media, local universities, mu-sicians, poets, chefs, basketball players—all contribute to a city being cool or not. Since each person is unique and weights amenities differently, an urban-level analysis only captures aggregate effects shared across classes of individu-als. The null hypothesis is that amenities add nothing beyond more standard migration measures. We are still near the beginning of amenities research, but

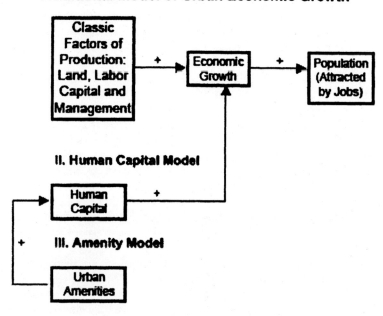

Traditional Model of Urban Economic Growth

Figure 3.1. Three Successive Models of Urban Development

introduce several new amenity measures and analyses that add more subtlety than in past work. The core idea of this amenity approach is contrasted with two past approaches in Fig. 3.1. Classically, a location rich in production factors would generate more jobs, which in turn would attract people. Human capital theory stressed that talented persons create innovations and jobs. Amenity theory builds in turn on these and suggests that amenities attract especially talented and innovative persons, who are more mobile. Still, all three models are nested and each still no doubt explains something. But what and how much? To answer this we build on past research.

There is a huge literature on migration and urban dynamics. Past studies classically analyzed how jobs attracted people, esp. across metro areas. Often separate was how persons chose locations inside metro areas, where jobs might be less deterministic. The traditional models have weakened. Berry and Horton (1970: 301) showed this in repeating the same analysis of determinants of land value from 1910 to 1960; they found a consistent decline in the power of each individual coefficient (distance from downtown, population density, etc.) and in the whole equation. What then drives growth?

Human capital has been a main thrust of economic development work in recent years, suggesting that locations whose residents have better education and creative skills will develop more. But human capital is often treated as a factor of production, implying it is either fixed in location as a stock like land, labor, and capital, or that it follows jobs and capital, and thus does not locate autonomously. Florida (2002) extends this tradition by labeling the "creative class" those thirty million-odd Americans who work in occupations whose creativity is distinctly valued. But as Florida, Glaeser (below) and I maintain, amenities act jointly with human capital. Why? They are the cheese, or correction, the three star meal, attracting talent. They transform a location into a scene. Sometimes a cool scene. Human capital theory is thus not incorrect, but contextually incomplete, underspecified, in that it does not explain where and why human capital locates. And since talent is in fact highly mobile, our amenities theory enters critically to close the causal loop, joining jobs with human capital.

This shift has deep policy implications. Fiscal stress, cuts in grants, and market-sensitive management led many local governments to seek to expand their tax bases in recent decades. Most used subsidies to firms like tax incentives, land consolidation, and so forth. Still, most studies find that these traditional firm-oriented incentive strategies do not work or have very weak effects (e.g. Walzer, 1995; Walzer & P'ng, 1994).

Some local policy makers have changed. Amenities are increasingly recognized as critical (see the review in Clark et al., 1986; Green, 1997; Miranda & Rosdil, 1997). Efforts to improve the "quality of life," via festivals, bicycle paths, or culture are recognized as central not just for consumption but for economic development, which is increasingly driven by consumption concerns. How? Many amenities are Samuelson-type public goods; they do not disappear like a payment to one firm if the firm goes bankrupt. Amenities benefit all firms as well as citizens in the area. They often enhance the local distinctiveness (of architecture or a waterfront) by improving the locality, rather than just making it cheaper for one business. Human capital development of the local workforce, like other amenities, is a public good for the location, aided by better schools, worker training programs, and the like (Clarke & Gaile, 1998; Clarke & Moss, 1990). Public goods policies imply fewer zero-sum conflicts of the sort featured in class or race conflict or growth machine paradigms. Even less developed countries are discovering the huge value of clean vacation areas (across Latin America), and historic sites (e.g. in China), which rise in salience with global tourism. Tourism by some counts is the largest industry in the world. Interpretations are clouded by the fact that many local residents act "as tourists" in supporting nearby amenities. If many localities adopt amenity strategies, competition can continue nationally and internationally, but the focus is less the firm and its location and more the citizen as consumer/tourist/workforce member. Culture and entertainment are the largest industry in Chicago and second only to finance in New York (Kleiman et al., 2002; Clark, 2003).

Symphonies, Pavement, and Bank Clearances: Boosterism is a Staple of American Novelists

Culture has become as necessary an adornment and advertisement for a city today as pavements or bank-clearances. It's Culture, in theaters and art-galleries and so on, that brings thousands of visitors to New York every year and, to be frank, for all our splendid attainments we haven't yet got the Culture of a New York or Chicago or Boston—or at least we don't get the credit for it. The thing to do then, as live bunch of go-getters, is to capitalize Culture; to go right out and grab it.

Pictures and books are fine for those that have the time to study 'em, but they Don't shoot out on the road and holler "This is what little old Zenith can put up in the way of Culture." That's precisely what a Symphony Orchestra does do. Look at the credit Minneapolis and Cincinnati get. An orchestra with first-class musickers and a swell conductor—and I believe we ought to do the thing up brown and get one of the highest-paid conductors on the market, providing he ain't a Hun—it goes right into Beantown and New York and Washington; it plays at the best theaters to the most cultured and moneyed people; it gives such class-advertising as a town can get in no other way; and the guy who is so short-sighted as to crab this orchestra proposition is passing up the chance to impress the glorious name of Zenith on some big New York millionaire that might establish a branch factory here!

– Chum Frink

Lewis, Sinclair. Babbitt. New York: Harcourt, Brace & World, Inc. (1922) 1950. p. 261 The boosterism theme is detailed historically in Boorstin (1973).

More attention to amenities flows from the gradual recognition that people choose their place of residence often before or simultaneous with their choice of job. No longer is the prime mover the job-seeking migrant from rural areas, although this continues for some jobs, especially lower positions. But increasingly important is a pattern I illustrate with Sally, who moved to San Diego to surf. Sally stayed a year until mom said no more money. Then Sally opened a veggie burger stand. Her personal move came first, the job followed. Urban economist Richard Muth (1971) modeled this pattern with simultaneous equation models, which show that the traditional path from jobs to people is sometimes weaker than the Sally-type path from people to jobs (details are in Clark & Ferguson, 1983, Chap. 8 and Clark et al., 1986). The key result: both types of migration are statistically important, and in some studies the new Sally-type is more important for the total U.S. workforce.

Florida (2002) and some others stressing human capital focus not on the entire workforce, but on innovation, patents, leaders in gentrification, and smart risk capital. These involve more educated and affluent persons, who we explore below. But consistent with the last chapter, our goal is to develop an analytical framework including all types of persons—rich and poor, more and less talented. And, we suggest, all are driven by private goods concerns (jobs, income) as well as by urban amenities. It may be that the most affluent, and those who do not work at all (like retired persons) are driven primarily by amenities, while persons with fewer job opportunities are driven more by jobs (and thus fit more the traditional economic model of Fig. 3.1). But the talented workforce should be driven by a combination of jobs and amenities, and more often make decisions where these are jointly determined. Similarly, as the entire economy, or a subsector of it, generates more jobs than can be filled by the available workforce, this should both increase more job offers, higher wages, and permit more amenity considerations. Conversely, as the economy or a sector declines, so should job offers and amenity considerations.

Still amenities count for everyone, to some degree. If some are considered frills, others are essential to stay alive (like low crime) and others enhance job opportunities (like contacts or education). The amenities particularly stressed for low income persons by Chicago's Mayor Daley in campaign speeches around 2000 were public education and less crime (Clark, 2003). For Hispanics and many immigrants, the most critical amenity is often family and personal contacts that channel migrants from villages to a U.S. city and then help them find lodging and jobs. Large immigrant neighborhoods with information about jobs, as well as churches, music, food, and nightlife are narrowly concentrated. Moving to another neighborhood or city lacking these amenities would be unthinkable for many recent migrants, for whom the "ghetto economy" drives economic development (cf. Portes & Rumbaut, 1996 who explore the ghetto economy argument). The last chapter reports distinct leisure activities like shopping or visiting bars by African-American men, women, and other DDB respondents. Below we contrast patterns for the young, for college graduates, and also for the elderly and non-college graduates—recognizing that while these are rough analytical categories, they are numerically important and, critically, available in the Census. We then analyze how these population changes are related to constructed and natural amenities. This chapter does not seek to detail more precise subsets of amenities for each population subcategory. Indeed, to try to do so would be mistaken since it implies looking for consistent preferences across Census-defined social groups. Mistaken, since these groups are too broad and rough to warrant more than simple preference classifications, such as natural and constructed amenities. This is heightened by the growing recognition that social background characteristics like age and education are only modestly related to consumption preferences. We thus proceed with a limited number of amenities and social groups since no one previously assembled or examined such amenities for population impacts. Some powerful results emerge, despite these caveats.

Urban Amenities in a Low-Income African-American Neighborhood
Overall Goals

- To develop Bronzeville into an international African American Heritage Tourism Destination that will generate a billion dollars in Revenues
- To ignite a public/private dialogue around broad based civic engagement, public trust and citizen involvement from all sectors of the community in the Restoring Bronzeville Campaign
- Bronzeville by the year 2020, evolves to become a self-sustained predominantly African American community that generates wealth for its citizens through heritage tourism entrepreneurial business enterprise development . . .

In order to take full advantage of the tourism development potential of Bronzeville, the community must identify viable tourism assets, evaluate those assets, and set goals and priorities for tourism development.

Continue to support the five Principles of Heritage Tourism (National Trust for Historic Preservation)

Save the Sites
Focus on Authenticity
Make the Sites come alive
Find the fit in the community
Collaborate, Collaborate, Collaborate

From: Keynote address Toward the Bronzeville Arts Trust, January 25th, 2003 by Harold L. Lucas, President & CEO, Black Metropolis Convention & Tourism Council, Chicago, Illinois.

Notes: "Greater Bronzeville" refers to the African-American South Side of Chicago, extending the designation from Drake and Cayton (1945).

Clark and Ferguson (1983, Chap. 8) was an early study of the dynamics of jobs and population that documented the reversal in causal direction, and the distinctive importance of amenities and public decisions shifting individual migration. It showed that people did not just move to jobs, but many chose cities and their amenities. Separate models were estimated for blacks and whites which documented amenity impacts consistent with other more focused studies. In the 1990s, economists reported many other examples of amenity-driven behavior (cf. Glaeser et al., 2000), even if political scientists and sociologists have been slower to catch up to this the reversal of past causality. (Many still follow the older Logan and Molotch (1987), even though both Logan and Molotch themselves have moved closer to our newer view.) As this last sentence has been queried, I add brief evidence: Molotch et al. (2000, p. 816) embrace a multi-causal approach highlighting amenities to explain growth. Their illuminating comparison of Santa Barbara and Ventura, California shows how the two adjacent cities were very similar a hundred years ago. Both had oil and beaches. But they used them differently. Amenities and the beachfront were stressed in Santa Barbara, while oil pumping dominated in Ventura. Comment: "By reformulating character of place as the mode of connection among unlike elements, and tradition as the mode of perpetuating these links, we gain a way to explain how place differences develop and persist.[2] Methodologically, locating character and tradition requires keeping the agenda open, rather than focusing for example on the economic versus the political versus the ideational versus the natural. History occurs across all the realms, all the time, with no time out."

John Logan and two coauthors completed a masterful review of twenty years of research on the growth machine hypothesis. They conclude: "after two decades of research, we are still unsure whether growth machines make a difference to urban development. Much greater attention needs to be given to consideration of the efficacy of local regimes and formal polices. As we have shown, this is not a simple question. Researchers should probe variations in regimes, explore how growth coalitions are brought together and operate, investigate the sources of opposition, and determine how policies are implemented or obstructed. Field studies, even those using a single case, can make conceptual contributions to these questions. Assessing the net effects of the local regime and its policies will require large sample studies with stronger designs, including explicit measures of the influence of various constituencies, studying effects over time, and estimating reciprocal causal relationships. Few comparative studies have been reported. No study has been specifically designed to deal comprehensively with all these aspects of the question." Logan, Bridges and Crowder (1997, p. 624). Weaknesses of growth machine and business-regime approaches are detailed in Clark and Goetz (1994) and Chapter 9 (this volume).

Unfortunately we have not found any work to date which uses simultaneous equation methods to measure the relative effects of jobs on people and of people on jobs and which looks at such effects separately by subpopulations and incorporates amenities. The closest seems to be work by Mathur (e.g. Mathur & Song, 2000).

AMENITIES: NATURAL, CONSTRUCTED, AND OTHER

The amenity items in this chapter include:

- Natural physical amenities (climate, humidity, temperature, water access, overall natural attractiveness).

- Constructed amenities (numbers of bigger institutions like research libraries, museums, and opera or small firms like used and rare bookstores, juice bars, Whole Foods stores, Starbucks, and bicycle events).
- Socio-economic composition and diversity (income and education of residents, foreign born, Hispanics, African-Americans and a special focus on percent gays, specifically self-reported gay male households).
- Values and attitudes of residents (friendliness or hostility, tolerance, risk taking, individualism, and other items, explored in the last chapters and briefly below and in Chapter 7) which are amenities or disamenities for potential new residents.

We explore these several categories of amenities and find differential impacts on different subpopulations, change in key industries, and innovations as measured by patents.

Amenities have gradually come into the radar scopes of public officials as a tool to attract new residents. Governments have spent billions on convention centers, stadiums, malls, light rail, and other facilities they hope will attract people and firms. Related are the "big ticket" cultural items like concert halls and art museums. These large amenities have won most funding, and had some dramatic successes like the Guggenheim Museum in Bilbao, Spain. But they are criticized for generally low impact by Florida (2002). He suggests other amenities are more important: smaller items like cafes which change street life. These are similarly favored by New Urbanism architects and planners who seek to recreate the vital street life of pre-automobile cities, lauded earlier by Jane Jacobs (1961). The leading public official promoting New Urbanism policies was Mayor James Norquist (1998) of Milwaukee, who started tearing down freeways into his city to demonstrate commitment to street life, even if it weakened suburban connections.

Enhancing the lives of citizens via better education and job training are increasingly recognized as critical in making cities attractive not only to citizens, but to investors and mobile firms (Clarke & Gaile, 1998). Indeed, the core of the human capital interpretation of work, as applied to cities, stresses such improvements of the workforce (e.g. Glaeser et al., 2000). The newest addition to this argument is culture, not just as an elite consumption item, or tourist attraction—widely recognized functions—but also as enhancing the lives of average and disadvantaged persons, and potentially improving their life chances (Stern, 2002).

Related are amenities comprised by the types of people who live in the location, in terms of how they add (or subtract) value to their neighbors. Since Hobbes, the breakdown of social order is the classic negative amenity; crime is the main urban example. Some persons like social diversity, others prefer homogeneity. Florida and Gates in this volume argue that diversity and tolerance are key concerns of the "creative class," and use percent gays as an urban diversity marker. But they define the creative class as over thirty million Americans, so clearly not all seek such diversity; others prefer homogenous neighborhoods or suburbs, characterized by labels like "safe for children to play," or "a good place to raise a family." Kotkin (2001) terms these "nerdistans" and maintains that if they attracted "square" professionals and high tech persons in the 1980s, by the 1990s, the truly creative more often preferred to rub shoulders with artists, musicians, and the more socially diverse. Bohemian was the older label for social diversity advocates (cf. Lloyd, 2002). But the classic distinctions of bourgeois/bohemian, central city/suburb, and left/right have been superseded by new amalgams. This is the main point of our New Political Culture analysis (e.g. Clark & Hoffmann-Martinot, 1998). Closely similar ideas are pursued on a lifestyle/amenity level by Brooks (2000), who argued that bohemians and bourgeois merged in the 1990s into the "bobo," a new American cultural amalgam, which Florida (2002) elaborates as a "Big Morph." Unlike Kotkin, Florida and others, however, Brooks invokes *suburban* illustrations as "cutting edge," like Wayne, Pennsylvania, the Philadelphia Main Line suburb. He does not stress classic themes of churches, clubs, or ethnicity, but consumption in shops marketing personal identity—consistent with our last chapter.

Examples: organic food stores, gourmet coffee houses with poetry readings, peasant styles like Moroccan crafts, replacing French aristocratic restaurants and furniture. Wandering through these shops are "vineyard-touring doctors, novelist-writing lawyers, tenured gardening buffs, unusually literary realtors, dangling-earring psychologists, and the rest of us information-age burghers" (Brooks, 2000, p. 61).

These are his "bobos." While Brooks does not, I stress that these style changes are not distinctly suburban, but similarly popular in central city neighborhoods, like New York's Soho, or Chicago's Wicker Park or the LA suburb of Santa Monica—the semi-bohemian zones admired by Kotkin, Lloyd and others. "Nerdistan" is an anti-utopia from people who do not dig beneath the surface, albeit an image continued in popular songs, Hollywood films, and one-liners: "I've been to Irvine and I have to say, there is nothing there," states Kotkin, quoted in Kleiman et al., 2002).[3] Kotkin continues, "This is why they and Silicon Valley are having a tough time right now. They're areas I typically call Nerdistans—they only thrive on technical know-how. New York has culture and a mix of industries that the new economy thrives on." I applaud the focus on culture and diversity but question the Nerdistan labeling and geographic turf wars. Complementing Brooks' ethnography, and reporting similar moves toward social diversity and political support of new social roles are results from, of all places, Irvine. In fact, it is the epicenter of a systematic urban change study. Repeated annual surveys of citizens, mayors, and council members in each municipality of Orange County, California were conducted over more than a decade by Baldassare (1998) who documented with painstaking precision the emergence of variations and subtlety in taste and politics. Old style Reaganism was increasing-

Table 3.1. Natural Amenities by County

	County	Natural Amenities Index	Land	Percent of Water Area	January Temperature	January Sunlight	July Temperature	July Humidity	Topography
1	Ventura CA	7.00	21.00	16.41	1.73	2.18	4.67	-.82	1.84
2	Humboldt CA	7.00	21.00	11.84	1.19	.50	6.50	-.27	1.84
3	Santa Barbara CA	7.00	21.00	27.74	1.68	2.18	4.24	-.82	1.84
4	Mendocino CA	7.00	20.00	9.52	1.24	.50	6.50	-.27	1.69
5	San Francisco CA	7.00	16.00	75.00	1.49	.59	6.22	-1.23	1.08
6	Los Angeles CA	7.00	21.00	14.57	1.79	2.18	3.84	-.82	1.84
7	San Diego CA	7.00	21.00	7.10	1.85	2.18	3.60	-.82	1.84
8	Monterey CA	7.00	21.00	11.91	1.42	.59	5.23	-1.23	1.84
9	Orange CA	7.00	16.00	16.69	1.77	2.18	2.95	-.82	1.08
10	Lake CO	7.00	21.00	1.83	-1.22	2.15	3.90	1.44	1.84
11	Santa Cruz CA	7.00	16.00	26.65	1.32	.59	4.91	-1.23	1.08
12	Contra Costa CA	7.00	16.00	10.21	1.36	.59	5.25	-1.23	1.08
13	Calaveras CA	7.00	20.00	1.61	.33	1.01	2.58	2.33	1.69
14	Mono CA	7.00	21.00	2.79	-.01	1.46	1.76	2.53	1.84
15	San Mateo CA	7.00	16.00	39.40	1.38	.59	4.35	-1.23	1.08
16	Marin CA	7.00	16.00	37.24	1.16	.59	3.67	-.27	1.08
17	Summit CO	7.00	21.00	1.79	-1.39	.86	3.99	2.40	1.84
18	Sonoma CA	7.00	20.00	10.87	1.10	.50	3.57	-.27	1.69
19	San Luis Obispo CA	7.00	16.00	8.61	1.58	.59	4.64	-1.23	1.08
20	Napa CA	7.00	20.00	4.37	1.20	.50	3.55	-.27	1.69
21	Grand CO	7.00	21.00	1.07	-1.49	.86	3.76	2.40	1.84
22	Nevada CA	7.00	21.00	1.73	.12	-.44	3.45	1.92	1.84
23	Stanislaus CA	7.00	20.00	1.34	1.01	1.01	0.93	2.33	1.69
24	Cochise AZ	7.00	12.00	.79	1.22	3.27	0.29	1.92	.47
25	Tuolumne CA	7.00	21.00	1.71	.91	1.01	0.64	2.33	1.84
26	Gilpin CO	7.00	21.00	.26	-.50	1.88	3.01	1.37	1.84
27	Clear Creek CO	7.00	21.00	.25	-.50	1.88	3.01	1.37	1.84
28	Douglas OR	6.00	21.00	1.89	.67	-.95	2.75	2.05	1.84

Table 3.1. (Continued)

	County	Natural Amenities Index	Land	Percent of Water Area	January Temperature	January Sunlight	July Temperature	July Humidity	Topography
29	Washoe NV	6.00	12.00	3.19	-.08	1.46	1.68	2.53	.47
30	Riverside CA	6.00	21.00	1.31	1.59	2.18	1.62	-.82	1.84
31	Clallam WA	6.00	21.00	34.79	.47	-3.12	5.85	-.48	1.84
32	Chaffee CO	6.00	21.00	.15	-.36	2.15	2.30	1.44	1.84
33	El Dorado CA	6.00	21.00	4.46	.62	-.44	1.28	1.92	1.84
34	Deschutes OR	6.00	17.00	1.20	-.22	-.77	3.28	2.40	1.23
35	Lincoln OR	6.00	20.00	17.94	.86	-3.09	5.94	-.96	1.69
36	Monroe FL	6.00	1.00	73.32	2.71	2.18	1.09	-1.10	-1.19
37	Fresno CA	6.00	21.00	.91	1.03	1.01	-.21	2.33	1.84
38	Placer CA	6.00	21.00	6.39	1.00	-.44	.62	1.92	1.84
39	Santa Clara CA	6.00	20.00	1.02	1.38	.59	3.44	-1.23	1.69
40	Solano CA	6.00	16.00	8.68	1.00	-.44	1.09	1.92	1.08
41	Mohave AZ	6.00	12.00	1.17	.29	2.36	.83	1.71	.47
42	La Plata CO	6.00	21.00	.46	-.58	.86	1.65	2.40	1.84
43	Boulder CO	6.00	21.00	1.19	.01	1.88	.54	1.37	1.84
44	Shasta CA	6.00	21.00	1.61	.07	-.44	1.97	1.92	1.84
45	Tulare CA	6.00	21.00	.31	1.05	1.01	-.05	2.33	1.84
46	Larimer CO	6.00	21.00	1.24	-.50	1.88	.84	1.37	1.84
47	Jefferson CO	6.00	21.00	.77	-.08	1.88	.66	1.37	1.84
48	Archuleta CO	6.00	21.00	.39	-1.08	.86	1.98	2.40	1.84
49	Davis UT	6.00	21.00	51.94	-.34	-.35	-.32	2.53	1.84
50	Coos OR	6.00	20.00	11.40	.97	-3.09	5.54	-.96	1.69
51	Dade FL	6.00	1.00	19.97	2.84	2.03	1.22	-1.10	-1.19
52	Teton WY	6.00	21.00	5.07	-1.78	-.44	2.90	1.92	1.84
53	Martin FL	6.00	1.00	26.19	2.69	2.03	1.10	-1.10	-1.19
54	Jefferson WA	6.00	21.00	16.95	.55	-3.12	4.46	.00	1.84
55	Sublette WY	6.00	21.00	1.10	-1.77	.53	2.37	2.19	1.84
56	Routt CO	6.00	21.00	.27	-1.49	.86	2.28	2.40	1.84

Table 3.1. (Continued)

	County	Natural Amenities Index	Land	Percent of Water Area	January Temperature	January Sunlight	July Temperature	July Humidity	Topography
57	Whatcom WA	6.00	21.00	15.32	.31	-3.00	4.10	.48	1.84
58	Lee FL	6.00	1.00	33.70	2.53	2.18	.85	-1.10	-1.19
59	Yavapai AZ	6.00	17.00	.06	.24	2.36	1.07	1.71	1.23
60	San Benito CA	6.00	20.00	.12	1.31	.59	3.88	-1.23	1.69
61	Klamath OR	6.00	17.00	3.12	-.26	-.77	1.87	2.40	1.23
62	Douglas CO	6.00	21.00	.31	-.44	1.88	1.03	1.37	1.84
63	El Paso CO	6.00	21.00	.14	-.35	2.15	1.02	1.44	1.84
64	San Miguel CO	6.00	21.00	.15	-.82	.86	1.77	2.40	1.84
65	Palm Beach FL	6.00	1.00	14.76	2.70	2.03	1.18	-1.10	-1.19
66	Alameda CA	6.00	16.00	10.20	1.05	.59	2.32	-1.25	1.08
67	Butte CA	6.00	20.00	2.24	1.02	-.44	.40	1.92	1.69
68	Charlotte FL	6.00	1.00	19.27	2.58	2.18	.98	-1.10	-1.19
69	Yolo CA	6.00	20.00	1.02	1.04	-.44	.80	1.92	1.69
70	Crook OR	6.00	16.00	.27	-.16	-.77	3.13	2.40	1.08
71	Pinellas FL	6.00	1.00	53.90	2.43	2.00	.71	-1.10	-1.19
72	St. Lucie FL	6.00	1.00	16.80	2.53	2.00	1.20	-1.10	-1.19
73	Collier FL	6.00	1.00	12.13	2.68	2.18	1.02	-1.10	-1.19
74	Broward FL	6.00	1.00	8.40	2.81	2.03	1.22	-1.10	-1.19
75	Clatsop OR	6.00	20.00	23.74	.64	-3.09	4.93	-.96	1.69
76	Eddy NM	6.00	15.00	.37	.81	2.85	-.62	1.44	.93
77	Summit UT	6.00	21.00	.58	-.78	-.35	1.91	2.53	1.84
78	Skagit WA	6.00	21.00	9.64	.39	-3.00	3.94	.48	1.84
79	Gunnison CO	6.00	21.00	.64	-1.84	.86	1.83	2.40	1.84
80	Utah UT	6.00	21.00	6.66	-.56	-.35	.37	2.53	1.84
81	Coconino AZ	6.00	8.00	.23	-.20	2.36	1.53	2.05	-.13
82	Wasatch UT	6.00	21.00	2.34	-1.01	-.35	1.36	2.53	1.84
83	Albany WY	6.00	16.00	.82	-1.01	1.16	2.06	1.64	1.08
84	Maricopa AZ	6.00	17.00	.23	1.52	2.91	-2.55	2.46	1.23

Notes: These amenities scores were converted to normalized z scores and summed to create the Natural Amenities Index in the first column. Data come from the US Department of Agriculture. Only high scoring cases shown of the 3,111 total US counties.

ly superseded by styles closer to Wayne, PA. One mayor of Irvine, Larry Agran, joined hands with hundreds of residents to create a human chain and stop rush-hour traffic on the expressways, to press the case for mass transit. The national style-setters in cool eyeglasses are at the Oakley Company, in Irvine. Just look at the *New York Times* fashion section, or read the *Wall Street Journal* on the ultra-hip Oakley Company. See Clark and Hoffmann-Martinot (1998, p. 150ff.).

The strength of these creative concepts is also their weakness. They are original in capturing a new phenomenon and articulating its specifics. But their weakness is to assume implicitly that their core, critical lifestyle or outlook (bohemian, bobo, diverse, creative) is the touchstone of innovation and urban development. There is a lack of analytical diversity or relativism; they do not incorporate a *conceptual diversity of multiple specific lifestyles*—as outlined in the last chapter. All the above writers are smart and sensitive enough to note variations and exceptions, but their main emphasis is not here.[4] Consequently, since "urban growth dynamics" and even "innovation" are so vast, each of the above concepts captures only part of them. Edward Glaeser, Harvard urban economist stresses multiple factors as driving urban growth dynamics, like amenities and consumption patterns, religion and civilization, innovation and creativity, and how these interact with size and density (e.g. Glaeser, 2000a, b), which cumulatively bring more perspective and balance—the opposite of what many expect from economists!

Much past policy concern focused on large infrastructure amenities—convention centers, malls and the like (e.g. Boschken, 2002; Spirou & Bennett, forthcoming; Strom, 2002). We consequently explore in more detail what is new in these broader interpretations and for which we have new data: natural and constructed amenities, and their distinct impacts on subgroups and subcultures. How?

The items are from our new data files, discussed in the Introduction. The simpler ones appear in past work, the more subtle are new. Our natural amenities items are in Table 3.1: temperature and humidity are classic, but newer are water area, topography (such as hills and mountains vs. flatlands) and overall natural attractiveness—a sum of the previous measures. It sums six measures that most people prefer: warm winter, winter sun, temperate summer, low summer humidity, topographic variation, and water area. The locations ranking highest are the California coast and mountains, then Utah, Florida, Colorado, Texas, and "Sunbelt" locations. Often with smaller populations, these natural amenity measures come from multiple sources, assembled by the U.S. Department of Agriculture.

Our constructed amenities are very different. The main "big ticket" item here is operas, found especially in older Northeastern locations, but also San Francisco and Houston. Culturally related are research libraries and used and rare bookstores. By contrast the smaller, more commercial amenities like juice bars, Starbucks, brew pubs, and Whole Foods are more concentrated in newer

Who Performs in (those Eastern Establishment?) Opera Houses?
The Homeric battle for honor continues in new Forums:

"The nations call, thy joyful people wait
To seal the truce, and end the dire debate.
Paris, thy son, and Sparta's king advance,
In measured lists to toss the weighty lance;
And who his rival shall in arms subdue,
His be the dame, and his the treasure too."

The Iliad of Homer, Translated by Alexander Pope. London: Penguin Books, 1996, Book III, lines 320–330.

"Just as Homer was the greatest composer of serious poetry . . . he constructed the *Odyssey* around a single action . . . and the *Iliad* similarly . . . Poetry should represent universals, not particulars." Aristotle, *Poetics.* Translated by Richard Janko. Indianapolis: Hackett (1987, pp. 5, 11, 12).

"(In 1898) Jenkins defeated Farmer Burns at the Grand Opera House in Indianapolis. The setback was one of only a handful Burns suffered in a career that included some six thousand matches, and it stamped Jenkins as the American heavyweight champion . . . The Farmer, weighing in at 165 pounds, simply couldn't cope with the brute strength of Jenkins, who was forty pounds heavier."

From: The WAWLI Papers (Wrestling As We Liked It), edited by J Michael Kenyon, Issue No. 595, Sunday, October 3rd, 1999, oldfallguy@aol.com.

By 1997, more Americans attended opera performances than National Football League games (16.5 vs. 14.7 million http://www.oper aam.org/quick.htm and http://chl.ca/FootballNFL97Review/BC-FBP-STAT-NFLATTEND-R.html).

locations in the West, like Los Angeles, San Diego, or Santa Clara Country (including Palo Alto, Stanford, Silicon Valley). Bicycle events (road and mountain) are more common in smaller towns, although New York City and Los Angeles also rank high.

The constructed amenities were painstakingly assembled from address lists and websites, then aggregated to generate county scores. This is the first analysis of these constructed amenity data. The top-ranked counties on opera are listed in Table 3.2, but look near the bottom: San Diego has little opera but many juice bars. Among café-chic aesthetes, Starbucks and juice bars may be faulted as upper-middle brow, but we chose these mainstream locales since their national distribution is more normal; the more chic would be heavily skewed toward a few ultra cool locations like Burlington, Boulder, or Palo Alto, which Brooks

Table 3.2. Constructed Amenities

	County	City	Operas	Starbucks	Juice Bars	Brew Pubs	Museums	Whole Foods Stores	Bicycle Events
1	Richmond NY	New York	12	56	0	6	0	0	14
2	Bronx NY	New York	12	56	2	6	2	0	14
3	Kings NY	New York	12	56	3	6	2	0	14
4	New York NY	New York	12	56	9	6	8	1	14
5	Queens NY	New York	12	56	8	6	0	0	14
6	Los Angeles CA	Los Angeles	6	84	114	21	7	11	36
7	San Francisco CA	San Francisco	5	37	13	13	3	3	2
8	Cook IL	Chicago	5	24	7	11	8	4	8
9	Fort Bend TX	Houston (Southwest Suburbs)	5	4	0	3	0	0	13
10	Harris TX	Houston	5	4	12	4	1	4	14
11	Montgomery TX	Houston	5	2	0	3	0	0	13
12	DuPage IL	Chicago (West Suburbs)	4	27	1	15	5	1	10
13	Middlesex MA	Urbanna	4	10	2	6	2	0	4
14	Philadelphia PA	Philadelphia	4	2	1	7	6	0	2
15	Alameda CA	Alameda	3	22	10	10	3	1	2
16	Cuyahoga OH	Cleveland	3	13	2	7	3	0	1
17	Norfolk City VA	Richmond (Southeast Suburbs)	3	2	0	0	0	0	5
18	Denver CO	Denver	3	1	3	13	3	1	6
19	Santa Clara CA	San Jose	2	33	12	12	3	4	10
20	Dade FL	Miami	2	9	0	4	0	0	6
21	Fresno CA	San Jose (Southeast Suburbs)	2	8	4	3	0	1	0
22	Riverside CA	Los Angeles (Southeast Suburbs)	2	8	10	5	2	0	13
23	Suffolk MA	Boston	2	8	1	9	1	0	1
24	Allegheny PA	Pittsburgh	2	6	2	6	2	0	4
25	Essex NJ	Newark (Northwest Suburbs)	2	5	2	2	1	0	4
26	Westchester NY	New York (North Suburbs)	2	4	0	1	1	0	13
27	Arlington VA	Arlington	2	3	0	1	0	0	3
28	Jackson MO	St. Louis (South Suburbs)	2	3	0	9	2	0	1

Table 3.2. Constructed Amenities

County	City	Operas	Starbucks	Juice Bars	Brew Pubs	Museums	Whole Foods Stores	Bicycle Events
29 Providence RI	Providence	2	3	1	3	0	0	1
30 Summit OH	Columbus	2	3	1	2	0	0	2
31 Cass MO	St. Louis (North Suburbs)	2	2	0	8	0	0	1
32 Clay MO	St. Louis (North Suburbs)	2	2	0	8	0	0	1
33 Dane WI	Madison	2	2	2	7	1	1	7
34 Mercer NJ	Trenton	2	1	0	1	3	0	4
35 Platte MO	Kansas city	2	1	0	8	1	0	1
36 Delaware PA	Philadelphia (Northwest Suburbs)	2	1	1	2	0	0	0
37 El Paso CO	Denver (South Suburbs)	2	1	4	7	4	0	32
38 Ingham MI	Lansing	2	1	1	2	0	0	0
39 Ramsey MN	St. Paul	2	1	1	4	1	1	15
40 St. Louis City MO	St. Louis	2	1	1	3	1	0	3
41 Broome NY	New York (Northwest Suburbs)	2	0	0	0	0	0	8
42 Eaton MI	Lansing (Southwest Suburbs)	2	0	0	0	0	0	0
43 McLennan TX	Dallas (East Suburbs)	2	0	0	0	0	0	2
44 Osage OK	Tulsa (North Suburbs)	2	0	0	0	0	0	7
45 Otsego NY	Albany (West Suburbs)	2	0	0	2	0	0	0
46 Rogers OK	Tulsa (East Suburbs)	2	0	0	0	1	0	6
47 Tulsa OK	Tulsa	2	0	0	0	3	0	7
48 El Paso TX	El Paso	2	0	1	1	1	0	0
49 San Diego CA	San Diego	1	23	16	18	6	2	16
50 District of Columbia DC	Washington	1	20	0	5	0	2	2
51 Nassau NY	New York (East)	1	15	2	1	2	0	1

Notes: These items were assembled from websites, electronic telephone books, and similar sources, then aggregated to the county level. Some items are repeated for several counties, especially New York, where opera and bicycle events are summed for all five boroughs. Only high scoring cases shown of the 3,111 total US counties.

Table 3.3. Factor Analysis of Natural and Constructed Amenities

	Structure Matrix Component			
	1	2	3	4
Brew pubs	.66	.31	.09	.10
Rare and used bookstore	.82	.15	.11	.26
Research libraries	.56	−.17	−.07	−.03
Whole foods store	.79	.20	.14	.31
Opera	.62	−.10	.23	.03
Starbucks	.83	.09	.28	.17
Juice bars	.81	.27	.02	.38
Natural amenities	.20	.76	−.02	.72
Bicycle events	.69	.06	−.14	.27
Museums	.60	.03	.14	.05
Land	.06	.90	−.37	.17
Water area	.11	−.05	.83	−.06
January temperature	.19	.26	.04	.85
January sunlight	.19	−.11	−.22	.82
July temperature	.19	.74	.40	.10
July humidity	−.08	.27	−.60	.14
Topography	.06	.90	−.37	.17

Notes: Date are for U.S. counties, $N = 3,111$. Key items are in bold.
Extraction Method: Principal Component Analysis.
Rotation Method: Oblimin with Kaiser Normalization.

aptly terms "latte towns." Whole Foods is selective and thus borderline in this regard. Ideal for comparative purposes are indicators that vary across the entire U.S., and not just score zero in many locations.

Grand Ole Opry

Dance announcer George D. Hay, who called himself "The Solom Old Judge" . . . had originated the National Barn Dance on WLS in Chicago in 1924 . . . Immediately after a broadcast of the NBC Music Appreciation Hour . . . Hay opened the program by saying: "For the past hour, you have been listening to Grand Opera. Now we will present Grand Ole Opry!"

The name stuck, and in succeeding years, as the live audience grew, the program moved, first to a newly built studio that accommodated about five hundred, then to the Hillsboro Theatre, and East Nashville Tabernacle, and later to the auditorium of the war memorial, which seated about 1,200. Two years after the Opry became a network show, with a half hour broadcast coast to coast, it moved to the famous Ryman Auditorium where it remained until 1974.

With the opening of Opryland U.S.A. and amusement park dedicated by

President Nixon on March 16th, 1974, the Opry moved into a new $15 million Theatre, the largest broadcasting studio in the world, with a seating capacity of 4,400.

From: Southern Music in the Twentieth Century,
http://www.southernmusic.net/grandoleopry.htm.

Are these different amenity types patterned by city or county? Do some cluster together? Very much so. This is clear in a factor analysis (Table 3.3). It shows that all the constructed amenities cluster on the first factor, so we summed them in a Constructed Amenities Index. See the Chapter Appendix.

Do amenities drive urban growth? If so which amenities? To this we turn next.

THE MAIN FINDING: CONTEXTUAL RELATIVISM

The main results in this chapter extend those in the last: different kinds of people move to different locations with distinct amenities. What attracts one person canrepel others. There is no "silver bullet" for urban dynamics. Different subsets of persons want different things from cities, and move to some, or leave others, for distinct reasons. While this is a relatively simple idea, it is again the opposite of the more standard approach, which is to analyze the sources of growth or decline for the total population over a decade, usually using just census data or basic social background items from surveys—as in countless reports. (Some of the best are by Edward Glaeser and Shapiro (2001), Roy Bahl and George Peterson, reviewed in Clark and Ferguson (1983, Chap. 3 and passim). We also include total population to contrast with our more refined analyses. Sharp differences emerge. This is because "total population growth" is a summation of all kinds of different, and contradictory, dynamics—subtypes of migrants move for different reasons. More useful for many policy or analytical purposes is to specify how distinct subpopulations (like elderly, college graduates) act—rather than generalizing from one of these to the whole. Subcultures differ. Unfortunately the U.S. Census does not measure population change using culture subcategories like those in the last chapter, so we are constrained to several that are available and that link with more specific ideas. College graduates are one leading subsector of Florida's (2002, p. 327ff.) creative class which he defines very broadly as including over thirty million Americans who do creative work of some sort, measured broadly and roughly by summing classes of occupations from the

Table 3.4. OLS Regressions of Change in Total Population and its Components: Core Model Results

					Dependent Variables						
Core Model-Independent Variables	Change of Population (Ratio 2000/90)	Change of Population (Ratio 90/80)	Change of Percent with Some College (Ratio 90/80)	Change of Percent with a Bachelors Degree or Higher (Ratio 90/80)	Change of Percent of Elderly, Non-Working Age (Ratio 90/80)	Change of Percent of All Hispanics (Ratio 90/80)	Change of Percent of Asian/Pacific Islander (Ratio 90/80)	High Tech Patents 1975–1999	Change of Percent of Finance, Business/Professional Services, Personnel/Public Admin (Ratio 90/80)	Change of Percent of Entertainment Services (Ratio 90/80)	Change in Percent Young (Age 22–34, Ratio 90/80)
Percent gay households pergay00	+	+	+	0	0	0	0	0	0	0	0
Percent White residents p80white	0	0	+	–	0	+	+	–	+	+	–
Natural Amenities index natramen	+	+	–	–	+	0	–	+	–	+	–
Median family income @3AMEDFM	+	+	–	+	+	+	0	+	–	+	0
Constructed Amenities index Zcamnte	+	+	–	0	–	0	0	+	–	+	0
Total population size @3aPop	–	–	+	0	+	0	0	–	+	+	+

Notes: Combined data from DDB, Census, US Dept of Agriculture, US Patent Office for US counties, *N* is approximately 3100.
+ or – assigned to *t* values; 0 assigned when sig. > 0.05.

Census. We can find more meaningful variations by analyzing such subpopulations.

- As a baseline, we still start with total population growth (or decline), as it is the focus of most studies of urban growth or decline. We include the 1980–1990 and 1990–2000 periods, and find more growth in locations with more amenities, both natural (sunlight, water, etc.) and constructed (opera, juice bars and more). Similarly, counties with more gay male households have more growth, as did locations with smaller populations and higher median family incomes. Table 3.4 shows specifics. Results are identical for both decades (1980–1990 and 1990–2000), which suggests that using the 1980–1990 period is reasonably predictive of later years. We use only 1980–1990 for subgroups below since the 2000 data by county were not available except for total population when this analysis was completed (December, 2002).

- If we shift from total population to growth in the percent of residents with bachelors degrees or more, results change: college graduates increased more in locations with *fewer* natural amenities; constructed amenities were insignificant. Growth was higher where there were higher incomes but fewer white residents. Growth was unrelated to percent gays or population size. As some of these results do not square well with hypotheses about the culturally sensitive moralists and individualists from the last chapter, or Brooks, Florida, et al., just above, we also analyzed the percent of college graduates in 1990 (thus studying the *level* of college graduates in a county rather than *change*). Using the same regression model, we found more expected results: higher percentages of college graduates resided where gays and constructed amenities were higher, although population size was negative, which fits the latte-college town image, but not the imagery of the New York/LA as the (past?) destination of young talent.[5]

Chicago Tribune, December 18th, 2002
Those Who Coulda Been Mayoral Contenders
By Cate Plys, a Chicago journalist

Thank God somebody actually filed to run against Mayor Richard M. Daley . . . Still, every four years Daley should have to come up with new excuses to avoid debating his opponents. I was beginning to think he'd get out of it this time. Old-line politicians took a pass, preferring less public forms of humiliation, or were they just afraid of angering Daley? . . .

Political neophytes faced a different problem: the Herculean signature total required by the Chicago Board of Elections to get on the ballot for a citywide office since the Illinois legislature turned Chicago's mayoral elections into nonpartisan contests in 1997. It's still unclear whether any of the four candidates who filed really have enough signatures. That gave me the idea to form the Alternatives to Potter Committee, and recruit my own candidates.

Unfortunately, I wasn't able to get enough signatures for any of them.

Still, I present them here as a vision of what might have been.

—Rich Melman. Founder of Lettuce Entertain You, Melman is as successful as New York Mayor Michael Bloomberg, so he'd probably serve for free too. The city budget could use the help.

Disasters like Millennium Park and Soldier Field already had me thinking of a businessperson, and then I spoke with University of Chicago sociology professor Terry Nichols Clark, who specializes in urban finance. "The city's No. 1 economy now, as they label it, is entertainment," said Clark. "That's driven by residents, but also many tourists, from suburbs and conventions . . . Critical to that is making the city a fun place, a lively place. Sculpture, roses. People sometimes make fun of this, but this is being done around the country, and do we want to be Detroit or Cleveland?"

Melman is just the guy to entertain tourists. "I think the best thing I could do is hire the mayor as a consultant," said Melman, after he stopped laughing. But he quickly came up with his campaign's cornerstone. Melman recalls the Catskills Mountain resorts used to have a singles week. He's aware that many people come to Chicago from Detroit and Cleveland—see above—for job opportunities as well as marriage prospects. "So my idea is that we should have a singles week where we invite singles from all across the country, and it's sort of a big party for people to meet and hopefully settle in Chicago in the future,"he said.

"I want to be careful to not let the mayor think we're serious," he added. "That wouldn't be so smart."

- Percent residents with only some college education increase more in localities with *fewer* natural and constructed amenities, but more gay and white residents, larger populations, and lower incomes. These results and those for analysis of the level of percent residents with some college are nearly the converse of those for college graduates. Indeed they broadly correspond to the patterns associated with the traditional political culture index of the last chapter, which is negatively associated with education for example, as discussed further below.
- Many past analyses use professionals and persons working in finance as cutting edge sectors (e.g. Kasarda, 1985; Sassen, 2001, p. 156ff.) but surprisingly perhaps, these increased more in locations with *fewer* natural and constructed amenities, which were *lower* in income, and larger in population. These contradict the Wall Street image. If we analyze levels rather

than change, we find quite different results, suggesting a shift in the factors driving growth of such jobs, probably high land value and rental costs which skyrocketed in the 1990s (Kotkin & DeVol, 2001). The level analysis, which captures the residue of past decades, showed that there were more persons working in finance and professional jobs if the county had more gays, fewer whites, more natural and constructed amenities, higher income, and smaller population. These differences between the level and change results flag the beginnings of moves by firms away from locations like Manhattan, which seem to have accelerated in later years. The scarce Census data to date do not permit analysis of their recent dynamics with the sorts of multi-causal methods that demographers prefer.

- To contrast with persons in finance and professionals, we analyzed persons employed in entertainment and recreation activities, again from the Census. These include Hollywood and Disney staff, but the majority in these occupations perform basic tasks like cleaning swimming pools or waiting on tables. We find growth in entertainment jobs higher in locations with more natural and constructed amenities, higher income, more white residents, but unrelated to percent gays. The levels analysis was generally similar, but showed entertainment jobs more numerous in locations with fewer constructed amenities and smaller populations. The dynamics of such occupations have been little studied and deserve more attention.[6]

- Young persons (age 22–34) were more numerous in 1990 in locations with more constructed but fewer natural amenities, more gays, fewer whites, higher incomes, but smaller populations. They grew in numbers in 1980–1990 in locations that were larger in population, and had fewer constructed amenities, but otherwise results were similar to those for 1990 levels. Unfortunately these data do not permit us to distinguish for instance young with and without college degrees and other characteristics, so results are for the entire age cohort. A related study of migration by young persons shows the importance of amenities in a manner generally similar to our results (Gottlieb, 2003).

- The non-working elderly are an important group as they are large, growing, and potentially driven more by amenities than job characteristics in location decisions. We find that they increase *more* where there are natural amenities, but *less* with constructed amenities, and change is unrelated to gays or percent white residents. They increase more in larger and higher-income locations, so they are not just moving to the country. This is consistent with related work on the elderly (Frey & de Vol, 2000). The analysis of the level (percent of elderly in 1990) suggests the operation of more traditional forces in the past: the percent elderly persons in 1990 was higher in counties with fewer gays, more whites, fewer natural and constructed amenities, and lower family incomes. The contrasts of the level and change results indicate a shift in the kinds of locations where the elderly are moving. They suggest that choices in the 1980–1990 period were of a more up-scale elderly popu-

lation than the earlier decades of choices which (along with those made in
the 1980–1990 decade) are captured in the level of elderly residing in a
county in 1990.

- To assess two critical immigrant groups, we included percent Hispanics and
  Asian-Pacific Islanders. Hispanic growth is *unrelated to any* of the amenities, but Asian-Pacific Islanders increase more where there are more natural
  amenities. Both are unrelated to gays and most other variables, but Hispanics increase more in areas with higher income. Japanese, Koreans, and
  Asian-Indians are explored further with Other Variables below.
- To explore urban innovation and creativity hypotheses, we analyzed locations of persons who take out patents registered with the U.S. Patent Office.
  We created three patent measures, for high tech, entertainment, and other
  inventions, based on all 1.1 million patents issued from 1975 to 1999. In-
  ventors of all three types are far more likely to live in locations richer in
  natural amenities *and* constructed amenities like Starbucks, Brew Pubs, and
  Whole Foods. There are also more patents in counties with fewer whites,
  higher incomes, and smaller populations. This is broadly consistent with
  Florida's (2002) hypotheses, except that gays are insignificant. This analysis was of levels only since change seemed more affected by patent-specific
  factors than these general urban factors.

OTHER VARIABLES AND OTHER AMENITIES?

There is so much literature on job and population growth that we reviewed some
of the best recent work and added fourteen other variables to supplement those
in our core model above (in Table 3.4). These fourteen were used in related studies and widely discussed (e.g. Frey & Liaw, 1998; Glaeser et al., 2000; Glaeser
& Shapiro, 2001 and the review of Bradbury et al., 1982). We did not include
the fourteen in the core due to intercorrelations among some of the variables and
to simplify the presentation. The "Other Variables" included population density,
percent working in construction and manufacturing, percent college graduates
(as an independent variable at the county level), years of education completed
(from the DDB for individual respondents), homeownership, FBI crime rates,
fear of crime (DDB survey), percent unmarried households, Democratic voting,
change in percent gay residents, percent Koreans, Asian-Indians, and Japanese
(as these are discussed as driving high tech growth), net migration, and strong
and weak network ties.

Many such "other variables" had significant effects, generally consistent
with past work. But our main concern here is not to build a bigger or more comprehensive model, but to explore new variables, especially amenities, and how
they differ by subpopulations. The key question we thus posed about the "other
variables" was: do they suppress or shift the impacts of the amenity variables

from those of the core model? The answer is usually no. Specifically we calculated the percent of the fifty-four coefficients in the core model that shifted with the addition of each of the fourteen other variables, and found that most changed 0, 2 or 4 percent. The apparent exception was fear of crime as reported by DDB respondents, which suppressed twenty-eight percent of the core coefficients. But this DDB item was available for less than half of the counties which seems to have been important. By contrast the Census measure of serious crimes per 100,000 residents suppressed none of the core variables. Details are in the Appendix.

Performing Miracles
Mark J. Stern

As an economic tool, culture is a hot ticket.

Across the nation, cities have turned to the arts as an economic development strategy. At last count, no fewer than ninety U.S. cities had put forward plans to useculture to revitalize distressed areas. For the most part, such plans focus on the direct economic impact of large-scale institutions and planned cultural districts. In New York, for example, the Brooklyn Academy of Music LDC is developing a fourteen-block, $560 million "cultural district" in Brooklyn's Fort Greene.

But what if a handful of homegrown, community-based arts groups could have just as dramatic an effect on a neighborhood as a planned cultural district or major arts institution? What if a church-basement theater troupe were actually just as important for a struggling area as a MOMA or a Lincoln Center?

Over the past eight years, the University of Pennsylvania Social Impact of the Arts Project has studied the ways in which the arts and culture influence Philadelphia's neighborhoods. We learned that culture does have a powerful effect on neighborhood revitalization—but it is one that has little to do with tourists, jobs or even revenue. In Philadelphia, the average community arts group had only a few hundred people register for its classes per year; the average annual budget of a cultural organization in a low-income neighborhood was $150,000; the average group employed no more than two or three full-time employees. In short, even when considered as a sector, whatever direct contribution these groups were making to their local economies was quite small. Nonetheless, these same community cultural programs seemed to have a substantial impact on the economic fortunes of their respective neighborhoods.

During the 1980s, for example, Philadelphia neighborhoods with an active arts scene (measured by the number of cultural providers within one-half mile) were nearly three times more likely to see their poverty rates decline and their populations increase.

The connection between culture and community vitality continued into the 1990s. During that decade, the city of Philadelphia lost over 65,000 residents—a decline of thirty-eight people per "block group" (approximately six city blocks). The results, however, varied widely from one neighborhood to another, and these variations were strongly linked to cultural participation. In the quarter of census block groups with the lowest cultural participation rate, the numbers were far worse than those for the city overall; these areas lost an average of ninety residents during the decade. Among block groups with higher-than-average cultural participation rates, the news was much better; these neighborhoods gained population, an average of nearly twenty residents per block group.

The impact of culture on population change was not restricted to well-off neighborhoods. A low-income neighborhood's chance of experiencing population growth more than doubled if it had a higher-than-average cultural participation rate. The results also held across ethnic lines: Older white ethnic neighborhoods such as Fishtown, established African-American neighborhoods such as Germantown and East Oak Lane, and emerging Latino areas such as Oxford Circle all used high levels of cultural engagement as one way of attracting new residents.

Culture had a positive impact on housing prices as well. Between 1995 and 2000, the average sale price of a home in Philadelphia increased from around $49,000 to $59,000. In neighborhoods with few cultural organizations, the increase was much smaller—only about $3,000. By comparison, in neighborhoods with many cultural organizations, the average price increase was nearly $30,000.

What's more, these boosts in neighborhood economic fortune generally occurred without substantial gentrification. Certainly, in some neighborhoods the speculative housing market was so strong that neighborhood revitalization quickly became wholesale displacement, but for every "hot" neighborhood there were, and still are, dozens of communities eager to attract new residents and new investment. Here, urbanist Jane Jacobs' classic distinction between "cataclysmic money" and "gradual money" makes all the difference. Although we can point to some neighborhoods where a flood of speculative money pushed longtime residents out, a lively cultural scene was more likely to attract smaller and slower redevelopment efforts. Fishtown, for example, continues to attract new development gradually. It has also emerged as a diverse area with people of different economic and ethnic backgrounds living together as neighbors.

The connection between diversity and culture is one of the keys that explains the impact the arts have on neighborhood revitalization. We've discovered that neighborhoods that are economically and ethnically diverse are most likely to have high levels of cultural engagement. Neighborhoods that have higher-than-average poverty rates and large numbers of professionals living in them—what we call pov-prof neighborhoods—consistently have more cultural organizations and high participation rates. The cultural institutions in these neighborhoods serve as anchors, preventing diversity from becoming a transient state. That is why economically and ethnically diverse neighborhoods with high levels of cultural engagement were much more likely to remain diverse over time. Cultural organizations simultaneously stimulate population growth in and the stabilization of diverse neighborhoods.

How do small, perennially cash-strapped local arts and cultural programs perform all this magic? The answer is simple: Culture stimulates revitalization not through direct economic impact, but by building the social connections between people.

A lively cultural scene appears to contribute to neighborhood vitality in two important ways: It increases the inclination and ability of residents to make positive changes in their community, and it increases the connections between neighborhoods of different ethnic and economic compositions.

Mark J. Stern is Professor of Social Welfare and History at the University of Pennsylvania School of Social Work, and co-directs the Urban Studies program. The Social Impact of the Arts Project's research is available on its web site: http://www.ssw.upenn.edu/SIAP. This report is excerpted from: www.nycfuture.org/

One much discussed concept is social capital, including strong and weak ties, considered in Chapter 9. Do these shift population or job growth? Putnam (2000) holds that strong ties can reinforce political coordination and encourage trust. Florida (2002) takes the other side, suggesting that weak ties are more important, at least for high tech job growth and innovation as measured by patents. We thus analyzed both strong and weak ties, adding them to the core regression model in Table 3.4 to assess their impact on population change. Results? Zero impact on any; all relations were insignificant. Components of the strong and weak ties indexes are detailed in the Chap. 2 Appendix.

We analyzed change in the percent of persons in poverty as a dependent variable, but found none of the Table 3.5 model variables significant.

What of the three types of political culture from the Chapter 9? They are linked with distinct amenities, broadly consistent with their overall cultural outlooks. The Moralists are in locations with more natural amenities and most created amenities. The Individualists are in the middle, in locations with fewer amenities than the Moralists, while Traditionalists reside in locations with the fewest natural and created amenities. One might wonder if these are driven more by income than culture, but when we recomputed controlling income, the same patterns hold (see Table 3.5).

Table 3.5. Moralists Live Nearby More Amenities of All Sorts, Traditionalists Least: Correlations of the Three Political Cultures with Amenities and Related Characteristics

	Moralistic Political Culture MORAL2	Individualistic Political Culture INDLS1	Traditional Political TRAD1
Natural Amenities index—NatrAmenS	.121**	-.031**	-.074**
Constructed Amenities index—Zcarnnte	.105**	.014**	-.0198**
Sunlight—SUNLIT	.082**	-.008*	-.015**
January temperature—TMPJANZ	.36**	.009*	.021**
July temperature—TEMJULZ	.103**	-.29 **	-.090**
Humidity—HUMIJZ	-.006	-.016**	-.006**
Topography—TYPOGZ	.031**	-.047**	.046**
Water—WATERZ	.096**	.025**	-.075**
Number of used and rare bookstores	.085**	-.005	-.057**
Number of Whole Foods	.049**	-.005	-.044**
Number of Brew pubs	.073**	-.002	-.065
Number of Operas	.044**	.043**	-.064**
Number of Starbucks	.093**	.016**	.092**
Number of Juicebars	.076**	-.01	-.049**
Number of bike event (SCCA, NORBA by city originally) Agreg country	.073**	.00	-.050**
Number of museums MUSEUM_1	.083**	.023**	-.069**
Number of research libraries	.072**	.014*	-.055**
What is your political affiliation?	(a)	-.050**	-.054**
Are you a registered voter?	(a)	-.071**	-.031**
Respondent's age	-.037	-.101**	.123**
Size of city of residence	.113**	.040**	-.105**
Education level of respondent's spouse	.183**	.124**	.100**
Level of education completed	.216**	.160**	-.125**
Employment status of R (merged)	-.040**	-.088**	.070**
Owns residence	-.003	-.009**	.067**
Which one of the following best describes your marital status?	.100**	.018**	.100**
Ownership of residence	-.006	.010**	-.050**
Sex of respondent	.058**	-.055**	-.116**
Democrat (DDB, DEMOC)	(a)	.023**	-.070**
2000 Percent gay households	-.032	.008	.006
90 Percent Non-Hispanic white	.027	-.059**	.00
Blacks, all yrs, DDB	.013**	.075**	-.025**
Percent education wkforce	-.025	-.01	-.066
90 Percent born in state of residence	.107**	.033*	.142**
90 South	.032	.001	-.047
90 Percent foreign born	.034	-.005	.017

(a) Cannot be computed because at least one of the variables is constant.

Sources: DDB survey combined with amenities, Census, and other items. The three political culture indexes are defined in the Appendix to Chap. 2. The survey items are from the DDB, for items like homeownership, education, spouse's education, age, etc. That is these are individual responses not county averages for all residents as in the Census. The amenity items are county level as in earlier tables in this chapter. *N* for individual respondents is as high as 88,000 but most are far less as the items were not repeated in all years. *N* for counties = 3,111. These are Pearson correlation coefficients (*r*'s).

* Correlation is at significant at the 0.05 level (one-tailed).

** Correlation is at significant at the 0.01 level (one-tailed).

CONCLUSION

Amenities differ, as do responses to them by different types of persons. Distinct amenities explain different types of population growth. We introduced two new amenity measures, *natural amenities* such as moderate temperature, hills, and nearby water, and *constructed amenities* like the numbers of opera, research libraries, used and rare book stores, juice bars, Starbucks, and bicycle events.

For the total population, the simple proposition "amenities attract people" holds: growth is higher in counties with more natural and constructed amenities. These relations hold even while controlling up to twenty variables in multiple regressions.

But when we deconstruct total growth into components, results markedly change. College graduates are more numerous where there are fewer natural but more constructed amenities. Conversely, the elderly seem attracted *more* by natural, but *less* by constructed amenities. Residents filing high tech patents, however, live in places with *more* natural and constructed amenities.

Percent gays has been stressed in recent work on urban growth, but we found it had inconsistent or near zero relations with many factors plausibly explaining its dynamics. For instance, percent gays is unrelated to high tech patents and growth in college graduates using data for all U.S. counties.

Still, the main goal of this chapter is to encourage researchers and policy makers to give serious attention to amenities in future thinking. It was hard work for us, but conceptually simple, to count up the numbers of different amenities. Yet they take on meaning only in the minds of persons reacting to them, and such reactions, as this chapter and the last have shown, are complex but still interpretable.

ACKNOWLEDGMENTS

Thanks to some key persons who are themselves great amenities: Bill Bishop, who found the bike events and organized a circus; Bob Cushing, who created files of natural amenities, patents and more; Richard Florida, fellow cycling theorist; Gary Gates, Census tyro; Aaron McCright, Stephen Appold, Alex Chandler, Jennifer Novak, and Ray Hutchinson, who questioned all; Erica Coslor, Ms. Nightlife; Joshua McFeeters, a real programmer; Carl Pickerill and Marie Ann Ramos, the table team; Konrad Siewierski, logician.

APPENDIX

The Constructed Amenities Index. Summed the normalized values (z-scores) of nine amenities: brew pubs, used and rare bookstores, research libraries, museums, Whole Foods stores, operas, Starbucks, juice bars, and bicycle events. We were concerned about aggregating such diverse indicators, since different persons might react to them in distinct ways. Thus we constructed two smaller indexes, one more cultural and intellectual, of bookstores, libraries, opera and museums, and the second of the five more physical amenities. But the Pearson r's among the three indexes were so high—0.97, 0.87 and 0.96—that they were virtually interchangeable when compared across U.S. counties. We thus retained the single larger Constructed Amenity Index in most subsequent work. We constructed the index after finding that many individual items generated quite similar results. This is clear in high intercorrelations and the factor analysis among them (e.g. Table 3.3). The first component shows that brewpubs, used and rare book bookstores, research libraries, Whole Foods stores, Starbucks, juice bars, opera, and bicycle events all tend to be more numerous in broadly similar locations. Second are land and overall natural amenities. Third is water access. Fourth is temperature and sunlight. After also analyzing the items separately, to simplify we report just the two indexes, of Natural and Constructed amenities.

Absolute vs. Per Capita. Should amenities be adjusted by dividing them by population size to create per capita measures? To do so implies a quite different conceptualization with drastically different rankings than the absolute numbers we use. For some purposes per capita measures are appropriate, such as helping leaders in a smaller town assess "how well" they are doing compared to larger locations. But in this context, many adjustments might be added in addition to population size—like income, citizen age, other measures of citizen demand for an amenity—if the concern is to assess whether the supply and demand for a given amenity are close to local market equilibrium in economic terms. Still, from the standpoint of potential migrants (citizens or firms) choosing among alternative locations based on their overall amenity market basket, the absolute scores provide a more comprehensive sense of the richness or poverty of a location. If I move to Los Angeles, Table 3.2 shows, I will be in the capital of juice bars and Starbucks, while New York is where I should go for opera (and theater and related entertainment). This is more critical for the citizen or tourist who wants to know the options for opera than knowing the Iowa City per capita opera rating. We analyzed per capita items, and found many interesting patterns, but they capture other aspects of localities that are distinct from and generally less powerful than the absolute scores we report.

Why These Amenities? As a simple strategy we sought to include some major amenities discussed in past work as distinguishing locations in their attractiveness, especially to younger and more mobile populations (e.g. Florida, 2000). These are clearly intended to serve as indicators only of the many other components of amenity-rich localities. They are only samples of the local amenity infrastructure. The high interrelations suggest that if we had added say symphony orchestras or swimming pools we would have found these more numerous in the same general locations as score high on our Constructed Amenities Index. Natural and constructed amenities indexes are less tightly intercorrelated at $r = 0.56$.

Percent Change and Net Migration. Concerning the form of the dependent variables: demographers distinguish local growth due to differential birth rates from net (in minus out) migration, but given the high rates of migration for many subgroups, and the non-availability of net migration data by subgroup, we use simply percent change of the size of subgroups like college graduates. However, we added Net Migration to the county as an Other Variable to see if it shifted the effects of the core model.

N's. The number of cases (*N*) varies for different variables. The *N* is about 3,111 for the counties surveyed by the U.S. Census in 1980, 1990, and 2000. The DDB Lifestyle Survey includes 84,989 interviews, but only 14,444 respondents as many were resurveyed to permit over-time panel analysis. The same items were not posed each year, so the *N*'s vary by item. The DDB survey was stratified by county population size, so the number of interviews was higher in large counties. We checked the DDB survey results for possible sample selection bias against the Census using the male/female ratio and found the two near identical in the larger countries, but sometimes disparate in smaller counties. The natural amenities data were from the U.S. Department of Agriculture for 3,111 counties. The constructed amenities we assembled from electronic telephone books, web sites, and similar sources for individual institutions by street address, then summed to the county level. While all U.S. counties were included in principle, these amenities were more geographically concentrated and none were reported for many locations. The lowest *N* was forty-one for Whole Foods; that is forty-one counties had at least one store, although LA County included eleven Whole Foods stores. Opera was next lowest; 113 counties had at least one opera per our sources, but New York's five boroughs had twelve operas. The skewed nature and low *N*'s of these individual amenities were two reasons that we summed them in an index for all the constructed amenities; the distribution for the Constructed Amenities Index across all U.S. counties was more normal than its components.

File Merging. The data from these several sources were merged, first at the county, and second assigned via the county ID number to the individual DDB response case. Certain county-level analyses were completed, such as the factor analysis of amenities. But for regressions including both DDB individual and county level data, we used the largest merged file with up to 84,989 cases. Every individual respondent in each county was assigned the county scores; all residents of LA County, for instance, had identical merged scores for LA County on all the Census and amenity items.

Pairwise Analysis. Given these uneven N's for several variables, we used pairwise analysis of missing cases, which computes a correlation matrix of r's with as many cases as are available for each pairwise combination of two variables. From the r matrix, regressions and other analyses are in turn computed. While the N's thus appear huge for some variables, the presence of others with lower N's constrains the robustness of the analysis. Consequently we were cautious about including too many independent variables in regression models; we noted instability as the number of variables grew. For important tables, we replicated models with larger and smaller numbers of variables to assess whether they remained consistent, as illustrated most explicitly below with our metro area replications of the gay results. We generally report just plus and minus signs to ease communication about regressions in the text. More detail is available from the author.

Other Variable Analysis. As discussed in the text, we extended the core regression model (of Table 3.4) with fourteen other variables, suggested mainly by past work on population change. They were added to the core model one at a time using the "enter" SPSS regression command which forces the inclusion of all variables. That is, the core variables plus one other variable were entered simultaneously to estimate the nine equations explaining each of the nine dependent variables (like total population change, change in college graduates, etc.). An example of the method is shown in Table A.3.1, where Panel A shows the Core regression and Panel B adds one Other Variable. We did not use a stepwise method which treated the first six variables differently from the seventh or all other variables. The same nine equations were reestimated fourteen times (for $9 \times 14 = 126$ total equations), each time including a different one of the fourteen "other variables." Then we looked for two patterns. First which other variables had "direct effects," that is was the regression coefficient for the single "other variable," population density for instance, significant in explaining any of the nine dependent variables? The percentage of times that the nine dependent variables were significantly related to the other variables is reported in the far right column of Table A.3.2. It shows that most of the other variables did have significant effects, in addition to the six core variables. This is consistent with much past work. But second, we looked to see if these fourteen other variables changed the results of the six core variables—did the core variable regression coefficients rise, fall, or change sign when the other variables were added? Here we found minimal impacts, usually just 0, 2, or 4 percent of the fifty-four core model coefficients (6 independent × 9 dependent variables) were changed when the other variables were added. The exceptions were variables that had much lower N's and came from the DDB survey, FAMCRIME (fear of crime) and DEMOC (percent Democrats). Because these were so unusual, and we were concerned that the results may have been due more to the lower N than to their substantive meaning, we added two similar variables from the Census: serious crimes reported to the police per 100,000 residents, and percent Democratic voting in the Presidential election. For these two Census variables, with the full number of cases, there were just eight percent changes in the core coefficients. To distinguish the impact of 1. the lower N from 2. fear vs. crime rates, we reestimated the core model twice. First, including all cases, and second omitting those cases for all variables that lacked FAMCRIME data—since FAMCRIME was missing for 56 percent of the cases. Results from the two methods differed dramatically: there was zero suppression and zero direct effects of FAMCRIME using the lower N. This indicates that the 28 percent suppression using the first method was essentially an artifact of changes in the cases analyzed. The zero suppression using the second method is more meaningful. Percent young and the level variables were added after completing the main Other Variable analysis, so they are not reported in Table A.3.2.

In brief, adding fourteen other variables suggested by related work did not suppress the core, including the amenity variables.

Table A.3.1. Illustration of Core and Other Variable Regressions

	Unstandardized Coefficients		Standardized Coefficients		
	B	Std. Error	Beta	t	Sig.
Panel A: Core analysis of six independent variables, shown for one dependent variable					
(Constant)	1.02	.08		12.68	.00
2000 percent gay households	-.07	.10	-.04	-.68	.50
Pct 1980 White	.00	.00	-.01	-.23	.82
Natural amenities—NatrAmenS	.03	.00	.56	9.75	.00
80 Median family income in 1979	.00	.00	.14	2.80	.01
Constructed amenities—ZCAMNTE	.00	.00	.22	1.25	.21
80 Total population	.00	.00	-.48	-2.86	.00
Panel B: Adding one other variable (density) to the of six core independent variable, shown for one dependent variable					
(Constant)	.96	.03		37.84	.00
2000 percent gay households	.14	.03	.08	5.06	.00
Pct 1980 White	.00	.00	.00	.05	.96
Natural amenities—NatrAmenS	.03	.00	.53	26.23	.00
80 Median family income in 1979	.00	.00	.14	8.58	.00
Constructed amenities—ZCAMNTE	.00	.00	.20	3.62	.00
80 Total population	.00	.00	-.44	-8.74	.00
90 population density—people per square kilometer of land	.00	.00	-.05	-2.92	.00

Notes: (a) Dependent Variable: Change of Population (ratio 90/80). These two panels illustrate the Other Variable method, of adding one additional variable at a time to the Core model. The printout for all Other Variables is so large that a summary is in Table A.3.2. In Panel B we see that the t of -2.9 indicates a significant direct effect. Density had a similar significant direct effect for six of the nine dependent variables, which appears as 67 percent in Table A.3.2. Comparison of each individual core coefficient of Panel A against Panel B shows that one moved up, percent gays, when density was included as an Other Variable. However, in results for all other dependent variables, no other independent variable moved up, so Table A.3.2 shows 2 percent in the Up column.

Table A.3.2. Other Variables Analysis: Many Direct Effects but Minimal Change in the Core

Other Variables (OVs)	% Change in Core Model Variables			% of Dependent Variables (DVs) Significantly Affected by the OV = Direct Effects on the nine DVs
	Up	Down	Change in Sign	
Percent construction and manufacturing PERIND2	2	2	0	89
Percent unmarried households PERUMH90	2	0	0	22
DDB level of education EDUC	0	0		11
WORKHARD—DDB item	0	0	0	0
HOMEOWNR—DDB item	0	0	0	0
Percent Democrats—DEMOC DDB item	0	56	0	0
Change in percent gays from 1980 to 1990 CHGAY	0	5	0	56
Population density—popdens	2	4	0	67
Fear of crime—FAMCRIME DDB item	0	28	0	89
Percent college graduates—CENSUS 80 percoll	0	5	2	78
Percent Japanese, Korean and Asian-Indian residents Asia3	0	4	0	44
Number of high tech patents (log) lghitec1	2	4	2	67
Democratic presidential voting—census	1	2	0	89
Serious crimes known to police, 1985: total crimes per 100,000 population	0	0	0	22
Net migration	6	6	2	67

Notes: The first three columns show the percent change in the original core coefficients when each other variable was added to the regression. There were six core independent variables and nine dependent variables, so 6 × 9 = 54 original core coefficients could change when each other variable was added. The logic of the table is explained further in the text. Down is defined as shifting from significant to statistically insignificant at the 0.05 level, Up is from insignificant to significant. Change of Sign is changing the direction of the *b* coefficient from significant at least the 0.05 level. High tech patents were added as other independent variables to eight models but not to the model where they were a dependent variable. Strong and Weak ties are defined in the Appendix to Chapter 2.

Sources: US Bureau of the Census, mainly from CD roms of the decennial census, unless noted. Patents from US Patent Office, assigned to counties by Bob Cushing. Gays and unmarried household data obtained by Gary Gates: DDB Lifestyle survey. The nine dependent variables included were: change from 1980 to 1990 in total population, college graduates, some college, elderly, Hispanics, Asian/Pacific Islanders, finance and professions, entertainment, and patents.

NOTES

1. This is the definition of two leading amenity economists: "A pure amenity is a non-produced public good such as weather quality that has no explicit price. In practice, previous empirical studies include some government services such as education and public safety," Gyourko and Tracy (1991, p. 775), building on Samuelson (1969).

2. And continue to differ in Ventura and Santa Barbara—TNC

3. The Kotkin line is appropriately quoted in a cultural policy statement for New York City (Kleiman et al., 2002).

4. Yes there are partial exceptions. Kotkin discusses big cities, Nerdistans and Valhallas, etc.

5. Indeed, commenting on the post September 11th, 2001 context, the same Kotkin (2002) faults New Yorkers for falling short of smaller competing locations on amenities: "Sure, New York is still 'The Greatest City in the World.' And Elizabeth Taylor is still 'The Most Beautiful Woman in the World.' Just ask her publicist."

6. See the overview of work to date in an email exchange by sociologists including Herb Gans, Sharon Zukin, Harvey Molotch, Richard Lloyd and others in the Urban and Community Section Listserve (2002) discussion, summarized in Chap. 8. It focused on amenities and factors encouraging artists and wannabe entertainers to locate in cities where they can actually live—since most must work in other jobs to support themselves. To explore such interdependencies of flexible yet culturally desirable jobs that are ancillary to, and geographically proximate to, art and entertainment is important for future work. Waitress and bartender are two explored ethnographically by Lloyd (2002).

BIBLIOGRAPHY

Baldassare, M. (1998). Citizen Preferences for Local Growth Controls: Trends in U.S. Suburban Support for a New Political Culture Movement of Clark and Hoffmann-Martinot, pp. 261–276.

Benjamin, W. (1999). Paris, Capital of the Nineteenth Century. In: *The Arcades Project* (pp. 14–26). Cambridge: Harvard University Press.

Berry, B. J. L., & Horton, F. E. (1970). *Geographic Perspectives on Urban Systems.* Englewood Cliffs, NJ: Prentice-Hall.

Boorstin, D. (1973). *The Americans.* New York: Random House.

Boschken, H. L. (2002). *Social Class, Politics, and Urban Markets.* Stanford: Stanford University Press. Bradbury, K., Downs, A., & Small, K. A. (1982). *Urban Decline and the Future of American Cities.* Washington, DC: Brookings Institute.

Brooks, D. (2000). *Bobos in Paradise.* New York: Simon and Schuster.

Clark, T. N. (2000). Old and New Paradigms for Urban Research: Globalization and the Fiscal Austerity and Urban Innovation Project, Featured Essay. *Urban Affairs Review,* 36 (1) (September), 3–45.

———(2003). *Trees and Real Violins: Building Post-Industrial Chicago.* Book MS.

Clark, T. N., Curtis, K. L., Fox, K., & Herhold, S. H. (1986). Business and taxes in Chicago. A Report to the City of Chicago. White Paper for Discussion (April), 130 pp.

Clark, T. N., & Ferguson, L. C. (1983). *City Money.* New York, NY: Columbia University Press.

Clark, T. N., & Goetz, E. G. (1994). The Anti-Growth Machine. In: T. N. Clark (Ed.), *Urban Innovation: Creative Strategies in Turbulent Times* (pp. 105–145). London— Newbury Park—New Delhi:Sage.

Clark, T. N., & Hoffmann-Martinot, V (Eds) (1998). *The New Political Culture.* Boulder, CO: Westview Press.

Clarke, S. E., & Gaile, G. (1998). *The Work of Cities.* Minneapolis: University of Minnesota Press.

Clarke, S. E., & Moss, A. K. (1990). Economic Growth, Environmental Quality, and Social Services. *Journal of Urban Affairs,* 12 (1), 17–34.

Drake, St. C., & Cayton, H. R. (1945). *Black Metropolis.* New York: Harper and Row.

Florida, R. (2000). Competing in the Age of Talent: Quality of Place and the New Economy. Report Prepared for The R.K. Mellon Foundation, Heinz Endowments, and Sustainable Pittsburgh.

———(2002). *The Rise of the Creative Class.* New York: Basic Books/Perseus.

———(2002, in press). The Economic Geography of Talent. *Annals of the Association of American Geographers,* 92 (4), 743–755.

Frey, W. H., & de Vol, R. (2000). *America's Demography in the New Century.* Santa Monica: Milken Institute.

Frey, W. H., & Liaw, K.-L. (1998). Immigrant Concentration and Domestic Migrant Dispersal. *Professional Geographer,* 50 (2), 215–232.

Glaeser, E., & Shapiro, J. M. (2001). *City Growth and 2000 Census: Which Places Grew, and Why?* Center on Urban Metropolitan Policy, The Brookings Institution, Survey Series, Census 2000, May 2001. http://www.brookings.edu/dybdocroot/es/urban /census/whygrowthexsum.htm

Glaeser, E. L. (2000a). Cities and Ethics. *Journal of Urban Affairs,* 22 (4), 473–494.

———(2000b). The Future of Urban Research: Non-Market Interactions. Brookings— Wharton Papers on Urban Affairs 2000, pp. 101–149.

Glaeser, E. L., Kolko, J., & Saiz, A. (2000). *Consumer City.* National Bureau of Economic Research, Working Paper 7790 (July).

Gottlieb, P. D. (2003). Economy Versus Lifestyle in the Inter-Metropolitan Migration of the Young. Draft Paper. Rutgers University/Brookings Institution.

Green, G. P. (1997). Structuring Locality: Economic Development and Growth Management in Wisconsin Cities and Villages. In: Norman Walzer (pp. 15–180).

Gyourko, J., & Tracy, J. (1991). The Structure of Local Public Finance and the Quality of Life. *Journal of Political Economy,* 99 (4), 774–806.

Harvey, D. (1990). *The Condition of Postmodernity.* Cambridge: Blackwell Press.

Jacobs, J. (1961). *The Death and Life of Great American Cities.* New York: Vintage Edition.

Judd, D., & Fainstein, S. (1999). *The Tourist City.* New Haven: Yale University Press.

Kasarda, J. D. (1985). Urban Change and Minority Opportunities. In: P. E. Peterson (Ed.), *The New Urban Reality* (pp. 33–68). Washington, DC: Brookings.

Kleiman, N. S. et al. (2002). *The Creative Engine.* New York: Center for an Urban Future. Report on website http://www.nycfuture.org/content/reports/reportview.cfm?re pkey =90&area=buspol

Kotkin, J. (2001). *The New Geography: How the Digital Revolution is Reshaping the American Landscape.* New York: Random House.

————(2002). New York State of Blind. http://www.nycfuture.org/content/reports/report view.cfm?repkey=70&area=ecopol

Kotkin, J., & DeVol, R. (2001). *Knowledge-Value Cities in the Digital Age*. Santa Monica: Milken Institute.

Lloyd, R. (2002). University of Chicago, Ph.D. thesis.

Logan, J. R., Bridges Whaley, R., & Crowder, K. (1997). The Character and Consequences of the Growth Regimes: An Assessment of 20 Years of Research. *Urban Affairs Review*, 32 (5) (May), 603–630.

Logan, J. R., & Molotch, H. L. (1987). *Urban Fortunes*. Berkeley: University of California Press.

Mathur, V., & Song, F. (2000). A Labor Market Based Theory of Regional Economic Development. *The Annals of Regional Science*, 34, 131–145.

Miranda, R., & Rosdil, D. (1997). Development Policy Innovation in American Cities. In: Walzer (pp. 181–208).

Molotch, H., Freudenburg, W., & Paulsen, K. E. (2000). History Repeats Itself, but How? City Character, Urban Tradition, and the Accomplishment of Place. *American Sociological Review*, 65 (December), 791–823.

Muth, R. F. (1971). Migration: Chicken or Egg? *Southern Economic Journal*, 37 (January), 295–306.

Norquist, J. (1998). *The Wealth of Cities*. Reading, MA: Addison-Wesley.

Portes, A., & Rumbaut, R. G. (1996). *Immigrant America: A Portrait* (2nd ed.). Berkeley: University of California Press.

Putnam, R. (2000). *Bowling Alone*. New York: Simon and Schuster.

Samuelson, P. A. (1969). Pure Theory of Public Expenditure and Taxation. In: J. Margolis & H. Guitton (Eds), *Public Economics* (pp. 28–123). New York: St. Martin's Press.

Sassen, S. (2001). *The Global City*. Princeton: Princeton University Press.

Spirou, C., & Bennett, L. (2003). *It's hardly sportin': Stadiums, neighborhood development, and the new Chicago*. Northern Illinois University Press (forthcoming).

Stern, M. J. (2002). Performing Miracles. Center for an Urban Future, http://www.nycfuture.org/content/about/mission.cfm

Strom, E. (2002). Converting Pork into Porcelain: Cultural Institutions and Downtown Development. *Urban Affairs Review*, 38 (1) (September), 3–21.

Urban and Community Section of the American Sociological Association, Listserve (2002) Starbucks, Bicycle Paths, and Urban Growth Machines: Emails Among Members. October–November, Compiled by Terry Nichols Clark, tnclark@uchicago.edu

Walzer, N. (Ed.) (1995). *Local Economic Development: Incentives and International Trends*. Boulder, CO: Westview Press.

Walzer, N., & P'ng, P. (1994). *Economic Development Strategies*. Presented to International Sociological Association, Bielefeld, Germany, July 1994, published as Chapter 7 of Walzer (1995).

Zukin, S. (1982). *Loft Living: Culture and Capital in Urban Change*. Baltimore: Johns Hopkins University Press.

Chapter Four

Consumers and Cities

Edward L. Glaeser, Jed Kolko, and Albert Saiz

INTRODUCTION

The future of the city depends on the demand for density. If cities are going to survive and flourish, then people must continue to want to live close to one another. Agglomeration effects—the effects of density—naturally determine the extent to which urban density is attractive. Most urban scholars think of cities as offering positive agglomeration benefits in the productive sphere, and as having negative agglomeration effects (or congestion effects) on non-work consumption. After all, firms and workers earn more in cities. In cities, workers pay higher rents, commute longer, and face more crime.

This basic viewpoint—that cities are good for production and bad for consumption—colors most of urban economics and has influenced most thinking on the future of cities. The critical questions about the future of cities have always been: (1) whether cities can maintain their productive edge in the world of information technology and speedy transportation; and (2) whether the service industries that currently drive urban employment will stay in cities or follow manufacturing plants out to the non-city areas.

But we believe that too little attention has been paid to the role of cities as centers of consumption. In the next century, as human beings continue to get richer, quality of life will get increasingly critical in determining the attractiveness of particular areas. After all, choosing a pleasant place to live is among the most natural ways to spend one's money. As Costa (1997) shows, between 1950 and 1990 the share of personal income in the United States spent on transportation and housing rose from 24 to 35 percent. This increase can be seen as spending to get a desirable place to live. If these trends persist, then we must think that

135

the future of cities depends on the ability of particular urban areas to provide attractive places for increasingly rich workers, who are less and less fettered by constraints on employment location.

This paper argues that there are four particularly critical urban amenities. First, and most obviously, is the presence of a rich variety of services and consumer goods. The Internet, and before it the revolution in catalog sales in the 1980s, means that manufactured goods really are national goods. However, restaurants, theaters and an attractive mix of social partners are hard to transport and are therefore local goods. Cities with more restaurants and live performance theaters per capita have grown more quickly over the past twenty years both in the U.S. and in France. In cities with more educated populations, rents have gone up more quickly than wages since 1970—the natural interpretation of this fact is that while productivity has risen in places with more educated workers, quality of life has risen faster.

The second amenity is aesthetics and physical setting. We have little evidence on the role of architectural beauty, but it does seem that more attractive cities have done better since 1980 (e.g. San Francisco). However, weather—measured by January temperature or precipitation—is the single most important determinant of population or housing price growth at the county level in the United States. Physical attributes of a community that make life more pleasant appear to be increasingly valued by consumers.

The third critical amenity is good public services. Good schools and less crime are also linked with urban growth. In a cross-section of cities, Berry-Cullen and Levitt (1999) show that an exogenous increase in crime is associated with lower population growth. Dropout rates among teenagers (controlling for the education level of adults and the poverty rate) are strongly negatively correlated with growth from 1970 to 1990. Schools and low crime also appear to be important in attracting a highly educated workforce. If education then creates further growth (as suggested by Glaeser, Scheinkman & Shleifer, 1995), there will be multiplier effects on these amenities.

The fourth vital amenity is speed. In a sense, the range of services (and jobs) available in a metropolitan area is a function of the ease with which individuals can move around. As time becomes more valuable, individuals will particularly avoid areas where transport costs are high. Indeed, the movement to edge cities and the decentralization of employment have increased commuting distances but often decreased commuting times relative to traditional downtowns. But this increasing value of time has also produced a radical shift within traditional cities. Areas close to the central business district (CBD) have succeeded as outer areas (still within the city) have failed. For example, within New York City, areas close to Wall Street have done extremely well since 1980 particularly in terms of income of residents and housing prices. The outer boroughs have continued in their century long-decline.

The importance of transport speed pushes us towards two visions of the urban future that are likely to coexist for decades to come. These two alternative future cities are based, ultimately, on transport modes. Essentially, the cities of the future will either be car cities with decentralized employment or walking/public transport cities with extremely high levels of density. In both of these models, transport times can be low, and different types of cities will succeed in different areas. In the U.S., where public transportation is less important and where gas taxes are low, low density "car cities" will continue to thrive. In cities where car transport is difficult because of older infrastructure, and in Europe where the infrastructure predates cars and where gas taxes are high, high density areas will also succeed. However, not all (or even most) high density centers will do well. Traditional cities will only succeed when they provide amenities that are attractive to high human capital residents. In principle, it may be beneficial for the poorer residents of a community for that community to attract wealthier residents. After all, it cannot help the poor to live in isolated communities filled with poverty.[1]

Our paper has strong implications for how local governments should stimulate growth. The sovereignty of the consumer is inescapable. Trying to keep manufacturing is probably useless and because of the negative amenities related to manufacturing (see Kahn, 1997) possibly even harmful. The key is to educate and attract high human capital individuals. This means providing strong basic services like safe streets and good schools. In the United States, as the desire for private schools continues to rise, allowing people who are paying for private schools to opt out of a fraction of public school taxes may be a good means of attracting better educated urban residents. Naturally, policies that ensure an attractive city that is easy to get around will also be beneficial . . .

Consumption in Cities

These functions of cities all focus on the production side. However, cities can also be desirable because of consumption amenities. Even at the same wage, some consumers may actually prefer denser cities. The lower transport costs in cities that make firms more productive may also make life outside of work more enjoyable.

For example, the low transport costs created by urban density may facilitate enjoyable social contact. The wide range of people living within a small geographic area means that big cities offer access to desirable interpersonal relationships. Glaeser and Sacerdote (1999) document that individuals who live in denser buildings and big cities are more likely to socialize with their neighbors. Of course, big cities can also create less desirable social contacts. Parents may wish to isolate their children from some peers, which will be harder in a city. The ease of interpersonal contact in cities also helps to explain higher levels of crime in urban areas (Glaeser & Sacerdote, 1999).

One area where this appears to be particularly important is the location decisions of young single people, who live disproportionately in the densest urban areas. A natural explanation of this phenomenon is that crowding makes meeting other single people easier and facilitates the operation of the marriage market (see Costa & Kahn, 1999, for more discussion). Alternatively, married people may live disproportionately in suburbs so that they can consume more space.

Lower transport costs for people in large urban areas may also create benefits for households in the consumption of non-manufactured goods. Above, we argued that service industries will benefit from the agglomeration of people in cities and the reduced transport costs that this agglomeration creates. Of course, the incidence of reducing transport costs will surely affect both producers and consumers. Some of the benefits of reduced transport costs will go to the producers, but the consumers will also benefit. This benefit can be seen in the range and proximity of services available in large cities.

Large urban markets may also increase the welfare of consumers because of goods which appear to have substantial scale economies. For example, baseball teams, opera companies, and comprehensive art museums all need large audiences to be successful. For consumers who want to be able to go to the Opera regularly or go to live major league baseball games, living in large cities is a necessity. The advantages from scale economies and specialization are also clear in the restaurant business where large cities will have restaurants that specialize in a wide range of *cuisines*—scale economies mean that specialized retail can only be supported in places large enough to have a critical mass of customers.

The consumption value of some cities may be a product of their possession of a valuable stock of buildings that are considered to be aesthetically pleasant. Paris' attraction as a consumer city comes in part from the advantages of its service sector (restaurants) and its products which rely on scale economies to function (the *Louvre*), but also from its large stock of buildings which are considered by many (including the authors) to be beautiful. Several American cities also have an aesthetic edge which makes them desirable to consumers. An aesthetic edge can clearly come from a good stock of buildings, but more generally some people may actually prefer city living itself for aesthetic reasons (of course, many people dislike city living on aesthetic grounds as well).

The Success of High Amenity Cities

Population has grown fastest in high-amenity areas. The key point is that consumer sovereignty is pushing the population towards areas with attributes that consumers value. Our interpretation is that the constraints on business location have decreased substantially and that the cities of the future must cater to consumers.

Table 4.1 shows the results from a multivariate regression of county population growth 1977–1995 on a vector of county-level characteristics in the U.S. All data sources are described in the Data Appendix. The dominant factors in county and city population growth since World War II have been natural features. This regression shows the extreme power of: (1) temperate climate (inverse of average deviation from 70 degrees); (2) dryness (inverse of average precipitation); and (3) proximity to the coast. All three of these variables are strong predictors of local growth. They are normalized so that a coefficient of 0.35 indicates that a one standard deviation increase in the temperate climate variable drives growth up by 0.35 standard deviations. These effects are much stronger than standard regional effects.

The second set of effects that we show in this regression illustrates the role of consumer goods. We use the presence of five different consumer amenity variables in 1977 as proxies for different forms of consumer amenities. We find that the presence of live performance venues and restaurants both significantly predict later growth at the county level. We find no connection between art museums and county growth. Interestingly, amenities appealing to less educated workers—bowling alleys and movie theaters—are both negatively associated with later county population growth.

Thus, not all consumer goods matter. The more basic consumer goods have non-spatial substitutes. Video machines and television reduce the need to go to a movie theater. Perhaps video games or other activities have substituted for bowling. The important consumer amenities are more difficult to duplicate and cater to higher human capital workers.

A final significant relationship is between initial human capital and later county growth. The human capital—city growth connection is among the strongest in the local growth literature (see Glaeser et al., 1995). One interpretation of this fact is that high human capital workers increase city productivity growth. An alternative, equally plausible interpretation is that high human capital areas are pleasant to live in. Higher human capital areas are relatively free of social problems and offer better schools.

Indeed, the literature on the importance of schools and crime appears to be quite strong. As mentioned earlier, Berry-Cullen and Levitt (1999) show a strong negative relationship between crime and city population growth. Rappaport (1999) looks at the effects of government spending. He finds that spending on schools predicts city growth and the spending on redistribution is negatively associated with growth. Again, it appears that catering to high human capital consumers is particularly critical.

Amenities attract population in Europe, too. For France, we examine the relationship between growth and restaurants per capita and hotel rooms per capita. We do not think of hotel rooms as an amenity, but rather a proxy for tourist demand for the city. Cities with more hotel rooms are presumably more attractive to visitors and potential residents as well. There is a strong positive relationship between both of these variables and city population growth in France. Indeed, the restaurant-growth connection is as important in France (quantitatively, if not statistically) as the climate-growth connection in the U.S. In England, there is also a connection between tourist demand for the city and city growth.

Table 4.1. Population Growth and Amenities

	Population Growth	
	Estimate	t-Value
United States (1977–1995)		
Temperate climate	0.35	17.8
Proximity to ocean coast	0.24	12.5
Live performance venues per capita	0.14	6
Dry climate	0.12	6.5
Restaurants per capita	0.05	2.9
Art galleries and museums per capita	−0.03	−1.5
Movie theaters per capita	−0.05	−2.6
Bowling alleys per capita	−0.19	−11.3
France (1975–1990)		
Restaurants per capita	0.45	5
Hotel rooms per capita	0.33	4
England (1981–1997)		
Tourist nights per capita	0.31	2.7

Notes: Each coefficient is the result of a separate regression of population growth on each amenity and other controls. The values of the variables were transformed to have standard error = 1. The temperate climate variable is the inverse of average temperature per year minus 70 degrees. All temperatures are measured in Fahrenheit degrees. Dry climate stands for the inverse of average precipitation. US regressions included controls for county density, share of college educated, and a shift-share industry growth measure. France observation units are the "Zones d'Emploi." France regressions included controls for participation rate and population in 1975. The England regression is for counties. The England regression included a dummy for Northern counties and initial population as controls.

NOTES

1. Adapted from Edward L. Glaeser, Jed Kolko and Albert Saiz, Consumer city, *J. Econ. Geogr.*, 2001, (1), 27–50.

2. However, it is not obvious that if cities increasingly work to attract the highly educated the poor on net will be better off. The outcome would depend on whether positive spillovers arising from the presence of highly educated neighbors outweigh rent increases for the poor. This calls for better social policies on the national level.

BIBLIOGRAPHY

Berry-Cullen, J., & Levitt, S. D. (1999).Crime, Urban Flight, and the Consequences for Cities.*Review of Economics & Statistics*, *81*(2), 159–169.

Costa, D. L. (1997). Less of a Luxury: The Rise of Recreation Since 1888, National Bureau of Economic Research Working Paper: 6054 (June).

Costa, D., & Kahn, M. (1999). Power Couples: Changes in the Locational Choice of the College Educated: 1940–1990, National Bureau of Economic Research Working Paper: W7109 (May).

Glaeser, E., &Sacerdote, B. (1999). Why is There More Crime in Cities? *Journal of Political Economy, 107*(6), 225–258. Part 2.

Glaeser, E., Scheinkman, J. A., &Shleifer, A. (1995). Economic Growth in a Cross-Section of Cities.*Journal of Monetary Economics*, 36 (1), 117–143.

Kahn, M. E. (1997).Particulate Pollution Trends in the United States.*Regional Science & Urban Economics, 27*(1), 87–107.

Rappaport, J. (1999). Local Growth Empirics. Development Working Paper No. 23, Harvard University, Center for International Development.

Chapter Five

The New Political Culture and Local Government in England

Anne Bartlett, Terry Nichols Clark, and Dennis Merritt

INTRODUCTION

While theoretical and empirical attempts to map the nature of economic global-ization are considerable, the shift in the nature of political decision-making has received rather less attention. To be sure, there have been attempts to theoreti-cally engage with changes to political discourse and strategy over recent years (Bobbio, 1996; Gamble, 1996; Giddens, 1998, 2000; Marquand, 1993), but they are rarely accompanied by an analogous empirical effort. While changes such as "the decline of the nation-state" are pervasive in much of the theoretical global-ization literature, most data still reflects a national bias. Yet a local focus is ar-guably more powerful to identify persistent differences within nations, to chart actual change processes, and to sort out the key dynamics of change.

From a British politics and policy perspective, this paper is an assessment of change associated with the "Blair Project," or the Third Way. The aim of this paper is to adopt a more wide-ranging approach, locating British dynamics in a broader global analytical framework. This is facilitated by working with con-cepts and data that emerged from debates that often originated outside the U.K. These debates, enlivened by the emergence of Blair as political leader, have sought to identify just how much of the change has a specifically British charac-ter and how much can be attributed to dynamics which are instead, international.

Radical changes to the economy and social structure over recent decades have presaged a paradigmatic shift in the way contemporary politicians think about the nature of their business. These changes in the substance and rhetoric of politics follow themes that are found elsewhere in this volume: differences in socio-economic context; the stress on consumption versus production; the battle

between new and more traditional social policy objectives. It is these factors that
differentiate between political cultures and form the basis for the analysis in this
chapter.

For England, like many neighbors, the global economy has encouraged a
profound reconfiguration of the socio-economic landscape, leading, for some
commentators, to a stark geography of have's and have-nots. Sassen (2001) suggests that disparities assume both spatial and economic dimensions, as sectors
focused toward the global market fare disproportionately well, while others dependent on older employment sectors, such as manufacturing, stagnate and decline. Consistent with trends in other countries, we might expect industrial areas
generally to decline relative to others that have "natural" amenities like a waterfront or attractive landscape. Localities in the London area also enjoy the
"amenity" of cosmopolitan migrants, shops, and tourists. These in turn may lead
local governments to encourage such activities further, through parks, festivals,
museums, sports stadiums, etc. (other chapters of this book). London, entrenched firmly in these dynamics, is a byword for the type of changes we describe. Yet it is not only London that is affected by these trends. In every part of
England similar changes are making themselves felt: while some localities make
the leap to new levels of growth and prosperity, others slip quietly yet irrevoca-
bly further down the road to economic and social decline.

If these disparities suggest a complicated economic picture, they certainly
create an uncomfortable paradox for England's political actors and solutions
open to them. In recent years, the difficult process of balancing the concerns of
diverse and unequal communities while simultaneously participating in a modernization agenda has produced many a headache for both politicians and their
administrative counterparts in local government. The need therefore, to "square
the political circle" and provide an alternative *modus vivendi* for twenty-first
century politics, now underscores much of contemporary debate, as does the
need to reformat policy so that localities can appear both symbolically and
pragmatically involved in generating their own outcomes.

A NEW POLITICAL CULTURE
FOR ENGLISH LOCALITIES?

New Labour offers a visible agenda for political modernization and regeneration
which places it squarely at the center of this debate. Characteristic of worldwide
moves toward a "new political culture," the modernization agenda seeks to bring
England, its local governments, and its mode of governance in line with changes
elsewhere.[1] As John Prescott, has pointed out, the modernization agenda "seeks
nothing less than a radical refocusing of councils' traditional roles."[2] This requires a fundamental shift in political culture, away from insular bureaucracy
building and vested interests, towards a responsive outward looking agenda for
change. The new framework for community leaders, which includes cabinet

systems and directly elected mayors, is designed to promote new and innovative approaches to local democracy. This is accompanied by a new language of government of generic, globally acceptable phraseology related to fiscal responsibility, accountability, and openness to investment and capital flows. The move is designed to bring the twenty-first century to the door of English localities: to encourage autonomy, flexibility and political innovation, while providing meaningful governance that takes advantage of, rather than held hostage to, the vagaries of the past industrial conflicts and the new global economy.

Needless to say, this agenda is a challenge and not without critics. The project is accused of political window dressing and inability to deliver anything substantive to the people who really need it. It is criticized that the middle class have been wooed by a syncretic mix of policies favoring economic development with a compassionate hand, while lower echelons of society have yet to reap tangible rewards. A new format for English politics is by no means a "done deal."

Most such debate has been rhetorical. An attempt to engage with this new political agenda empirically is long overdue. This paper therefore examines how the new political project—at least commitment to its goals—has been implemented throughout England, using a new methodological approach based on analysis of language and performance information in official documents. By grouping distinct types of local governments, we examine whether there has been a noticeable change in the way the "new political culture" has been incorporated into policy making, according to context, location, and economic structure. We assess whether a new political culture is evident, the extent to which it varies by local authority area, and how this might be explained, according to demographic, political or economic factors.

THE NEW POLITICAL CULTURE: DEFINITIONAL COMPONENTS

What is "new political culture?" For many commentators, the face of politics is changing (Clark & Hoffmann-Martinot, 1998; Giddens, 1998, 2000; Kreiger, 1999). The meaning of socialism and its alternatives once seemed clear: no longer. Class and unions, Labour and Tory, long characterized central conflicts in British politics. How much has changed? This question has generated a huge debate, as some of the most vigorous critics of New Labour suggest that class politics still generally operates as in the past, especially in Britain (contrast the Oxford vs. Chicago debate in Clark & Lipset, 2001). We suggest that a hybridized political culture has emerged, less adequately explained by traditional variables, such as social class. Many changes variously labeled the "Third Way," "post-materialist" or "post-modern" in their values, capture overlapping parts. All suggest movement towards a political culture that explicitly moves beyond the limitations of historically bounded ideology and embraces change, social diversity, and lifestyle issues.

The muddying of traditional political culture occurs in a number of distinct ways. A simple left-right continuum, for example, no longer typifies contemporary politics (Clark & Hoffmann-Martinot, 1998; Giddens, 1994, 1998, 2000). Whereas socialism traditionally signified a redistributive "big government" approach and neo-liberalism, a minimalist state, the "new political culture" combines elements of each. Voters from left and right background have grown more fiscally conservative, irrespective of their long-held political ideologies.[3] Markets are no longer perceived in so negative of a way by one side of the political arena; rather, they are lauded as a tool with the potential to overcome inequality (Giddens, 2000, p. 33). Globalization and the collapse of communism have served to re-negotiate left and right parameters. This has meant a rearticulation of political categories and a level of pragmatism uncharacteristic of most twentieth century politics.

Why the changes? The overall move toward fiscal conservatism seems driven by globalization, trade competition, markets, received international economic wisdom, and investors. But distinctly new is combining this with social tolerance and broader acceptance of rights and social diversity, driven by more education. The political joining of these apparently inconsistent approaches is driven by a general increase in affluence, but also it seems by the decreasing salience of rigid class lines. Alternative sources of identity, besides class, also have less obvious attachments to established political parties, including ethnicity, gender, disability and sexuality, which are increasingly important ways by which people define themselves (Kreiger, 1999; Sanders, 1998).

A further point: consumption issues, rather than production, and a highly specific issue politics become more salient relative to a party-driven conflict politics. A key element of Blair's New Labor is that it is not formally allied with trade unions, facilitating alliances with many other groups. Perhaps consistent with Inglehart's assertion that greater prosperity produces heightened concern for post-material values, we see increased support for environmental protection, animal welfare, food safety and a variety of other social movements, internationally. In the U.K., in particular, there are Eco-Warriors, road demonstrators, and protests against genetically modified foods. Roadblocks at British ports to prevent the live exports of animals to Europe are lined by middle-aged housewives as well as seasoned animal rights protesters.

If consumption, lifestyle, and identity issues suggest a greater listening role for government, and greater participation of the people, then the move towards less hierarchical governance echoes this move. At the heart is a belief that local service delivery is better accomplished near the arena where needs are articulated. Gone are the days when central government was seen as an acceptable mouthpiece for citizens, and central control was the unspoken leitmotif. Instead, there is now greater dialogue around such ideas as civil society, of the ability of citizens to interact intelligently with their legislators, and act in concert to produce desired outcomes.

This goes hand in hand with the resurrection of "community" the attempt to regenerate localities and bring a sense of involvement back to local residents.[4] As Blair has stated, community represents that arena where "we develop the moral power of personal responsibility for ourselves and for each other" (Blair, 1996; Kreiger, 1999) It is at the level of community, that the rise in "individualism" that so many commentators argue accompanies new political culture (Clark & Hoffmann-Martinot, 1998; Giddens, 1998, 2000; Kreiger, 1999) meets the mutuality and interdependence which characterizes a new socialism, or as some say, communalism.[5]

All of these moves underscore a greater sharing of responsibility, and an attempt to increase levels of accountability and transparency. Integral to such "governance" is a heightened belief in the potential for citizen reflexivity—a citizenry both conscious of its values and prepared to organize around them. This willingness to share in the responsibility of policy and decision making is then encouraged by the positive engagement of the state as "enabler," rather than "all knowing" central body. This does not imply withdrawal of the state from many areas; rather, it suggests a partnership where power is ceded, conditionally, so that effects of change are mediated and carefully monitored. Britain remains far from Swiss decentralization.

The New Political Culture in sum is based on a policy platform that is more responsive, more accountable, more reflexive, less centralized, less bureaucratic, and less hierarchical. It is more consumption and less production focused. It builds less on a national party program, and instead presents a more syncretic appearance, incorporating ideas on distinct issues willingly from a variety of established political canons. Increasingly, the central government role is one of strategist, rather than planner.[6] The aim is to increase local autonomy for the reasons outlined, but this devolved power should, when needed, feed back to central government, so that its responsiveness to both national and global challenges can be augmented.

Measuring Political Changes in the U.K.

While many such changes are easily discussed in an abstract, theoretical way, measuring attitudinal and policy shifts is more complicated. How can one confirm or deny claims that a new political culture is or is not emerging in Britain or elsewhere? The solution we propose builds on a new methodology, designed to link to theoretical propositions and to provide data for comparisons across localities and national boundaries.

The content analysis used a stratified sample of sixty-eight local authorities. Since a central hypothesis is that political culture is changing due to the reconfi-

LONDON DECLINE	POST-INDUSTRIAL	INDUSTRIAL
⬇	⬇	⬇
BARKING AND DANGENHAM	BASKINGSTOKE	BRADFORD
BARNET	BATH	COPELAND
BEXLEY	BRIGHTON	DERBY
BRENT	BRISTOL	KINGSTON-ON-HULL
CAMDEN	CAMBRIDGE	KNOWSLEY
EALING	CHELTENHAM	LUTON
ENFIELD	EXETER	MIDDLESBROUGH
GREENWICH	GUILDFORD	NORTHLINGS
HACKNEY	IPSWICH	NOTTINGHAM
HAMMERSMITH & FULHAM	LIVERPOOL	PETERBROUGH
HARINGEY	MANCHESTER	RESTORMEL
HAVERING	MILTON KEYNES	ROCHDALE
HILLINGDON	NEWCASTLE-ON-TYNE	ROTHERHAM
ISLINGTON	OXFORD	SANDWELL
KENSINGTON & CHELSEA	PORTSMOUTH	SHEFFIELD
KINGSTON-ON-THAMES	SWINDON	STOKE-ON-TRENT
LAMBETH	WINCHESTER	SOUTHTYNESIDE
LEWISHAM	YORK	STEVENAGE
NEWHAM		THURROCK
REDBRIDGE		WALSALL
RICHMOND-ON-THAMES		
SOUTHWARK		
SUTTON		
TOWER HAMLETS		
WLATHAM FORREST		
WESTMINSTER		
WANDSWORTH		

Figure 5.1. U.K. Local Authorities Studied by Group

guration of the economy and the rise of new political values, the sample should reflect the economic and geographic diversity of the country. London, with its strong attachment to the global economy (Sassen, 1991, 2001), is an obvious candidate. We therefore included as many London borough councils, as had available data, twenty-eight.[7] Then we added twenty post-industrial local authorities, selected for their high levels of service and financial industries.[8] Finally, twenty local authorities were selected with a declining industrial base and high levels of unemployment (see Fig. 5.1).[9] Overall, this selection offers considerable diversity and a base for testing the new political culture thesis.

The methodology starts with coding local government performance plans, available both in hard copy and in PDF format from U.K. local authority websites. Performance plans, for those not familiar with them, require each council to produce an annual document, which provides a "clear practical expression of an authority's performance in delivering local services" and its goals for the future.[10] Each plan must specifically address the borough's corporate objectives—environmental, economic, social, equality, anti-crime, transport, accountability, best value and efficiency—and join them under the aegis of one central plan.[11] Beyond elucidating corporate objectives, the onus falls on each borough to make clear the linkages between their service provision and that of other public and community agencies. Although there is flexibility, the intention is clear: each borough must publish key performance information in a format that allows comparisons to be drawn with their competitors across the country.[12]

Comparing local authorities (and distinct areas within the U.K.) is therefore considerably facilitated by these plans. Any initiative deemed important to a borough's overall strategic agenda should—given government instructions—be flagged within the body of the performance plan. Issues that are representative of a "new political culture" style of thinking such as quality of life, environment, accountability and efficiency are clearly identified, as are issues that typify a more traditional political approach, such as welfare and redistribution, general service provision, housing and the like. Performance indicators for each substantive area support the written content of each plan. In aggregate, the plans generate a fairly clear picture of the extent to which the "new political culture" is emerging in the U.K. Localities differ quite clearly and explicitly on these themes. Results thus highlight distinct patterns across the U.K.

The actual process of coding the performance plans starts with a count of every word in the plan, which is assigned to a category.[13] Care must be taken to read the performance plan carefully, identify initiatives common to all plans, and ensure that all governments are treated in a systematic and comparable manner.[14] Once all words in a plan are counted and allocated to categories, the categories are totaled and divided into two groups. This requires an assumption about which categories represent the new political culture and traditional political culture. Accountability, Best Value, Environment, Education, Leisure, Information Technology, Community and Crime and Decentralized Local Democracy are examples of categories that are treated as new political culture, whereas Social Services, Anti-poverty, Housing/Council Tax Benefits, Health Services, and General Council Infrastructure are not. A New Political Culture Score (NPC Score) is then generated by dividing the total number of words belonging to new political culture by the total words in the document.

RESULTS

We can identify distinct patterns in the local governments studied (see Fig. 5.2). There is considerable variation in the new political culture (NPC) scores across the sixty-eight cases. The lowest NPC score (percentage of words in a performance plan devoted to NPC issues) was 42 percent and the highest 84 percent. Considering the three groupings—industrial decline, post-industrial and London boroughs—distinct patterns emerge. The industrial decline group shows more homogeneity in scores (46–61 percent), and a lower median (56 percent) than

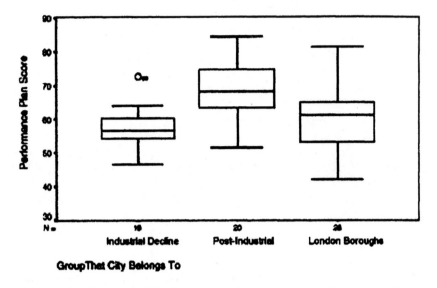

Figure 5.2. Box Plot to Show the New Political Culture Scores by Group: Industrial Decline, Post-Industrial and London Boroughs.

the other two groups. One outlier, Bradford (73 percent), deviates from the group.[15] The post-industrial group shows far greater variation (51–84 percent) and the median (68 percent) is higher.

The London boroughs, arguably the most global, exhibit the largest spread, with the lowest scores well below the minimum of the "industrial decline" group, and the highest near the maximum of the "post-industrial" group. The median score of the London Group falls between the two others, at 61 percent. Such a spread in political culture clearly follows the well-documented differences between the affluent areas of London involved in the service sectors, and those that suffer extreme deprivation. While the lowest scoring borough, Greenwich, devoted 42 percent of its plan to new political culture issues, affluent residential areas like Kingston-On-Thames, and Bexley, devoted 76 and 81 percent, respectively.

Where should we find the new political culture emerging? Inglehart suggests that greater affluence leads to a greater propensity to follow new political culture ideas and vice versa. One way to assess this is to consider the relationship between deprivation and adopting the new practices. Figure 5.3 plots new political culture scores against the Department of Environment Transport and the Regions (DETR) Deprivation Index.[16] This scatter plot confirms the hypothesis: while there is some overlay due to similar scoring, one can clearly identify Oxford, Swindon, Bexley, Bath, Kingston-on-Thames, and Cheltenham in the top left hand corner, which signals a high NPC score and low deprivation. Conversely on the bottom right we find Tower Hamlets, Greenwich, Camden,

Impact of Deprivation on New Political Culture Score

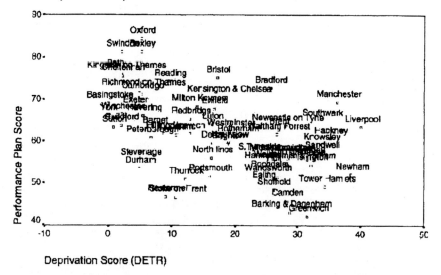

Figure 5.3. Relationship Between New Political Culture Score and DETR Deprivation Index. *Sources:* Individual performance plans for each local government unit and the DETR deprivation index.

Barking and Dagenham, Sheffield and Rochdale, all with high levels of deprivation and expectedly low NPC performance plan scores. Some authorities deviate from the predicted model—Manchester, Liverpool and Newcastle, for example—which have long traditions of urban blight, yet are also increasingly involved in both the consumption and service sector. These towns are moving toward a new political culture model, yet still have serious social and economic issues associated with their past labor structure.

Further investigation of the new political culture model using these results yields mixed support for the argument. Correlational analysis, first with all three groups then separately by group, shows that certain variables are consistently significant in explaining the new political culture, while others vary across the three groups. Starting with all three groups—London boroughs, the industrial decline and post-industrial groups—we find that the deprivation index shows a strong negative correlation with NPC scores (i.e. the lower the deprivation the higher the NPC score) yielding a correlation (Pearson r) of 0.50, and significance probability $p = 0.00$, consistent with the scatter plot in Fig. 5.3. Education is also significant, as expected: more educated locales have more NPC ($r = 0.28$, $p = 0.02$), but in the combined data set no other variables correlate significantly with NPC score (see Table 5.1A).

Table 5.1. Correlations of New Political Culture Performance Plan Scores with Socio-Economic Characteristics

	(A) All Three Groups: London Boroughs, Post-Industrial Group and Industrial Decline Group	(B) Two Groups: Post-Industrial Group and Industrial Decline Group	(C) London Boroughs Only
Performance Plan score	1.00	1.00	1.00
% Young 25–44	-0.13	0.18	-0.23
Average earnings	0.04	0.53**	-0.23
Deprivation score	-0.50**	0.34*	-0.70**
Percent higher education	0.28*	0.64**	0.04
% Ethnic group	-0.21	0.09	-0.33
	N = 68	N = 40	N = 28

Notes: Results are displayed separately for three groups of local authorities, as discussed in text. These are Pearson correlations (r's) with significance levels shown for two-tailed tests.

Sources: Performance Plan Score, Individual Local Authorities. 25–44 percent, ONS-Subnational Population Projections, Series p. 3, No. 10. Average Earnings, New Earnings Survey Deprivation Score, DETR. Higher Education, Census, 1991. Percent Ethnic Group, Individual Local Authority Data.
* Significant at 0.05 level.
** Significant at 0.01 level.

In the non-London boroughs—i.e. industrial decline and post-industrial groups—the NPC performance plan score is clearly positively correlated with both average earnings ($r = 0.53$, $p = 0.00$) and the percentage of people with higher education ($r = 0.64$, $p = 0.00$). This suggests that in these two groups, the more affluent and better educated the citizens, the more likely they are to pursue NPC objectives. The deprivation score is once again significant and negatively correlated with the performance plan score ($r = -0.34$, $p = 0.03$). The "percent of young people" and "percentage of ethnic residents" are insignificant (see Table 5.1 (B)).

Finally, considering just the twenty-eight London boroughs, deprivation is the sole variable showing a significant association with the performance plan score ($r = -0.70$, $p = 0.00$). Income and education no longer correlate with the new political culture plan focus. Quite why this is so is unclear, yet one may speculate that the latter two variables pale into insignificance alongside deprivation since this is so acute in urban centers such as London.

CONCLUSION

Although further work needs to be done with the performance plan data, preliminary results do appear to support the new political culture thesis. The theoretical predictions work well in the twenty Industrial Decline boroughs and twenty Post-Industrial boroughs. The performance plan scores are, as expected, positively correlated with education and earnings, and negatively with deprivation. While there is surely considerable variation in adoption of these new political culture objectives, there is no doubt that many local governments visibly feature this new approach is in framing the ways they do business.

The twenty-eight London boroughs do not conform neatly to the theoretical predictions of the new political culture. There is a huge spread in the scores with only one variable—the DETR deprivation index—that is significant. This is consistent with much recent research on London that suggests that it is unhooked from its immediate hinterland and more in tune with other locations worldwide. Further, London is a city of deep contrast—with five of the ten most deprived local authority areas in England. It is perhaps not surprising that deprivation is more politically important here than outside the London area.

The content analysis coding methodology is helpful to identify local authorities that perform according to entrenched political characteristics, and those that do not. The method of using websites and mandated government documents to identify political culture through language and priorities is a departure from standard theoretical approaches, but suggests a new approach distinctly useful for making comparisons. Besides confirming the values important to modernization of governance in England, it also highlights the significance of economic, social, and other local characteristics which shift how the modernization agenda plays out.

ACKNOWLEDGMENTS

Anne Bartlett (albartle@uchicago.edu) is responsible for most data analysis and writing of this chapter, and all the website content analysis. These are adapted from her longer MA thesis to feature the content analysis. The MA includes further coding details, multiple regressions, and discriminant analysis. Anne Bartlett is a British citizen with more than a decade of experience of working in British government. Terry Clark provided overall coordination and editing, and enlisted most British participants as part of the Fiscal Austerity and Urban Innovation (FAUI) project. Dennis Merritt provided technical assistance, with data from FAUI sources and the Census. Most data are currently available for others to analyze via the FAUI Project web site and FTP sites, see http://www.src.uchicago.edu/depts/faui/archive.html.

NOTES

1. This is particularly relevant to England's relationship to Europe, where "subsidiarity" has required governance processes to be devolved to the lowest workable level.

2. Modern Local government: In Touch with the People, Cm4014, July 1998, London, The Stationery Office. See Introduction.

3. In general, the trend toward new political culture is a socialist project, spawning center-left views.

4. Giddens (1998, p. 79).

5. Kreiger includes a quote from Blair in this regard, "Above all, it is about the union between individual and community, the belief that we are not stranded in helpless isolation, but owe a duty to others and ourselves, and are in a profound sense, dependent on each other to succeed," in the foreword to "Reclaiming the Ground: Christianity and Socialism" (Bryant, 1993).

6. Gamble (1996, p. 36).

7. A number of websites were "under construction" at the time the research was conducted.

8. This information was obtained from the Annual Employment Survey. The twenty highest "service oriented" English local authorities were used.

9. These cases were selected using 1991 U.K Census Data. Using a combination of "percent manufacturing decline between 1981 and 1991," and "level of male unemployment" we selected the twenty most hard hit councils.

10. Ibid., p. 73, paragraph, 7.31 et seq.

11. Ibid., p. 73, paragraph, 7.32 et seq.

12. Each plan is also externally audited for reliability, with guidance from the Audit Commission.

13. There are numerous categories to which these words could be assigned. The most common were Best Value, Accountability, Education, Environment, Infrastructure, Social Services, Local Democracy, Leisure, Housing, Health, Information Technology, Leisure, and Anti-Poverty. If a plan talked about school reform for a thousand words then these words would be assigned to the Education category. If a plan talked about fiscal responsibility and providing services in the most cost-efficient way, then these words would be allocated to the Best Value category.

14. This means, quite simply, that initiatives must be recorded in an identical manner, irrespective of whether they are called different things by the councils concerned. A good example of this problem is the treatment of the environment. Some councils argue that food inspections, dog fouling and cemetery maintenance should be treated as environmental issues. Others do not. There are lots of examples where council services are labeled incorrectly. This often occurs where councils attempt to make certain elements of their service delivery more akin to the government's modernizing agenda.

15. Speculating here, one could guess that this is due to the high ethnic group presence in the area. Later research will confirm whether ethnicity is a significant factor.

16. The DETR deprivation index is an amalgamation of twelve separate measures of deprivation rolled together to create one score. The higher the score, the greater the level of deprivation in the local authority area concerned.

BIBLIOGRAPHY

Blair, T. (1996). *New Britain*. Boulder, CO: Westview Press.

Bobbio, N. (1996). *Left and Right*. Cambridge: Polity Press.

Bryant, C. (Ed.) (1993). *Reclaiming the Ground: Christianity and Socialism*. London: Spire/Hodder and Stoughton.

Clark, T. N., & Hoffmann-Martinot, V. (1998). *The New Political Culture*. Boulder, CO: Westview Press.

Clark, T. N., & Lipset, S. M. (Eds) (2001). *The Breakdown of Class Politics*. Baltimore: Johns Hopkins University Press.

Gamble, A. (1996). *The Legacy of Thatcherism in The Blair Agenda*. In: M. Perryman (Ed.), London: Lawrence and Wishart.

Giddens, A. (1998). *The Third Way: The Renewal of Social Democracy*. Cambridge: Polity Press.

———(2000). *The Third Way and its Critics*. Cambridge: Polity Press.

Krieger, J. (1999). *British Politics in the Global Age: Can social democracy survive?* New York: Oxford University Press.

Marquand, D. (1993). *Labour's new model army in The Guardian* (May 26th).

Sanders, D. (1998). The new electoral battlefield. In: A. King (Ed.), *New Labour Triumphs: Britain at the Polls*. Chatham, NJ: Chatham House.

Sassen, S. (1991, 2001). *The Global City* (2nd ed.). Princeton, NJ: Princeton University Press.

Chapter Six

Technology and Tolerance: The Importance of Diversity to High Technology Growth

Richard Florida and Gary Gates

INTRODUCTION

The rules of the economic development game have changed. Companies were the force behind the old game. Cities and suburbs gauged their status by the number of corporate headquarters within their borders. Economic developers used financial and other incentives to lure companies to their communities. Now, however, people are the center of the action. High human capital individuals—or as we like to call them, talent—are the key to success in this new era of economic growth. Their ideas and creativity are the most important ingredients in the economic success of a firm or region.

Firms have always located near their key factors of production. In the past, companies located near raw materials or good transportation, to minimize costs. So, it is not surprising that firms in today's knowledge-based economy are increasingly making location decisions based on where the talent pool is located. According to the management-consulting firm, McKinsey and Company, the "war for talent" is the number one competitive issue facing companies in the United States and around the world, and it remains so even though the Internet bubble has burst.[1] As Hewlett Packard CEO Carly Fiorina told a conference of governors: "Keep your tax incentives and highway interchanges, we will go where the highly skilled people are."

The Nobel prize-winning economist Robert Lucas argues that the driving forces in the growth and development of cities and regions can be found in the productivity gains associated with the clustering of talented people or human capital.[2] Research by Harvard University economist Edward Glaeser and his collaborators provides ample empirical evidence of the close association between human capital and regional economic growth.[3] Glaeser finds considerable empirical evidence that firms gather in particular regions to gain advantages from common labor pools—not, as is more frequently argued, to gain advantages from linked networks of customers and suppliers. Related research by Spencer Glendon finds that a good deal of city growth over the course of the 20th century can be traced to levels of human capital at the turn of the century.[4] Places with talented people both grow faster and are better able to attract other talented people.

Not surprisingly, high-technology metropolitan areas contain more talent than other metropolitan areas. The statistical correlations between the percentage of the population with at least a college education and the strength of the high-tech economy are uniformly high and significant.[5]

What, then, brings talented workers to a particular metropolitan area? How do they make their residential location decisions? What sets high technology centers such as San Francisco, Boston, and Seattle apart from other metropolitan areas? Why have some metropolitan areas—many home to some of the nation's most prestigious university research centers and college graduates—been unable to attract a significant number of talented technology workers?

Our theory is that a connection exists between a metropolitan area's level of tolerance for a range of people, its ethnic and social diversity, and its success in attracting talented people and high-technology firms. People in technology businesses are drawn to places known for diversity of thought and open-mindedness. These places possess what we refer to as low barriers to entry for human capital. Diverse, inclusive communities that welcome gays, immigrants, artists, and free-thinking "bohemians" are ideal for nurturing creativity and innovation, both keys to success in today's economy. In fact, Florida argues that creativity has become so important to the economy that the "Creative Class" has emerged as the new driving force of economic growth and prosperity.[6]

This study examines the relationship between our measures of diversity and tolerance and high-technology success in the fifty most populated metropolitan areas in the United States.[7]

METHODOLOGY

We constructed four indices to attempt to capture the level of diversity and tolerance within the nation's most populous metropolitan areas. All indices utilize the 1990 U.S. Decennial Census Public Use Microdata Sample except the 2000 Gay Index, which utilizes data from the U.S. Census Bureau SF-1 data files:[8]

Gay Index: Constructed for both 1990 and 2000, this index measures the over- or under-representation of gay male couples in a metropolitan area relative to the population.[9] The index is constructed as the fraction of men in gay male partnerships who live in a metropolitan area divided by the fraction of the U.S. population who live in that area.[10] The value takes on the properties of an odds ratio whereby a value over one says that a gay coupled man is more likely to locate in the area than the population in general while values below one suggest that gays are under-represented.

Bohemian Index: Calculated in the same fashion as the Gay Index, this measures the over- or under-representation of artists and musicians in a metropolitan area. The index is based on the number of writers, designers, musicians, actors and directors, painters and sculptors, photographers, and dancers. Regions in which these "bohemians" are over-represented possess a milieu that favors openness to creativity and artistic expression.

Foreign-Born Index: The percentage of those within a metropolitan area who were not born in the United States or one of its territories

Composite Diversity Index: This index is a sum of the rankings of the three individual diversity measures: the gay index, bohemian index, and foreign-born index.

We compare our diversity measures to a measure of high-technology industry concentration and growth developed by the Milken Institute. In a July 1999 study titled America's High-Tech Economy, an index called the "Tech-Pole" was calculated to rank metropolitan areas (using 1998 data) based on a combination of two factors: (1) the output of an area's high-tech industries expressed as a percentage of the output of the nation's high-tech industries; and (2) a ratio of the amount of a metropolitan area's output from high-tech industries to the amount of the nation's output from high-tech industries.[11]

The first measure favors large metropolitan areas; the second favors small areas with large technology sectors. By multiplying them, the Milken Index creates a measure that favors neither. The term "tech-pole" refers to the relative technology gravitational pull that a metropolitan area exerts on high-tech industries. This measure is used throughout the study to compare a metropolitan area's technology prowess with our measures of talent, tolerance, and diversity.

Table 6.1. Milken Tech-Pole Ranking and Gay Index

Milken Tech-Pole Ranking	Metropolitan Area	Gay Index Ranking	
		1990	2000
Top 25 Regions			
1	San Francisco	1	1
2	Boston	8	11
3	Seattle	6	3
4	Washington	2	6
5	Dallas	19	13
6	Los Angeles	7	8
7	Chicago	15	23
8	Atlanta	4	4
9	Phoenix	22	16
10	New York	14	14
11	Philadelphia	36	30
12	San Diego	5	5
13	Denver	10	15
14	Austin	3	9
15	Houston	21	19
Bottom 25 Regions			
36	Cleveland	47	44
37	Miami	12	2
38	Rochester	13	39
39	Albany	30	41
40	Nashville	28	25
41	Greensboro	46	37
42	Oklahoma City	27	38
43	Las Vegas	48	10
44	Norfolk	37	47
45	Richmond	29	36
46	Buffalo	50	50
47	New Orleans	24	18
48	Honolulu	20	32
49	Memphis	33	40
50	Louisville	42	34

Notes: Top and Bottom Fifteen Out of Fifty Metropolitan Areas.
Sources: Milken Institute "Tech-Pole" Ratings; Gay Index constructed by Richard Florida and Gary J. Gates using data from 1990 U.S. Decennial Census Public Use Microdata Sample (5%) and Census 2000 STF-1 100% sample files.

Table 6.2. Correlations between Milken Tech-Pole and Growth Measures with Talent and Diversity Measures

	% College Graduates (1990)	Boho Index (1990)	% Foreign Born (1990)	Gay Index	
				1990	2000
Pearson Correlations					
Milken Tech-Pole	0.72 (0.001)	0.62 (0.001)	0.43 (0.002)	0.77 (0.001)	0.68 (0.001)
High-Tech Growth	0.25 (0.08)	0.19 (0.19)	-0.04 (0.78)	0.31 (0.03)	0.34 (0.02)
PPI New Economy Index	0.74 (0.001)	0.54 (0.001)	0.38 (0.005)	0.79 (0.000)	0.70 (0.000)
Spearman Rank Order Correlations					
Milken Tech-Pole	0.60 (0.001)	0.54 (0.001)	0.48 (0.001)	0.60 (0.001)	0.59 (0.001)
High-Tech Growth	0.20 (0.15)	0.24 (0.09)	0.07 (0.63)	0.26 (0.07)	0.36 (0.01)
PPI New Economy Index	0.78 (0.001)	0.56 (0.001)	0.49 (0.000)	0.62 (0.001)	0.61 (0.001)

Notes: Significance level shown in parenthesis. Bold cells are significant at 0.10 level or higher.

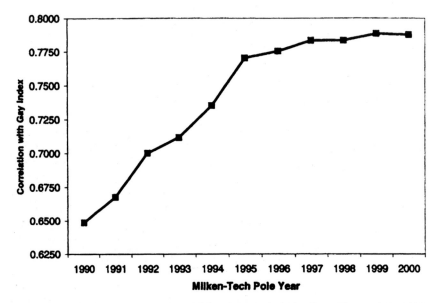

Figure 6.1. Pearson Correlation of the Milken Tech-Pole Index Over Time and the 1990 Gay Index

In order to test the sensitivity of our results to the technology measure, we also utilize the Metropolitan New Economy Index developed by the Progressive Policy Institute. This index, comprised of sixteen indicators that measure knowledge jobs, globalization, economic dynamism and competition, transformation to the digital economy, and technological innovation capacity, is designed to capture the extent to which a metropolitan area is prepared to compete in the New Economy.[12]

We also compare our measures with the Milken Institute's Tech-Growth Index.[13] This measures growth in output of high-tech industries within metropolitan areas from 1990 to 1998 relative to the national growth rate in output of high-tech industries during the same period.

All fifty metropolitan areas, ranked by our indices and the Milken measures, are shown in Appendix B. Appendix C details statistical techniques and modeling.[14]

FINDINGS

A Leading Indicator of a Metropolitan Area's High-Technology Success Is a Large Gay Population

The gay population can be thought of as canaries of the knowledge economy because they signal a diverse and progressive environment that fosters the creativity and innovation necessary for success in high tech industry. Gays are frequently cited as harbingers of redevelopment and gentrification in distressed urban neighborhoods. Studies also suggest that the presence of gays in a metropolitan area provides a barometer for a broad spectrum of amenities attractive to adults, especially those without children.[15] To some extent, the gay and lesbian population represents what might be called the "last frontier" of diversity in our society.

The Gay Index measures the concentration of gay coupled men in a community relative to the population in general.[16] Eleven of the top fifteen high-tech metropolitan areas (as measured by the Milken Tech-Pole Index) also appear in the top fifteen of both the 1990 and 2000 Gay Index (see Table 6.1).

The Gay Index is strongly associated with high-tech location (see Table 6.2). The correlations between the Gay Index (in both years) and both measures of high-tech concentration (Milken Tech-Pole and the New Economy Index) are high and consistently positive and significant.

Gays not only predict the concentration of high-tech industry, they are also a predictor high-technology growth from 1990 to 1998 rank in the top ten for the Gay Index in 1990. In addition, the correlation between the Gay Index (measured in 1990) and the Milken Tech-Pole Index calculated for 1990–2000 increases over time, as shown in Fig. 6.1. Figure 6.1 also suggests that the benefits of diversity may actually compound over time by increasing a region's high-tech prosperity.

Statistically, one might be concerned that the influence of San Francisco (which ranks unusually high, first in fact, on both the high-tech and gay indices) may create a false association between the two measures. To check for this, we removed San Francisco from the data and repeated the analyses. The basic findings remain virtually the same.[17] In fact, the influence of the Gay Index on high-tech growth strengthens slightly when San Francisco is not included. This increases our confidence in the strength of the concentration of gays as a predictor of high-technology concentration and growth.

While our findings on the link between the Gay Index and high-tech growth cannot be viewed as conclusive, the results are quite consistent with our theory that social and cultural diversity attracts talent and stimulates high-tech growth.[18] These findings support the view that encouraging diversity and lowering barriers to entry can help to attract human capital and generate technology-based growth.

High Concentrations of Creative People or "Bohemians" are also an Indicator of a Metropolitan Area's High-Technology Success

It has long been thought that talented people are attracted to amenities or a better quality of life. Terry Clark and Richard Lloyd argue that amenities are an increasingly important part of what cities have to offer, dubbing the new amenity-rich city "the Entertainment Machine."[19] The city as an entertainment machine is defined by a whole new cluster of amenities mainly revolving around a vibrant street level culture—from outdoor cafes and hip restaurants to art galleries and a pulsating music scene.

To get at the relationship between creativity and technology, we examine a metropolitan area's receptiveness to bohemians and artistic creativity. Again, we construct a new measure of our own.[20] We call it the Bohemian Index—or the "Boho Index." The index is based on the number of writers, designers, musicians, actors and directors, painters and sculptors, photographers, and dancers found in a metropolitan area. We believe this measure offers considerable improvement over traditional measures of amenities (such as restaurants, museums, symphonies and the like) in that it provides a direct measure of the producers of those amenities. Metropolitan areas that are over-represented by these bohemians are those with an appreciation of amenities that support and showcase creativity and artistic expression.

So what do we find? There is a strong correlation between the Boho Index and the concentration and strength of high-tech industry.[21] Ten of the top fifteen bohemian metropolitan areas also number among the nation's top fifteen high-technology areas, notably Seattle, Los Angeles, New York, Washington D.C., San Francisco, and Boston (see Table 6.3).[22] Thirteen out of the bottom fifteen high-tech metropolitan areas fail to appear in the top fifteen of the Boho Index.

Metropolitan Areas with High Concentrations of Foreign-Born Residents Rank High as Technology Centers

The growth and development of great cities comes from their ability to harness diversity, welcome newcomers, and turn their energy and ideas into innovations and wealth. The Milken Institute identifies immigration as one of the two most powerful demographic trends reshaping the nation's cities and regions. Its list of "Melting Pot Metros" ranks the most ethnically diverse regions in the country. Sure enough, highly ranked regions in California and Texas, as well as Chicago, Washington D.C., and New York City are also hot spots of economic growth. Not surprisingly, these metropolitan areas are also ranked highly as regions of technology and technological growth. Leading high-tech centers are places where people from virtually any background can settle and thrive. In Silicon Valley, the world's leading high-tech center, nearly a quarter of the population is foreign born; and almost one-third of the Valley's high-tech scientists and engineers hail from foreign countries, according to research by Annalee Saxenian of the University of California at Berkeley.[24] Roughly one-quarter of new Silicon Valley businesses established since 1980 had a Chinese or Indian-born founder, according to Saxenian's study. That figure increased to more than 30 percent between 1995 and 1999. And, these figures may actually underestimate the extent of immigrant influence, because firms started with a non-Asian co-founder are not counted.

Economists have long argued that diversity is important to economic performance. Generally speaking, they have been talking about the diversity of firms or regional industrial structures. John Quigley argues that regional economies benefit from the location of a diverse set of firms and industries.[25] In the knowledge-economy, ethnic, social, and cultural diversity is likely to be even more important.

To look more closely at the role of ethnic diversity in high-technology concentration, we examine the relationship between high-tech industry and the percent of a region's population that is foreign born. Nine of the top fifteen (and eight out of the top ten) metropolitan areas in terms of foreign-born residents were also among the nation's top fifteen high-technology areas: Los Angeles, New York, San Francisco, San Diego, Chicago, Houston, Boston, Washington D.C., and Seattle (see Table 6.4). Twelve of the bottom fifteen high-tech areas do not rank in the top fifteen on the Foreign-Born Index (although Miami ranked number one). The statistical correlation between percentage foreign-born and high technology success was quite strong.[26]

Table 6.3. Milken Tech-Pole Ranking and Boho Index

Milken Tech-Pole Ranking	Metropolitan Area	Boho Index Ranking
Top 15 regions		
1	San Francisco	8
2	Boston	9
3	Seattle	1
4	Washington	6
5	Dallas	15
6	Los Angeles	2
7	Chicago	20
8	Atlanta	13
9	Phoenix	24
10	New York	3
11	Philadelphia	35
12	San Diego	18
13	Denver	14
14	Austin	10
15	Houston	30
Bottom 15 regions		
36	Cleveland	47
37	Miami	27
38	Rochester	31
39	Albany	45
40	Nashville	4
41	Greensboro	21
42	Oklahoma City	49
43	Las Vegas	11
44	Norfolk	37
45	Richmond	26
46	Buffalo	48
47	New Orleans	41
48	Honolulu	17
49	Memphis	40
50	Louisville	33

Notes: Top and bottom fifteen out of fifty metropolitan areas.
Sources: Milken Institute "Tech-Pole" Ratings; Bohemian Index constructed by Richard Florida and Gary J. Gates using data from 1990 U.S. Decennial Census Public Use Microdata Sample (5%).

Table 6.4. Milken Tech-Pole Ranking and Foreign-Born Index

Milken Tech-Pole Ranking	Metropolitan Area	Foreign-Born Index Ranking
Top 15 regions		
1	San Francisco	4
2	Boston	9
3	Seattle	15
4	Washington	10
5	Dallas	16
6	Los Angeles	2
7	Chicago	7
8	Atlanta	31
9	Phoenix	21
10	New York	3
11	Philadelphia	25
12	San Diego	6
13	Denver	29
14	Austin	19
15	Houston	8
Bottom 15 regions		
36	Cleveland	22
37	Miami	1
38	Rochester	24
39	Albany	30
40	Nashville	47
41	Greensboro	48
42	Oklahoma City	36
43	Las Vegas	13
44	Norfolk	32
45	Richmond	39
46	Buffalo	27
47	New Orleans	26
48	Honolulu	5
49	Memphis	46
50	Louisville	49

Notes: Top and bottom fifteen out of fifty metropolitan areas.
Sources: Milken Institute "Tech-Pole" Ratings; Foreign-Born Index constructed by Richard Florida and Gary J. Gates using data from 1990 U.S. Decennial Census   Public Use Microdata Sample (5%)

Regions with High Growth in the Technology Sector are More Racially Integrated

While the relationship between immigrants and high technology is encouraging, it is often said that diversity in high-tech industry is somewhat narrow and that it does not include members of traditional racial minorities, such as African-Americans. To get at this issue, we explored the relationship between high-tech industry and the percentage of population that is non-white. The results here are frankly disturbing. We find no significant correlation between a large African-American population and technology.[27]

However, we do not posit that simply having diversity within the population creates a positive climate for technology and tech growth. Rather, our theory is that diverse communities within a region must interact to create the energy that drives innovation and creativity. To explore this, we examined the relationship between technology and racial segregation within metropolitan areas. We constructed a segregation index for each metropolitan area utilized data from Census 2000. This index increases with the amount of segregation in the region. While we do not find a strong relationship between either the Milken Tech-Pole Index or the New Economy Index and segregation, metropolitan areas with high technology growth rates are among the least segregated regions in the country.

Within the fifteen fastest growing tech regions from 1990 to 1998, nine were ranked in the bottom fifteen of metropolitan areas ranked by the extent to which they are segregated (see Table 6.5). Conversely, among the fifteen areas with the lowest technology growth rates, eight are in the fifteen most segregated metropolitan areas within our sample. Our argument about diversity is simple and straightforward. Diversity of human capital is a key component of the ability to attract and retain high-technology industry. To demonstrate this, we constructed a Composite Diversity Index (CDI) measure based on the three diversity indicators that we discussed earlier—the gay and bohemian indices and the percent of foreign-born residents. We ranked our fifty metropolitan areas by each indicator (low to high) and summed the three rankings.

The CDI strongly correlates with the Milken Tech-Pole Ranking. As Table 6.6 demonstrates, the top eleven metro areas on the CDI are also among the top fifteen Milken Tech-Pole regions. The statistical correlation between the Milken Tech-Pole rankings and CDI rankings is higher than the same correlation with rankings by any of our individual diversity measures, or by simpler measures such as the percentage of college graduates in the population.[28]

Even more compelling, the CDI strongly predicts high-tech growth. When we estimate the effect of the CDI on high-tech growth and factor in the percentage of college graduates in the region, population, and measures of culture, recreation, and climate, we find that our diversity measure has a positive and significant effect on high-tech growth from 1990 to 1998 (see Table 6.7).[29] These results offer strong evidence of the importance of the combined effects of

Table 6.5. Milken Technology Growth and Racial Segregation

Milken Tech-Pole Ranking	Metropolitan Area	Segregation Ranking
Top 15 regions		
1	Austin	47
2	Portland	41
3	Phoenix	50
4	San Antonio	44
5	Atlanta	24
6	Sacramento	42
7	Houston	29
8	Denver	22
9	Dallas	36
10	San Francisco	31
11	Kansas City	11
12	Charlotte	40
13	Chicago	3
14	Greensboro	34
15	Norfolk	45
Bottom 15 regions		
36	Boston	28
37	New York	13
38	Orlando	38
39	Dayton	8
40	Indianapolis	9
41	Albany	25
42	Oklahoma City	37
43	Milwaukee	2
44	Baltimore	20
45	St. Louis	6
46	Cincinnati	7
47	Honolulu	39
48	Buffalo	4
49	Cleveland	5
50	Los Angeles	35

Notes: Top and bottom fifteen out of fifty metropolitan areas.
Sources: Milken Institute "Tech-Pole" Ratings; Segregation Index constructed by Richard Florida and Gary J. Gates using data from Census 2000 STF-1 100% sample files.

Table 6.6. Milken Tech-Pole Ranking and Composite Diversity Indicator

Milken Tech-Pole Ranking	Metropolitan Area	Composite Diversity Ranking
Top 15 regions		
1	San Francisco	2
2	Boston	6
3	Seattle	5
4	Washington	3
5	Dallas	15
6	Los Angeles	1
7	Chicago	11
8	Atlanta	14
9	Phoenix	21
10	New York	4
11	Philadelphia	32
12	San Diego	7
13	Denver	17
14	Austin	8
15	Houston	18
Bottom 15 regions		
36	Cleveland	43
37	Miami	10
38	Rochester	22
39	Albany	36
40	Nashville	25
41	Greensboro	42
42	Oklahoma City	39
43	Las Vegas	24
44	Norfolk	37
45	Richmond	30
46	Buffalo	48
47	New Orleans	27
48	Honolulu	12
49	Memphis	44
50	Louisville	47

Notes: Top and Bottom fifteen out of Fifty Metropolitan Areas.
Sources: Milken Institute "Tech-Pole" Ratings; Composite Diversity Index constructed by Richard Florida and Gary J. Gates using data from 1990 U.S. Decennial Census Public Use Microdata Sample (5%)

social, cultural, and ethnic diversity for both high-tech location and growth.

We also examine how the concentration of gays in combination with other factors affects high-tech growth (as shown in Table 6.7). A metropolitan area's percentage of gay residents provides the only significant predictor of high-tech growth in a region when we factor in other regional characteristics such as talent, foreign-born residents, bohemians, several measures of lifestyle amenities, and population.[30]

Table 6.7. OLS Estimation of the Effects of Various Metropolitan Area Traits (Measured in 1990) on High-Technology Growth from 1990 to 1998

Independent Variables	Dependent Variable: High-Tech Growth	
Composite diversity index	0.005*** (2.91)	—
Gay Index	—	0.15* (1.70)
% College Graduate	-0.41 (0.29)	-0.24 (0.15)
% Foreign Born	—	-0.28 (0.34)
Bohemian Index	—	0.26 (1.23)
Culture	-0.00002 (0.27)	-0.00005 (0.69)
Recreation	-0.0002** (2.56)	-0.0001 (1.54)
Climate	-0.0001 (0.27)	-0.0004 (1.13)
Population	0.00 (0.80)	0.00 (0.001)
R-squared (N=50)	0.32	0.28

Notes: Absolute values of t-statistics are shown in parentheses.
*Significance < 0.10 level.
**Significance < 0.05 level.
***Significance < 0.01 level.

KEY FINDINGS AND POLICY IMPLICATIONS

The bottom line of our analysis is basic tolerance and diversity clearly matter to high-technology concentration and growth. Of our individual measures of diversity and tolerance, the top factor that correlates with a metropolitan area's high-technology success is a large gay population. Other significant factors include high concentrations of foreign-born people and bohemians. When we use a composite measure of overall social, cultural, and ethnic diversity, the results are even stronger.

We do not mean to imply that these results prove that a large gay population or concentration of bohemians directly causes the development of a technology industry; the theory is that people in technology businesses are drawn to places known for diversity of thought and open-mindedness, and that our measures potentially get at a broader concept of diversity and inclusiveness.

In this study, six metropolitan areas ranked in the top fifteen for each of our three individual indices of diversity. Four of these six metro areas were the top ranked high-tech regions on the Milken Index—San Francisco, Boston, Seattle, and Washington D.C. The two remaining metros—Los Angeles and New York—also ranked in the top ten on the Milken Index.

While more research is certainly required to get at the causal linkages between diversity and high-tech industry, we feel confident in the nature of the relationship our analysis has uncovered. We are convinced that tolerance and low entry barriers to human capital help to attract talent, and that talent is in turn associated with high-technology industry and regional growth among America's largest urban centers. In additional analysis not shown in this study, we have examined these trends in a broader group of metropolitan areas and find that the predictors of technology concentration and growth do vary somewhat depending of the size of the region. We certainly welcome more research designed to address this important issue.

The basic message to city leaders and economic developers is clear. Talented people go to places that have thick labor markets, are open and tolerant, and offer a quality of life they desire. Places that attract people attract companies and generate new innovations, and this leads to a virtuous circle of economic growth. Cities must begin to combine their goal of providing a better business environment with strategies aimed at improving their diversity and tolerance.

Austin has utilized such an integrated approach to capture high-technology talent. The region has made significant investments in research and development, higher education, and business incubation with major facilities like Sematech and MCC. But alongside this, the region also made considerable investments in its lifestyle and music scene—from the clubs and bars of Sixth Street to Austin City Limits and the South-by-Southwest film and music festival.

Austin Mayor Kirk Watson was a driving force between this and strategy that aimed to capitalize on the "convergence" between technology, talent, and tolerance, as he puts it. Watson was to his second term re-elected with 84 percent of the vote. "Austin has benefited from a convergence between technology and our laid back, progressive, creative, lifestyle and music scene," he says. "The key is that we continue to preserve the lifestyle and diversity, which enables us to lure companies and people from places like Silicon Valley. We are building the habitat to do that." That is a message other cities and regions should heed. Talent powers economic growth, and diversity and openness attract talent. Companies remain important, but no longer call the shots. The location decisions of people are just as important—potentially more important—than those of firms. In fact, companies increasingly will go where talented people are located.

Building a vibrant technology-based region requires more than just investing in R&D, supporting entrepreneurship, and generating venture capital. It requires creating lifestyle options that attract talented people, and supporting diversity and low entry barriers to human capital. These attributes make a city a place where talented people from varied backgrounds want to live and are able to pursue the kind of life they desire.

ACKNOWLEDGMENTS

The Brookings Institution Center on Urban and Metropolitan Policy would like to thank Surdna Foundation, Inc. and The Fannie Mae Foundation for their generous support of our work on central city competitiveness. Elizabeth Currid, Sam Youl Lee, and Ji Woong Yoon assisted with this article. The authors benefited from discussions and helpful comments provided by Ashish Arora, Mark Kamlet, and Ben Margolis.

APPENDIX

Table A.6.1. Rankings of Top Fifty Metropolitan Areas by Various Indices

Metropolitan Area	Milken Tech-Pole	Composite Diversity	Gay Index	Milken Tech-Growth Index	Foreign Born Index	Bohemian Index	Talent Index % College Degree
San Francisco	1	2	1	10	4	8	3
Boston	2	6	8	36	9	9	2
Seattle	3	5	6	20	15	1	6
Washington	4	3	2	24	10	6	1
Dallas	5	15	19	9	16	15	10
Los Angeles	6	1	7	50	2	2	23
Chicago	7	11	15	13	7	20	13
Atlanta	8	14	4	5	31	13	5
Phoenix	9	21	22	3	21	24	35
New York	10	4	14	37	3	3	9
Philadelphia	11	32	36	27	25	35	20
San Diego	12	7	5	25	6	18	14
Denver	13	17	10	8	29	14	7
Austin	14	8	3	1	19	10	4
Houston	15	18	21	7	8	30	12
Portland	16	16	23	2	23	5	17
Indianapolis	17	40	34	40	44	34	31
Kansas City	18	34	35	11	42	22	24
Minneapolis	19	19	17	29	35	7	8

Table A.6.1. (Continued)

Metropolitan Area	Milken Tech-Pole	Composite Diversity	Gay Index	Milken Tech-Growth Index	Foreign Born Index	Bohemian Index	Talent Index % College Degree
St. Louis	20	49	45	45	43	38	36
Orlando	21	9	11	38	17	12	32
Sacramento	22	20	9	6	14	39	22
Detroit	23	26	44	33	20	25	48
San Antonio	24	31	32	4	12	50	40
Pittsburgh	25	46	39	26	37	46	39
West Palm Beach	26	13	16	34	11	16	33
Tampa	27	23	18	18	18	32	49
Columbus	28	29	25	28	38	29	21
Salt Lake City	29	28	41	19	28	23	25
Birmingham	30	50	49	35	50	42	38
Baltimore	31	38	31	44	33	44	18
Cincinnati	32	33	38	46	40	19	28
Charlotte	33	45	43	12	41	36	37
Dayton	34	41	26	39	45	43	43
Milwaukee	35	35	40	43	34	28	30
Cleveland	36	43	47	49	22	47	42
Miami	37	10	12	30	1	27	46
Rochester	38	22	13	31	24	31	19
Albany	39	36	30	41	30	45	15
Nashville	40	25	28	17	47	4	29
Greensboro	41	42	46	14	48	21	41
Oklahoma City	42	39	27	42	36	49	27
Las Vegas	43	24	48	21	13	11	50
Norfolk	44	37	37	15	32	37	45
Richmond	45	30	29	22	39	26	11
Buffalo	46	48	50	48	27	48	44
New Orleans	47	27	24	32	26	41	34
Honolulu	48	12	20	47	5	17	16
Memphis	49	44	33	23	46	40	26
Louisville	50	47	42	16	49	33	47

NOTES

1. Chambers, E. G. et al. (1998). *The War for Talent, The McKinsey Quarterly, 3.*

2. Lucas, R. E. (1998). On the Mechanics of Economic Development. *Journal of Monetary Economics*, pp. 38–39. Lucas says: If we postulate only the usual list of economic forces, cities should fly apart. The theory of production contains nothing to hold a city together. A city is simply a collection of factors of production—capital, people and land—and land is always far cheaper outside cities than inside . . . It seems to me that the "force" we need to postulate account for the central role of cities in economic life is of exactly the same character as the "external human capital" . . . What can people be paying Manhattan or downtown Chicago rents for, if not for being near other people?

3. Glaeser, E. L. (2000). The New Economics of Urban and Regional Growth. In: G. Clark, M. Gertler & Maryann Feldmen (Eds), *The Oxford Handbook of Economic Geography* (pp. 83–98), Oxford: Oxford University Press. Glaeser, E. L. (1999). The Future of Urban Research: Non-market Interactions, Working Paper, Harvard University. Glaeser, E. L. (1998). Are Cities Dying? *Journal of Economic Perspectives*, 12, 139–160. Glaeser, E. L. (1997). Learning in Cities, NBER Working Paper, 6271. Glaeser, E. L., Sheinkman, J. A., & Sheifer, A. (1995). Economic Growth in a Cross-Section of Cities. *Journal of Monetary Economics*, 36, 117–143.

4. Glendon, S. (1998). Urban Life Cycles, Working Paper, Harvard University.

5. The analysis indicates a Pearson correlation between the Milken Tech Pole Index and the proportion of the population with a college degree at 0.72. The Spearman rank order correlation was 0.60—that is the relationship between the rank number of a region on the Tech Pole and the rank on the percentage of the population with a BA or above. Interestingly, talent explains more than 50 percent of the variation in high-technology concentration.

6. Florida, R. The Rise of the Creative Class and How It's Transforming Work, Leisure, Community and Everyday Life, Basic Books, May 2000.

7. We combine any MSAs that are also part of a consolidated metropolitan statistical area (CMSA) as defined by the U.S. Census Bureau. As a result, the following areas are constituted as a single metropolitan area:

San Francisco: San Francisco, Oakland, San Jose
Los Angeles: Los Angeles, Anaheim, Riverside
Miami: Miami, Fort Lauderdale
New York: New York, Bergen County, Newark, Middlesex County, Nassau County, Suffolk County, Monmouth County

8. The Census Bureau releases two public use samples of decennial census person-level data, the 1 and 5 percent PUMS. The 5 percent PUMS is a representative sample (3 in 10) drawn from the 1 in 6 sample of people who filled out a census long-form, which amounts to 5 percent of the U.S. population or approximately 12 million observations. The sample is representative of the entire U.S. population and also is considered representative within metropolitan statistical areas, the unit of analysis utilized for this work.

9. Black, D., Gates, G., Sanders, S., & Taylor, L. (2000) Demographics of the Gay and Lesbian Population in the United States: Evidence from available systematic data sources. *Demography*, 37(2), 139–154. They demonstrate that unmarried same-sex partners in the Census are comprised primarily of gay and lesbian couples.

10. The 2000 gay index uses the fraction of gay coupled households divided by the fraction of all households.

11. DeVol, R. C., Wong, P., Catapano, J., & Robitshek, G. (1999). America's High-Tech economy: Growth, Development, and Risks for Metropolitan Areas. Milken Institute.

12. See http://www.neweconomyindex.org/metro/overview.html for details on the construction of this index. We were able to obtain a New Economy Index for forty-seven of our fifty metropolitan areas. Those not included were Albany, Birmingham and Honolulu.

13. DeVol et al. (1999).

14. In addition to statistical research on the fifty metropolitan areas, the study was informed by interviews, focus groups and case studies the authors have conducted separately or together over the past several years.

15. There are a number of reasons why this conclusion makes sense. Gay males are less likely to have children. In addition, if they couple with another male, their household income will be on average higher than the income of male/female households since males on average earn more than females in our economy. With no children in the household and relatively high incomes, gay couples can devote larger portions of their income to the purchase and development of amenities. See: Black, D., Gates, G., Sanders, S., & Taylor, L. (2001). Why Do Gay Men Live in San Francisco, forthcoming, *Journal of Urban Economics*. Research has shown that gay male couples live in some of America's most sought-after urban areas and are more likely to live in distressed areas within cities and gentrify their surroundings more than any other household type. See: (Gates, Gary, 2000). Essays on the Demographics and Location Patterns of Coupled Gay Men, Doctoral dissertation, H. John Heinz III School of Public Policy and Management, Carnegie Mellon University.

16. Several cautions must be noted regarding the Census data and gays and lesbians. We are measuring only individuals in same-sex unmarried partner relationships. As such, these figures do not take into account non-partnered gays. In addition, we estimate that the Census only captured approximately 35 percent of all gay/lesbian partnerships (see Black, Gates, Sanders & Taylor, 2000).Also, the Gay Index from Census 2000 represents an improvement over Census 1990 for several reasons. First, the 1990 Index is constructed based on observations in the 5 percent Public Use Microdata Sample while the 2000 Index utilizes counts from the 100 percent Sample of all Census responses in that year. Further, the 1990 sample does not include gay couples who considered themselves "spouses" (only those who called themselves "unmarried partners"), while the Census 2000 counts include both same-sex "spouses" and "unmarried partners."

17. The only qualitative difference was that the Pearson correlation between percent college graduate and the Tech-Pole index was slightly higher than the same correlation with the gay index. However, the Spearman rank order correlation with the Tech-Pole index was higher for the gay index.

18. One question raised by this strong connection between gays and high-technology is the extent to which gays and lesbians are over-represented in the industry. If gays and lesbians make up large fractions of this industry, then it could be that the location of high-technology firms brings about a larger concentration of gays in a region. To look at this, we analyzed 1990 Census data to assess the extent to which gays and lesbians are over-represented in some high-technology fields and industries. Gay men are about 1.3 times more likely to be scientists and engineers than the population in general. Lesbians are as likely as the rest of the population to be in these occupations. If the gay men and

lesbians are combined, the result shows that they are 1.2 times more likely than the population to be scientists and engineers. We also examined those employed in the computer and data processing services industry. Gay men are 2.3 times and lesbians are 1.3 times more likely than the population to be employed in this industry. Together, gays and lesbians are 1.9 times more likely than the population to be employed in the computer services industry. While some of the correlation between gays and high-technology might result from their over-representation in the industry, it seems difficult to explain how their over-representation would predict growth. To do so would be to suggest that that gays and lesbians are somehow on average more productive or entrepreneurial than their heterosexual counterparts.

19. Clark, T., & Lloyd, R. (2000). *The Entertainment Machine*. University of Chicago.

20. Originally, we undertook a series of analyses using various measures of amenities. We looked at things like climate, and professional sports, and arts and culture, and many others. In most of this work, we found only a loose relationship between amenities, talent, and technology. A large part of the reason, we came to believe, was due to the measures themselves. They were based on combinations of different factors and were not very consistent or reliable. And many of the things we would have liked to measure—such as a city's music or art scene were simply unavailable.

21. The two measures are correlated at 0.62 using a Pearson correlation and 0.54 using a Spearman rank-order correlation. Both are significant at the 0.001 level.

22. While an association between the Bohemian Index and the Tech-Pole Index is observed, a similar connection between growth and this index is not noted. Alone, the Boho Index can explain nearly 38 percent of the variation in high-tech concentration. The combination of the Boho Index and our measure of talent account for nearly 60% of the high-tech concentration measure.

23. Frey, William, & Ross DeVol (2000). *America's Demography in the New Century: Aging Baby Boomers and New Immigrants as Major Players*. Milken Institute.

24. Saxenian, A. (1999). *Silicon Valley's New Immigrant Entrepreneurs*. Public Policy Institute of California.

25. Quigley, J. Q. (1998). Urban Diversity and Economic Growth. *Journal of Economic Perspectives*, 12(2), 127–138.

26. The Pearson correlation between percent foreign born and the Tech-Pole Index was 0.43 (significant at the 0.01 level) and the Spearman rank-order correlation with 0.48 (significant at the 0.001 level). We did not find a similar correlation with high-technology growth.

27. The Pearson correlation was—0.11 and the Spearman rank-order correlation was—0.20. Neither was statistically significant.

28. The Spearman rank-order correlation between the Milken Tech-Pole and the composite diversity measure was 0.63. See Appendix C for other correlations.

29. We did not include our measure of segregation as it does not temporally precede our dependent variable. However, if it is included, it actually has the strongest predictive power in the model.

30. The overall F-statistic for the model is also only significant at the 0.07 level. This means that the total predictive power of the combined variables is significant, but somewhat weak. There is also a strong relationship between the concentration of gays in a metropolitan area and other measures of diversity, notably the percent of foreign-born residents: San Francisco, Washington D.C., and Los Angeles all ranked highly. These results reiterate the impact of diversity on a broad section of society. Low barriers to entry seem to be good for the whole economy, not just high-skilled labor.

Chapter Seven
Gays and Urban Development: How are They Linked?

Terry Nichols Clark

THE GAY FACTOR: COMPETING INTERPRETATIONS

A striking recent finding is that local areas with more gay male households have more high tech growth. This is so new and controversial that it demands scrutiny. The type of specific relationship between gays and economic growth remains imprecise. Multiple alternatives are explored in propositions below, which both codify and extend the varied types of association, causality, or symbolic linkage from past discussions. The literature on the topic is sparse—a handful of papers (Chap. 6, this volume; Black et al., 2002; Florida, 2002, in press; Florida & Gates, 2001)—but its policy implications are powerful and are being actively explored by some developers, consultants, and city government officials as if the "finding" were established (for one example, see *The Boston Globe* story in the box). Whatever the precise nature of the linkage, most commentary on gay-growth linkages takes for granted that there is indeed a linkage of some sort. This foundational assumption is thrown into question by our results below.

The results show a far less clear association between gays, innovations, population growth, and high tech impacts than past work suggests. Why? Results differ substantially across units (big and smaller metro areas and counties) and as we added different variables (Census items, amenities, and DDB survey measures). Results from these new analyses refine and contextualize the Gates/Florida results. Their findings were from the fifty largest metro areas. The main problem here is that percent gays and percent college graduates correlate ($r = 0.7$), and when both are included in regressions, gays are suppressed. Still the modeling questions are complex and are pursued in the Appendix. The gay impacts also fall in smaller metro areas and in counties or when we introduce key amenity and tolerance-related measures. And they differ substantially when we look at distinct aspects of growth and innovation. These important differences across units make the catchment area critical.

FINDING HOPE IN GAY ENCLAVES

DETROIT AND SUBURB SAY SUCH NEIGHBORHOODS CAN REJUVENATE THE CITY
The Boston Globe, 1/15/2003

By Tatsha Robertson, Globe Staff

FERNDALE, Mich. One of Detroit's biggest developers has been advertising vacant lofts in local gay publications, taking a lesson from the economic rejuvenation of this nearby suburb and trying to lure gay residents to move into the city.

"It's very true that Ferndale hit its stride because of the positive influence of gays," said David Farbman, president and chief executive of the Farbman Group, a real estate corporation that advertised the lofts. "In order for Detroit to expedite what it can become, it has to have a strong gay community."

Since the riots of 1967, Detroit has tried several strategies to revitalize its downtown, including riverfront development and a new mass transit system. City leaders continue to hope that General Motors' move downtown in 1996 will bolster the city's comeback.

Now, some leaders are hoping that an influx of gay residents will help revitalize Detroit. Though the idea is buttressed by a growing body of research, the notion comes as a surprise, given the city's often prickly relationship with the gay community.

Research suggests there is a direct correlation between sizable gay communities and economically viable cities . . .

Richard Florida, a professor at Carnegie Mellon University in Pittsburgh, has traveled the country preaching to city managers, urban planners, and economic development specialists that one important indicator of how successful their city will be in the 21st century is the size of its gay population . . .

Gates said his research seems to confirm an old axiom, that the property values in fringe neighborhoods tend to increase after gay men move in. Anecdotal evidence, according to demographers, shows that other upwardly mobile professionals tend to follow gays into these areas, making them highly sought after neighborhoods, such as Minneapolis's Lorin Park, Boston's Jamaica Plain, and Chicago's Boystown . . .

Critics say that Florida has cause and effect reversed, but Gates said these cities never would have evolved into what they are today without the diversity and tolerance that gay communities have brought to them.

AMENITY CATCHMENT AREAS

Must you personally "consume" an amenity to appreciate it? And what does "consume" mean? How big a geographic area should amenity analysis cover? Florida and Gates (Chap. 6) favor metro areas and study the fifty largest in the U.S., reporting that gays in these areas are associated with tech growth. We explore specifics of how and why gays might relate to tech growth below, but here we use the example to bring out some complexities of access to amenities. An argument for studying larger aggregations like metro areas is that a gay subculture can be centered in San Francisco, yet stretch down to Silicon Valley to define it as "diverse" and tolerant (per Florida and Gates). They resist considering smaller units like counties or smaller metro areas. Symbolic association and geographic stretch are critical points, but it is far from transparent how large the "ideal" or "appropriate" impact zone is for one or multiple amenities. When we consider how much these issues are often based on the symbolism of a mountain or beach, thirty or sixty miles away, it is difficult to assess precisely how close or distant the amenities must be to have "impact." Real estate developers and their creative associates have vivid imaginations, which they market aggressively. But how successfully? Disney is the standard against which competitors and critics rail. Thousands of low income Chicagoans and New Yorkers regularly fly to Disney creations in Florida, California, and Las Vegas. Indeed the mayor and urban policy makers of Chicago are explicitly competing with these locations, trying to add amenities that will retain more persons locally. These are big urban policy decisions which affect where business conferences are held: the top four U.S. destinations for "overnight group meeting travel" are Chicago, Atlanta, Orlando, and Las Vegas in that order; New York ranks a distant thirteenth (Clark, draft). People may be willing to drive a hundred miles to an opera once a year, but they not willing to travel over five minutes for a juice bar. More importantly, the elderly, or teenagers on a quiet summer weekend, may be willing to travel much further for dinner than top executives will for a business lunch. And to push a step further toward symbolism, for most amenity measures here, the issue is not "consumption" of these items considered alone, but the more general aesthetics and imagery, the overall gestalt, like a dinner combined with a striking sunset and San Francisco's Bay Bridge. The gestalt-like reasoning is that if New York has opera, museums, and juice bars, it probably has a few more big and little things too. Our amenity indicators are meant to help capture such imagery of urban cultural landscapes. They indicate and flag a deeper and broader gestalt of lifestyle and culture, things to do, people to be nearby, with tastes, smells, and feelings. They are not ends in themselves. They are flags atop icebergs.

How far are such flags visible? We cannot answer this carefully yet. But we pursue some analyses in this direction below using the same top fifty metro areas as Florida and Gates, and three hundred metro areas (detailed in the Appendix), but our main analysis uses all 3,111 U.S. counties, as these are the smallest geographic unit for which the DDB Lifestyle Survey data are reported. We merged the DDB data for 84,989 individuals with Census and amenity data for counties (see Appendix on the data and analysis specifics).

Applying this reasoning to gays, one can hold that the diversity they symbolized encouraged foreigners or off-beat persons to move to Silicon Valley—as does Florida (2002). But how far is Silicon Valley from San Francisco—a half hour to over an hour by car, one way, varying with the time of day, and far more via public transit. Conversely, one might argue, there are many lamented "burbs" around New York or London that are arguably highly homogenous, family-values oriented places—where some young people feel "trapped." Even Florida recounts how he felt trapped inside the tight social networks of his boyhood Newark, New Jersey. Yet Newark is physically closer to bohemian Greenwich Village, just across the Hudson River in New York, than many Silicon Valley towns are to San Francisco. "How local is local?" is the hard question here.

Answers are best framed by recognizing that each amenity may have a different "catchment area," or business area, and that subclasses of individuals differ substantially in terms of how large or small this may be, first for actual regular use, second for occasional visits, and third, for symbolic association even if the amenity is never physically "used." The symbolic meaning may be the most important in terms of who locates and why, yet for that reason it is all the more in need of original research to determine its actual cultural power. We cannot gauge the power of the Big Apple by measuring the travel time from a thruway exit in New Jersey. Analogously, think of persons from "lesser" countries in Europe who call themselves "Europeans," while the French seldom do. To capture such concerns systematically demands another level of original research beyond the present frontier. Currently, we simply do not know how many residents of the New York or San Francisco metro areas are persuaded by the friendly homogeneity of their immediate neighborhoods versus the rich diversity of their metro area. Indeed the work by Fisher (1982) and others shows that we may react positively to both. That is even the same person can enjoy the Gemeinschaft of a few close friends and family members a few times a week (and maybe choose to reside in a more homogenous county east of Berkeley or a gay neighborhood in downtown San Francisco), but on a weekend travel over an hour to a concert on the other side of the metro area. This is the sort of subtlety that weakens regression coefficients and makes simple questionnaire responses hard to interpret. But it also suggests that there is seldom one right answer to a question like how big an urban unit should we analyze to assess the impact of amenities.

The approach we have thus followed here is to use multiple methods, including those advocated by proponents of different arguments. The metro area analysis follows the Gates/Florida example because it was important to replicate their results precisely to build on and extend them; the county analysis permits examination of amenity items with other Census characteristics; and the DDB individual responses permit assessing the impact of these multiple units and past histories on specific individuals (for instance for the DDB risk and political culture items, discussed below.) When in doubt, try multiple approaches and look for consistency of results. The gay factor generally falls substantially as we use larger *N* data.

We urge others to purse such catchment questions as they could extend neighborhood identity studies from Firey (1945) and Suttles (1972) as well as neo-Marxist and post-modernist theorizing about place meaning (Lefebvre, 1981; Soja, 1996).

URBAN PATTERNS ASSOCIATED WITH GAYS: COMPETING PROPOSITIONS

Which specific gay-related factors might drive population and job growth and related processes? The writings on the topic are few and casual enough that rather than seek to quote them carefully, I explore some of the most plausible, reasonable alternatives that have come out of reading, reflection, and discussion with persons working on these issues (especially Gates and Florida). These incorporate the main plausible processes in past writings and add some more. Consider these options and a brief assessment of how each of them stands up to simple tests. These initial results are for all U.S. counties from the Census and DDB survey (for attitude and value items).

(1) The more gays in a city (or locality), the greater the stress on amenities, public and private, such as parks, bicycle paths, and distinctive restaurants. This is suggested as association, not causality, driven in the short term by selective migration of gays.
(2) Persons working in high tech industries need have no contact with gays who just happen to live in the same city, but they may enjoy the same amenities as found in locations with many gays. Amenities may thus be the link between gays and high tech growth.

What do we find? Results are positive but modest: the correlation (Pearson *r*) of

percent gays with Natural Amenities is 0.27 while that with Constructed Amenities (opera, juice bars, etc.) is just 0.07. Here and in this section, we report only
simple correlations as the main result which (to our surprise) is that most are low
or essentially zero. Regression analyses are similar, available from the author.

(3) High tech persons are more risk-taking, entrepreneurial, and innovative in
     outlook, and thus tolerate gays more than do persons of more traditional
     outlook. The key factor thus may be risk-taking and tolerance of diversity.
     Cities high on these should encourage both gays and high tech growth.

The DDB had several risk-related items permitting us to see if residents of counties with more gays were more favorable toward risk. Relations were near zero:
r's were 0.01, 0.001, −0.02, and −0.011 with these items:

"I like to visit places that are totally different from my home"

"I am the kind of person who would try anything once"

"Everything is changing too fast today"

"I don't like to take chances"

Other items: counties with more gays have significantly higher crime rates, r =
0.12 but not significantly more fear of crime, r = 0.06 with the DDB item "I
worry a lot about myself or a family member becoming a victim of a crime."

(4) High tech persons may come disproportionately from foreign areas (like
     Asian-Indian engineers) and have more cosmopolitan tastes than found in
     most small U.S. towns with "traditional" residents and shops. High tech
     staff are thus likely to move to larger and especially more cosmopolitan lo-
     cations.

Here we do find a clear positive relation of r = 0.38 between percent Japanese,
Korean, and Asian-Indian residents in a county and the number of high tech
patents. But the correlation of gays with these three key Asian groups is barely
significant, r = 0.04; it is suppressed in multivariate analyses that add additional
variables.

(5) Localities with numerous college faculty and students may be distinctly
     tolerant on social issues, and implement correspondingly "politically cor-
     rect" policies of non-discrimination, encouraging more socially diverse per-
     sons who may work in high tech growth, as well as gays.

Results? Percent gays are unrelated to college town indicators—college dormi-
tories per capita (r = −0.009) and percent of the workforce in educational servic-

es ($r = -0.017$). Further, there was no significant relation between percent gays and DDB respondents who classified themselves as more liberal on the item: "Generally speaking, would you consider yourself to be . . .

(1) Very Conservative
(2) Moderately Conservative
(3) Middle of the Road
(4) Moderately Liberal
(5) Very Liberal

Surprisingly, there was even a zero relation between percent gays in a county and citizen support for same sex marriages on a DDB item, $r = -0.004$

"I am in favor of legalizing same sex marriages"

Still there was a slight positive relation ($r = 0.047$, just statistically significant) between percent gays and:

"I am interested in the cultures of other countries"

(6) Locations with several above characteristics (amenities, risk-taking, toler-ance, cosmopolitanism) might attract new residents to migrate there. These locations (like Palo Alto, Boulder, Austin, Portland, Santa Monica) may es-pecially appeal to young, free-wheeling persons who may also go into high tech jobs. The key factor here is thus differential migration of persons who constitute a local talented workforce.

This could be pursued with more subtlety, but using the simple measure of per-cent residents with a BA or higher degree, we find just $r = 0.07$ with percent gays.

Leisure is complex in the above propositions in its interpenetration with work, which demands decomposition as these patterns are different from those traditionally considered. The association of gays and amenities with high tech growth is intriguing since it is not logically transparent that more and better lei-sure causes more economic growth. Indeed, the normal view is the opposite: hard work should bring economic success, and at least many publicized accounts report hugely demanding hours and commitment by many high tech workers (e.g. Florida, 2002 reviews many studies). How explain this apparent paradox of hard work vs. the impact of leisure-related amenities? Just laying out some logi-cal alternatives, as just above, can help. One relatively simple resolution:

(7) The top staff in highly dynamic firms may themselves be weakly influenced by amenities and social characteristics of the town where they reside. They may be too busy with their work to notice, or too austere in personal life-

style to "indulge." But if the top staff sense that middle and lower-level staff do appreciate such amenities, the top staff may move to, or expand their corporate activities in locations with such amenities in hopes of attracting more talented staff. They could similarly offer flex time, casual clothes, Fridays off, and other job-related amenities presumably more critical to middle and lower-level staff. Another class of policies, like longer vacations or working full time at home, might cause potential communication problems and, *ceteris paribus*, reduce productivity. But they still may be embraced by top staff as carrots, which provide a comparative advantage over other firms in a competitive market for talent. If such carrots attract talent, and even permit paying lower salaries, then such carrots may be "sound business decisions."

Related thinking is articulated by top executives in many U.S. high tech firms. For instance, in creating a charitable foundation for Silicon Valley, a leading concern of many leaders was to preserve a respectable and even abstemious lifestyle so that their children would not be "spoiled" like those in Hollywood (National Public Radio Broadcast, 1999). High tech firms like Microsoft, Intel, and Hewlett-Packard have expanded in locations like the Portland and Seattle areas—more austere and moralistic than Southern California.

CONCLUSION

We pursued multiple options in analyzing relations between gays and other factors over many months. The main result with the larger N's and more complex models, however, is that gay impacts are severely reduced and often insignificant. We also analyzed measures of lesbian couples and unmarried couples living together from the same 1990 and 2000 census sources (supplied kindly by Gary Gates); generally they were highly related to gays, and to some variables like population size, but we did not find clear or distinctive results of gays separate from the other two groups, or from other variables like education. We then analyzed a series of attitudinal and value items from the DDB source on risk taking, social tolerance, social diversity, and the like, to assess possible additional impacts of citizens in locations with more gays. Some were moderately related, but usually other variables like population size or educated residents suppressed gays. Still these results are so new and so different from past work that we much encourage others to help clarify these complex dynamics.

ACKNOWLEDGMENT

Thanks to Joshua McFeeters for programming assistance.

APPENDIX: METHODS OF ANALYSIS

Gays and Metro Areas

Our initial reanalysis of the metro data generated results consistent with the Gates/Florida (2001) paper. Indeed one assistant reviewing the results reported that gays were important in almost all models. Correct. But closer inspection revealed a different story. We analyzed the identical data and variables used by Gates and Florida for the fifty metro areas, as supplied by Gary Gates. These included: Milken Tech Pole and Tech Growth as dependent variables, which are among the most widely used measures of high tech concentration (cf. Malpezzi, 2002). The Milken Tech-Growth Index measures growth in output of high-tech industries within metropolitan areas from 1990 to 1998 relative to the national growth rate in output of high-tech industries during the same period ("location quotients" from Census data). To explain growth we and they used: percent gays, population size, Bohemian index (proportions of artists, musicians, etc.), foreign born, composite diversity (combining Bohemian index, foreign born, and gays) college graduates, proportion of the workforce in recreation jobs, climate—census derived variables.

When we added or deleted most of the other variables Gates and Florida used in their analyses, the gay results held. That is, large metro areas with more gays also had more growth in high tech jobs, as summarized in the Milken indices. Including or omitting San Francisco, as well as repeating analyses with different combinations of the explanatory variables they had used, gays were significantly related to growth in high tech. With one important exception. College graduates and population size are so highly interrelated with gays that they distort the results for one another's effects in these regressions for just fifty metro areas. Specifically, the impact of gays falls to zero if we include college graduates and gays in the same analysis, as Table A.7.1 shows. The larger the number of independent variables with such few cases, the less stable and less robust the estimated coefficients. Thus Models 5 and 27 with just gays and college graduates are less biased ways to measure the gay impact than models with larger numbers of independent variables. And in these two models, gays are insignificant.

Instability and bias increase as more variables are entered. This is a classic statistical problem with strongly intercorrelated variables. How strong are the potentially biasing correlations? The most serious problems are between gays and college graduates (Pearson $r = 0.718$); and gays and the BoHo index ($r = 0.570$). Table A.7.2 shows the r's for all other variables in the regressions. A standard solution to this "multicollinearity" problem is to repeat the same analysis with a larger or different set of cases, as we did next.

Table A.7.1. Regressions of Variables in Gates-Florida Paper

	Gay Index	Culture	Recreation	Climate	Percent College Grads	Percent Foreign Born	Population	BoHo Index
Model 1	0.106**							
Model 2	0.132***	0.000*						
Model 3	0.122***		0.000**					
Model 4	0.143***			−0.001				
Model 5	0.091							
Model 6	0.148***				0.359	−1.028		
Model 7	0.130***						0.000 *	
Model 8	0.102 *							0.022
Model 9	0.140***	0.000	0.000**					
Model 10	0.164***	0.000*		0.000				
Model 11	0.087	0.000**						
Model 12	0.156***	0.000			1.256	−0.711		
Model 13	0.133***	0.000					0.000	
Model 14	0.108 *	0.000**						0.164
Model 15	0.146***		0.000**	0.000				
Model 16	0.135 *		0.000**					
Model 17	0.146***		0.000**	0.000	−0.300			
Model 18	0.135 *		0.000**					
Model 19	0.145***		0.000*		−0.300	0.609		
Model 20	0.139***		0.000**				0.000	
Model 21	0.010 *		0.000**					0.126
Model 22	0.141 *			−0.001				
Model 23	0.173***			−0.001	0.046	−0.868		
Model 24	0.157***			−0.001			0.000	
Model 25	0.132**			−0.001				0.071
Model 26	0.154*					−1.044	0.000*	
Model 27	0.113				−0.128			
Model 28	0.090				0.411			0.010
Model 29	0.148***				0.345	−0.636	0.000	
Model 30	0.139**					−1.051		0.058
Model 31	0.107*						0.000*	0.157
Model 32	0.070	0.000**						0.141
Model 33	0.101	0.000*	0.000*		1.139			0.230
Model 34	0.131*	0.000	0.000*	0.000	0.186			0.261
Model 35	0.111	0.000*		−0.001	−0.070			0.189
Model 36	0.146*	0.000	0.000	0.000	0.717	−0.276		0.261
Model 37	0.145*	0.000	0.000	0.000	−0.246	−0.278	0.000	0.261
Model 38	0.175***	0.000	0.000	0.000	−0.024	−0.428	0.000	
Model 39	0.171***	0.000	0.000	0.000		−0.295		
Model 40	0.162***	0.000	0.000**	0.000				

Notes: In Model 5, gays are suppressed by percent college graduates; in Model 27 by college graduates and populating size. In Model 28, by college graduates and the BoHo index, and in Models 32, 33, and 35 gays are suppressed by similar subsets of variables. But in a confusing way, in Models like 32, 33, 36, and 37 the gay coefficient rises again to "statistical significance" when these same variables—gays, college grads and population size are all included together. Model 37 with all eight variables included is identical to the Gates/Florida paper Table 7; every coefficient matches perfectly. Why this inconsistency in gay coefficients across models? It is a classic disease of low N regression to begin to "explode" as more independent variables are added and degrees of freedom are exhausted; then one or two individual data points can drive the statistical result, often in misleading ways just like this.

Dependent Variable: Milken Growth Index. Beta coefficients shown for different sets of independent variables testing robustness of gay index.

*Significant at 0.1 level. **Significant at 0.05 level. ***Significant at 0.01 level.

Table A.7.2. Correlations of Percent Gays in 2000 with Other Items

	Pearson Correlation—r—with Percent Gay Households in County, 2000
High tech patents—LGHITEC1	0.076**
Entertainment patents—LGENTM1	0.071**
Other patents—LGOTHR1	0.057**
High tech patents county per capita	0.01
Entertainment patents county per capita	0.050**
Other patents N county per capita	0.02
Moralistic political culture MORAL2	−0.03
80 percent residing in college dorms	0.00
80 percent college age 18–24	0.139**
Whole food stores—TOTWF_1	0.052**
Museums—MUSENU_1	0.046**
Brew pubs—BREWS_1	0.06
Juice bars—JUICEN_1	0.08
Starbucks—STARBN 1	0.02
Operas—OPERNU_1	−0.04
Rare and used bookstores—BOOKSU_1	0.086**
Research libraries—LIBRAR_1	0.049**

Notes: These are for up to 3,111 U.S. counties using the DDB, Census, and other sources as in other tables in this paper. The *N* is "lower" for some variables, mainly due to zero scores on items like Whole Foods Stores. Moralistic political culture is an index of DDB items that seek to capture the key elements in Elazar (1984). In multiple regressions using these and other variables to explain population and job change and patents, gays are usually insignificant. Results are available from the author or in other reports.
** Correlation is significant at the 0.01 level 1-tailed.

Other Models and Levels of Analysis

Gates and Florida mainly analyzed six characteristics of the fifty largest U.S. metro areas. The classic problem with such low *N* analysis is that one or a few extreme cases distort results. There is no single or clearly right or wrong solution. The approach we thus used was first to try out the different logically possible combinations of the six variables to see if the gay result held consistently, or if it was "suppressed" by any other variable(s) (in Table A.7.1). Then we repeated similar analyses using larger numbers of cases and using different units (all three hundred metro areas rather than the largest fifty, then all 3,111 counties).

We experimented with many variations on the analyses above to explore the gay impact: "jackknifing" by cumulatively increasing the number of metro areas by ten cases (sixty, then seventy, etc.), repeating the same analysis until we reached the total *N* of 300; adding additional variables like amenities, repeating analyses with 3,111 counties which lowers the distorting *r*'s and makes it easier to disentangle effects of interrelated variables. This is a major reason we often

Table A.7.3. Intercorrelations Among Variables for Fifty Largest Metro Areas

				Pearson Correlation				
	Gay Index	Percent College Graduates	Population	Milken Tech-Pole	Culture	Recreation	Climate	BoHo Index	Composite Diversity Index
Gay index	1.00								
Percent college graduates	0.72**	1.00							
Population	0.29*	0.23	1.00						
Milken Tech-Pole	0.77**	0.72**	0.48**	1.00					
Culture	0.29*	0.43**	0.85**	0.49**	1.00				
Recreation	0.16*	−0.05	0.22**	0.16**	0.25*	1.00			
Climate	0.45	0.22	0.30	0.46	0.21	0.29	1.00		
BoHo index	0.57**	0.54**	0.45**	0.62**	0.44**	0.28*	0.37**	1.00	
Composite diversity index	0.77**	0.60**	0.49**	0.69**	0.44**	0.40**	0.33*	0.76**	1.00

Notes: These data are for the fifty largest U.S. metropolitan areas. The variables are identical with those in the regression analyses of Gates and Florida (2001), and Table A.7.1. They illustrate the high intercorrelations among critical variables, especially gays and college graduates, and difficulties of disentangling them as the several other variables are also highly intercorrelated. The text elaborates.

Sources: Data kindly supplied by Gary Gates, The Urban Institute.

* Correlation is significant at the 0.05 level (one-tailed).

** Correlation is significant at the 0.01 level (one-tailed).

use counties. Counties are the smallest unit for which DDB survey results are available, and can be readily combined with Census and other data sources for counties. Having 3,111 cases is far more powerful for distinguishing interrelated causes than smaller *N*s, and resolving ambiguities like the gay association with college educated, which is so troubling at the large metro level. Several other variables correlate over 0.5, which suggests caution about model results as the number of independent variables mounts (Table A.7.3). We started from the position that the gay findings seemed robust, and initially sought to assess *why* they held rather than did they hold at all. We were surprised (and disappointed, to be frank) that this dramatic result grew so weak.

Richard Florida (2002, in press) uses path analysis to estimate separate causal paths of gays and education. But the paper uses the same fifty metro areas and main variables as the Gates/Florida paper, and thus has the same constraining statistical problems of a low *N* and highly interrelated variables. His solution is compelling if one accepts the causal framework he imposes on the data, and I am a sympathetic reader. But the limits of these data do not permit such an analysis to refute competing interpretations. Education or other factors may still swamp tolerance/diversity/gay effects. More fine-grained analysis is required to distinguish their interrelations. This still leaves unexamined or untested as well the working assumption that analyzing differences among the fifty largest metro areas is more compelling than other approaches. Why not compare analytical characteristics like talent or density using not just fifty but also other units, rather than just variations among the fifty largest?

Amenities and Patents Measures

The Natural and Constructed Amenities indexes and patents are discussed in Chap. 3; the Moralistic Political culture index is in the Chap. 2 Appendix.

BIBLIOGRAPHY

Black, D., Gates, G., Sanders, S., & Taylor, L. (2002). Why do Gay Men Live in San Francisco? *Journal of Urban Economics, 51*(1), 1–23.

Clark, T. N. (Draft). *Trees and Real Violins: Building Post-Industrial Chicago.* Book MS.

Elazar, D. (1984). *American Federalism.* New York: Harper and Row.

Firey, W. (1945). Sentiment and Symbolism as Ecological Variables. *American Sociological Review, 80,* 140–148.

Fisher, C. S. (1982). *To Dwell Among Friends.* Chicago: University of Chicago Press.

Florida, R. (2000). Competing in the Age of Talent: Quality of Place and the New Economy Report Prepared for The R. K. Mellon Foundation, Heinz Endowments, and Sustainable Pittsburgh.

———(2002). *The Rise of the Creative Class*. New York: Basic Books/Perseus.

———(2002, in press). The Economic Geography of Talent. *Annals of the Association of American Geographers, 92*(4), 743–755.

Florida, R., & Gates, G (2001). *Technology and Tolerance: The Importance of Diversity to High-Technology Growth*. Washington, DC: Brookings.

Lefebvre, H. (1981). *The Production of Space*. Austin: University of Texas Press.

Malpezzi, S. (2002). Urban Regulation, the "New Economy", and Housing Prices. *Housing Policy Debate, 13*(2), 323–349.

National Public Radio (1999). Silicon Valley Charitable Foundations.

Soja, E. (1996). *Thirdspace: Journeys to Los Angeles and other Real-and-Imagined Places*. London: Verso.

Suttles, G. (1972). *The Social Construction of Communities*. Chicago: University of Chicago Press.

Chapter Eight

Starbucks, Bicycle Paths, and Urban Growth Machines: E-mails Among Members of the Urban and Community Section of the American Sociological Association Listserv

Compiled by Terry Nichols Clark

Lots of enthusiasm is emerging among Comurbanists for urban biking, so I have to pass on a new table I am refining on amenities in cities (county data shown here). It shows that NYC, LA and some other urban locations rank very high nationally, and above many suburban and smaller population counties, even in bike events (for mountain and road bikes).

Opera and Juice Bars are added to show that we are multidimensional entertainment analysts. And the ranking is by Opera, so the list is truncated; there may be some biking capitals that have no Opera so got dropped here. Who can tell us more about Ramsey, MN and El Paso, CO? But look how low Cleveland ranks. More in the draft book: *The City as an Entertainment Machine.*

Terry Clark

As I understand it, from about 1960 until 1990 or so, the U.S. population moved out of the central cities of the larger metropolitan areas: (1) to the nearby suburbs; (2) down the urban hierarchy to smaller metropolitan areas; and (3) to the South and West. Despite small pockets of gentrification in some large cities, I think the general pattern has been for the relatively better off to leave the central cities faster than the population as a whole while the less well-off continued to move to the central cities (even if at a slower pace in the 1980s than previously). I believe that prior to 1960, the aggregate pattern of movement was very different—basically towards the places that population subsequently moved away from (even if the beginnings of some, if not all, of the post-1960 movements could be seen in the 1930s and 1940s).

With the exception of population growth in two central cities, New York and Chicago, I think the previous patterns still continue. The pattern of employment change is probably a bit more complex, because of the possibility of commuting and because of retirement, children, and a household division of labor, but broadly the same. (Anyone who knows more about urban history and trends, feel free to correct me.)

How much do amenities—natural physical amenities, constructed amenities, socio-economic composition and diversity, and values and attitudes of residents (these are the factors examined in Terry Clark's chapter)—have to do with the changes—specifically, the population changes between 1990 and 2000?

What do these have to do with the amenity argument? People "vote with their feet" but it's often difficult to tell what they are voting for. First, the effects of amenities might be "suppressed." Philadelphia might be a great place but it had a blue collar industrial base which disintegrated. For quite awhile, its amenities would be paired with population decline. (I think older industrial cities with pre-war suburbs are wonderful places to live (at least some of them). Apparently few Americans agree with me.)

It's not a fair test of the amenities argument to start looking in 1990. A lot of what happened in the earlier decades probably had an effect in the last decade. Moreover, to the extent that Starbucks has a team of crack geo-demographers on the job, that amenity measure is a result of the sort of population and employment base they think will support (yet) a(nother) branch. Same deal for juice bars, although probably minus the analysts. I don't think bicycling events are a fair measure either. Attendance tends to be low and, if you caught a cold, you might miss out on your reason for living in Chicago (or wherever) for a year. These indicators tap into a whole range of unmeasured variables besides the amenity factor and many such amenities come and go quickly. (The whole bubble tea phenomenon came and almost went and I barely got to taste any.) Most opera houses have been around longer, but then, relatively few people actually attend the opera. To the extent there is a correlation with population growth (even of limited sub-populations), the correlation is almost certainly spurious. (Like maybe most of the 1990s was good to the financial industry and banks still have a presence in the cities sufficiently established to have opera houses—Hugh McNoll's efforts to the contrary.)

In the second half of the chapter, Terry Clark raises a whole host of measurement and conceptualization issues in addition to the urban growth process issues (honesty to the point of painfulness). How will these be addressed?

Steve
Stephen J. Appold
Department of Sociology
National University of Singapore

I certainly do not want Stephen to think that he is the only one sitting back and scratching his head as he reads the posts about bicycling and Starbucks and other urban amenities leading urban growth in American cities. I too wondered exactly what Terry Clark had in mind with this series of notes. I'm not certain that the material from the associated website does much to clear up the picture.

But I wonder if starbucks creates the neighborhood, or whether starbucks follows other more general demographic trends within particular neighborhoods? Should cities offer starbucks urban homesteading credits to locate in depressed neighbor- hoods so that these and other urban amenities can encourage yuppies to move into the area? If Kokomo wants to increase the number of middle and upper-income households in the community, should it open new bike trails? or should it build an opera house? If urban amenities in fact drive a particular form of growth, as Terry Clark suggests, these sorts of proposals would make sense.

I can think of some examples that better follow Stephen Appold's discussion of urban amenities. And this is probably a good way to approach our debate now that the various positions have been staked out—just as we do in class: what examples can we think of to assess the positions taken?

Let's take a good-old down-home example: Green Bay has for a decade or so sponsored a marathon (and a bike race!). We just opened a 24-mile biking trail along the beautiful Fox River (thanks to the rails-to-trails initiative). Professionals use these events as warm-ups for larger races in larger cities. Persons from several states come here to compete. Some people from here in town participate in the events. Some others go to watch. Have these events done very much to change the community? More people are bicycling because they don't have to worry about getting smashed by cars, but this doesn't seemed to have changed the local character of the town and I certainly don't see an influx of young urban professionals moving to the community.

Several years ago one of our neighbors opened the first drive-by espresso shop in town (check out www.jotogo.com). I was talking to him about this when it was in the late planning stages: he had visited relatives in Seattle, saw drive-ins there, was tired of the family business, and decided to start the new business. (I did ask him if he thought Green Bay was ready for an espresso shop.) The business has been reasonably successful—enough so to support two branch stores and to nurture two copy-cat businesses. And we got our own first real-life starbucks a couple of months ago (or so my students tell me, I haven't seen it yet). But the question remains: are these urban amenities that suggest great changes ahead for the city? Is Green Bay going to experience a sudden growth because we got espresso drive-bys and starbucks before your town did? Are we going to see an influx of upwardly mobile households to the community because we have this and you don't?

Ray Hutchison

Sent: 11/2/02 4:35 P.M.
Subject: Growth Machines, and more, Harvey Molotch etc.

Terry indicates that John Logan and I may have "abandoned" the growth machine or "relativized" it. I don't think so. We have both gone on to other projects in our own work, dealing with other aspects of urban life that interest us.

The city is a big place, with many dimensions. I stick to the idea that growth machines are the critical element of power in U.S. cities and a rich basis for analytic and empirical work. More needs to be said not only about growth machines but about the rich contexts—of culture, nature, and biography—with which growth machine dynamics are in interaction.

But I like to do other kinds of work as well.

The beat goes on.

Harvey Molotch
Professor of Metropolitan Studies and Sociology
New York University
and Professor of Sociology
University of California, Santa Barbara

The artist as vanguard thing, quite evident and discussed in studies of SoHo and the East Village, and increasingly apparent in cities all over, needs some nuance with regards to the amenity discussion. Chicago's Wicker Park, where I have done some research, became well-known during the 1990's as the city's new bohemia. It also substantially gentrified during the decade, and attracted fairly significant presence in new media and graphic design firms. In 2000, it finally got a Starbucks on its main intersection.

So Starbucks did not drive gentrification, and indeed the funky neighborhood ethos may even have discouraged Starbucks arrival past the point where the residential demographic appeared to call for it, since even many professional residents considered outlets like Starbucks or the Gap too "mainstream" for a neighborhood whose value resided heavily in the aura of countercultural cool.

Still, artists were moving in throughout the 1980s without producing much notice or rent escalation. Indeed, they were having a hard time finding even each other. As one of my informants, fresh from art school when he moved to WP in 1988, told me: "Everyone said move down there, move down there, there's a lot of artists. But when I got there, there were no artists, I couldn't see them." Only after a handful of new venues opened, like Ricky Renier's gallery, or the Urbus Orbis Cafe, and some older places changed their strategies, from say featuring polka music to showcasing punk, was it possible for the scene to coalesce in a way that was visible to both insiders and outsiders. Thus, local consumption amenities like art galleries, meeting places, and performance venues proved crucial platforms from which an incipient scene could come into itself, as it were, and in the process become useful to property speculators and post-industrial enterprises. Therefore, if amenities do not drive urban growth, they still seem to be crucial intervening variables, without which certain path dependent trajectories would be short-circuited.

In a point I'd like to perhaps return to as the debate progresses, the amenities- growth relationship should probably be viewed as more dialectical than strictly causal—in either direction.

Richard Lloyd

Ray,

What puts Green Bay on the map for Americans and the world? Its machinery? Its banks? Or a major sports team? What industry is a sports team part of?

How many people visit Green Bay as tourists to ask about sports?

Is the Green Bay Machine about manufacturing? Is this all just fluff?

Tourism is the third largest industry in the world—bigger than computers.

The City of Chicago now counts its largest industry as "Entertainment" which includes the businesses that supported two of the 10 persons who earned the highest incomes of any in the U.S., Oprah and Michael Jordan. They earn more than any Chicago corporate or finance leaders; are they less "real" than stodgy tractor manufacturers or unemployed steel workers, who long for an older Chicago?

How much are baseball players paid?

How much of Green Bay's economy is driven by entertainment?

I love your Indianapolis oval track story, but how does the comparison you list with Jackson, MI deal with issues of spuriousness and "other variables?"

Alas, times change faster than sociologists like to recognize. Maybe if we were paid like football players we would work harder and think faster?

Terry

Terry and urbanists,

So, it's not about urban amenities (quality of residential life). Its export base after all. It's just that once it was "breadbasket," then it was "workshop," then it was "bean counters." Now it is "stars."

My neighborhood has the bike path used by people who would have lived here anyway (and it hasn't attracted many new residents). Indianapolis has the recreational amenity (that attracts a fair number of visitors a few weekends a year but few new residents). Chicago has, courtesy of television, the export base (Oprah and Michael Jordan) and its supporting industries that attract new residents.

The "entertainment machine" argument seems different from the amenity argument. "Entertainment" sounds more like export base theory—with a different industry (the theory always had difficulty specifying what could be base and what not). And maybe just like manufacturing in the U.S. created the ethnic immigrant neighborhoods, entertainment might produce "revived" urban environments. The panhandlers in Chicago are so polite, I almost thought they were hired   by   the   Chicago   Tourism   Board   to   provide   atmosphere.

Steve
Stephen J. Appold

From: "Richard Florida" <florida@andrew.cmu.edu>

Terry—

Thanks for your note. I wrote an undergraduate thesis paper on Habermas, O'Connor, Harvey, urban political economy and Terry Clark on financial markets and urban fiscal stress: Pretty cool, huh? :-)

Thank you for sending these threads. I think it is FANTASTIC that sociologists are having such an interesting and productive debate. And I am honored that my work in some way figures into this. I never expected this kind of attention either in the academic community or with a broader public audience. I'd like to thank all involved for their thoughtful comments.

But sometimes in this kind of debate things get misinterpreted or somehow contorted into a different shape than was intended. So let me take a few moments to try to clarify a few things.

My work is devoted, at its very bottom, to trying to get beyond the old (and rather knee-jerk) saw—What comes first, the chicken or the egg?—or in this case, jobs or Starbucks. There is no one way causality here. Life is multi-causal and complex. Years ago we had people like Myrdal or lord knows Robert Park arguing that industrialization or urbanization or just plain economic growth is a process of cumulative causation, not simply a linear process where one thing causes another, causes another.

So what can I say: Of course amenities do not drive growth. Of course gays do not equal high-tech. Of course bohemians do not cause innovation. But I say that all in the book—and in rather plain language.

My empirical work points to some consistent themes and findings. Our indicators of creativity (particularly the so-called bohemian index) continuously come up positive and significant in virtually every kind of model we can fashion whether it be for high-tech or innovation or economic growth. We like that indicator because it is a measure of the direct producers of cultural creativity as opposed to an indirect measure of some construct called amenities. Our recent research on Canadian regions undertaken with Meric Gertler and his colleagues at the University of Toronto indicate that the strength of this relationship is even greater for Canada than the U.S. I mentioned to you earlier that I try to use some path analysis to show the structure of the relationships between and among diversity, creativity, human capital, innovation and economic growth in a paper which is forthcoming in the Annals of the Association of American Geographers. This tries to ferret out the structure of direct and indirect relationships between diversity, creativity, innovation and so on. It seems to suggest that diversity works indirectly through human capital, and increases the ability of regions to attract and harness talent and that this in turn registers itself in higher rates of high-tech concentration and then higher growth.

But my work goes well beyond these indicators. I have never ever been the kind of person who searches for correlations or mines data or even puts a lot of credence in quantitative research. The key driver of my work is field study and observation. Like Jane Jacobs would say, or even Marx, we need to understand the world as it really exists and to do this in the social world requires real world observation. Sure quantitative data is useful and can illuminate some sorts of relationships, but it can NEVER alone specify causality. Only good theory can. And the theory here says urban life is complex and multi-causal.

My book and work is motivated by a strong—indeed, overwhelming and over- arching—theoretical position. That is: creativity—and its subcomponents, technological, economic and cultural—drive economic growth. For too long we have had super-reductionist theories that say economic growth is the product or technology, entrepreneurship or human capital. Of course!!! But this simply begs the question—what produces those things in the first place. That is what my work tries to address.

One of my students put it this way the other day. Human capital theories treat human capital as any other economic factor and thus their faith in some disembodied "stock." But what makes human capital are real people. People who can and do make choices and pick places to live and work. The real task is to understand better the real choices real people make. AMEN!!!

So these choices are messy and not uni-causal. People do not pick places simply to work. And they do not migrate simply to the highest paying jobs. People like places they like. They like to have fun. They like interesting high-paying jobs.

Driving this is the rise of creativity as an economic force. The fact that value is increasingly derived from creativity rather than manufacturing or rote service provision. And to mobilize and harness creativity requires a great deal of stimulation from the environment. Thus, lifestyle and amenities are not epiphenomenal but related directly and causally to the nature of the economy and of work. So to be productive and efficient these people tend toward interesting and stimulating and high amenity places. Not because they are "fun" but because these environments or habitats are productive.

It ain't jobs versus Starbucks. To compete, to be effective, to generate productivity advantages, cities have to have something for everybody. Lots of different everybodies. Lots of different kinds of work. Lots of different kinds of fun. Lots of different kinds of schools. Lots of different kinds of people. Lots of everything. This in turn is because all of this is required to harness creativity. And in an evolutionary sense, the firms, organizations and regions that do this best will win and those that don't will not.

There are so many other things I can say. That creative centers are highly unequal. That this age is rife with contradiction. That creative centers, we find, even controlling for occupation, are rife with mental stress. That these contradictions need much more study . . .

But I blather on too long.

Let us know what you think. And thanks so much for your collegiality.

Rich

I am greatly touched by the deep interest in the discussion of amenities and entertainment as motors of economic development, especially since I have tried for many years to understand just how it happened that the cultural base has (apparently) overtaken the industrial infrastructure. Though I have written about the goad to development, and material for development, provided by artists and other cultural producers, I am constantly surprised by how life imitates sociology.

Or does it? The major point I find most interesting in the current discussion, including Richard Florida's healthy contribution and the reference to John Logan's study, is that no one agrees on what causes economic growth.

While writing a paper recently on the redevelopment of Lower Manhattan—to be delivered as a keynote for a European conference on branding cities—I have been thinking about the willful processes of the growth machine of real estate developers and local elected officials in hyping the social reproduction of past growth patterns and excluding the possibility of change. Certainly my own preference (and, I think, Rich Florida's) for replacing the grieved upon Twin Towers with low-rise live-work studios and performance spaces is very far from local developers' minds . . .

Thanks to Ray Hutchison for mentioning Loft Living. Yes, the thread that runs through all this "creative"-led development, from SoHo to Wicker Park and Hoxton Square, is low-rent space—the incubators for development Jane Jacobs wrote about in the middle chapters of Death and Life. But there also has to be access to linked markets for housing, kaffee klatches or Starbucks, continued artistic training (visual, holistic, or otherwise), and some sort of compensating amenities (friendship, fashion, food, music, bike paths). As Ann Markusen shows in a paper she wrote on artists' careers in Minneapolis, and as Rich Florida would no doubt confirm, real people make real trade-offs in their decisions about where to live.

And let's not forget that Starbucks is not a "first-order" creative place the way some dive in a grungy urban neighborhood may be. It's the visible evidence of artists in consumption spaces that pulls in the tourist dollars and affluent residents. Which in turn raises the demographics that pull in chain stores.

By the way, for Herb and others, I recommend John Hannigan's *Fantasy City* (Routledge, 1998) as a meticulous examination of the business of real estate development that builds interchangeable urban entertainment destinations. Though John doesn't dwell upon the urban political machines, he does make clear the mutual deal-making between politicos and developers. Isn't this what the growth machine is all about?

Sharon Zukin

Subject: RE: How Do Growth Machines Respond to Amenities?

Terry, Terry

Please translate the whole message into English.

Robert J.S. Ross, Ph.D.
Professor of Sociology
Director, International Studies Stream
Clark University

Subject: Re: English: How Do Growth Machines Respond to Amenities?

We should add amenities to the "interests" of growth machine participants, who include politicians and media people as well as developers and bankers.

They did in Santa Barbara, but did not in Ventura.

If you want more, please just mark sections that are particularly vague. Although
the works cited are there with many pages of elaboration.

Thanks for trying to keep me honest. What if Hegel sent out a draft like this? Or
Habermas, who I listened to today after biking one hour north to Loyola. His
Ph.D. was on your favorite topic.

Terry

Why Terry, what an admirably clear proposition. I even agree—it incorporates
the otherwise uneconomical stadium/pro team along with cutesy Faneuil Hall
clones.

Bob

About Jurgen: there's a guy who never learned that less is more.

Robert J.S. Ross, Ph.D.

Two questions:
  (1) Has any Olympics planning ever been done with an eye to converting
      the facilities to help poor people, or at least non-rich people? And could
      it not be done now if the economic/political power structure were other
      than it is?
  (2) How much are the benefits of the culture industry shaped by the fact
      that so much of it is located in NY and LA—economics of scale, etc.
      that would not exist in countries in which said industry was more de-
      centralized. (I wonder to what extent jobs in NY's film, TV and adver-
      tising industries make it possible for actors (other than stars) to work
      (for peanuts) in the theater? Also the U.S. entertainment industry is in-
      ternational; the majority of the world's film audience goes to American
      films and has done so almost from the very beginning of the industry.

Herbert Gans

The standard progressive position is that tourism inevitably means bad, seasonal
jobs. This, however, is a product of labor organization, not of the inherent qualities of the industry, especially in cities where seasonality is much less of a prob-

lem than in resorts. There is no real trade-off between encouraging tourism and manufacturing, because there are no or few American cities that have much potential for increasing manufacturing jobs—especially not well-paying ones. Given that tourism is labor intensive and can absorb people with few skills and little English, we need to concentrate on improving the sector rather than on condemning it.

Whether entertainment is a driver of growth or simply a consumption good has already been answered in the dialogue that has transpired—it is both. To the extent that it is symbiotic with other industries its multiplier effect is fairly substantial.

Also, we need to be careful about seeing cultural industries as only meeting the consumption desires of the rich. Poor people also travel, and a lot of community-based arts activity is not the province of the YUPs. I like to cite the comment of an African American minister who lectured to my redevelopment class on the revitalization of New Brunswick, NJ. When I asked him whether his congregation, which mostly lived in public housing, resented the transformation of the main street by street furniture, brick sidewalks, etc., he looked at me as if I was crazy and told me that poor people liked to be in nice surroundings too. The point is to find ways of preventing displacement, not deciding that you will block any attempts at beautification because they make poor people feel that they don't belong there.

Incidentally for people who don't know that I have left Rutgers, please note my new address:

Susan S. Fainstein
Professor of Urban Planning
Graduate School of Architecture, Planning and Preservation
Columbia University

Eric Peterson and Herb Gans raise a point I would love to see clarified, or sources that document and measure. There is a huge migration literature I read closely years ago, but I am way out of date.

How well can we really answer what is "intra" and "inter-Metropolitan"? Yes these are separate data sources and traditions of work, but apart from that, what do the results show when we try to explain who moves and why?

The drive behind my question is which amenities reach how far? How can we answer this systematically?

I used the term "catchment area" to try to capture this and suggest we don't know so well, and to suggest a few hypotheses in the chapter I put up. Juice bars shorter, opera longer? But how long or short?

Rich Florida and Gary Gates suggest gays have a big impact using data for the 50 biggest metro areas, but this falls to near zero when we choose all counties in the U.S. They reply: metro migration is what drives the rest.

Are they right? Can anyone help?

Thanks!!

Terry

PS. I cannot resist adding the great first paragraph of Guido M's recent paper, which he will draw on in a presentation at the U of Chicago Nov 18th, 4–5:20 p.m. in 106 SS (1126 E 59 St).

If you are not in Chicago just glance at the below:

Space, Technologies and Populations in the New Metropolis
Position paper for the International Workshop of the Project MoVe
Università degli studi di Milano-Bicocca
Aula Rodolfi, U6, 4th floor 9.30 a.m. to 5.00 p.m.
Wednesday June 26th, 2002
Prof. Guido Martinotti

Once upon a time, in ancient times, writes Giddens, it was not possible to separate place from space time. Even gods could not do it. Take the turning point in the Odyssey of Odysseus, the prototypical traveler. This comes when Odysseus' protector Athena, taking advantages of his lazy reveille, bamboozles Zeus into up- lifting the travelling damnation imposed on Odysseus by Poseidon. Zeus decides to send Hermes, the messenger, to the island where the love affair with Calypsos, the Nymph, has kept Odysseus in stall for 7 years during his long way home. In the Internet era, the order would go instantaneously, but in the age of the unity of time and place in theatrical narrative, even imagination had to follow the rules. Hermes could go at dream speed, but still had to physically travel. "volò il potente Argheifonte. Piombò dal cielo sul mare; e si slanciò sull'onde, come il gabbiano che negli abissi paurosi del mare instancabile, i pesci cacciando, fitte l'ali bagna nell'acqua salata; simile a questo, sui flutti infiniti Ermete correva" Od,V,50. Later on Hermes complains of the fatigue of the travel. "E chi volentieri traverserebbe tant'acqua marina, infinita? Non neppure vicina qualche città i mortali che fanno offerte ai numi, elette ecatombe" Od,V,101. In short, a long trip with no food stops. No Macs, no Burger Kings nor International Houses of Pancakes. The story is very interesting precisely because it makes clear that even in the phantasmagoria world of the Odyssey, travel had to be real, confirming the sociological intuition of the disembedded nature of contemporary societies, in which mobility is not only a major social dynamic, but also a dominant cultural trait.

If Artists Bring Amenities, How Can Cities Attract Artists? These last few posts by Herb and Sharon in particular could fuel an intriguing set of hypotheses first, and maybe some testing later. I pose questions, not yet clear hypotheses, but ask for help from others more knowledgeable, like Sharon or her students, or Ann Markusen or Rich Florida or Harvey Molotch (whose new book has a chapter on artists cum designers).

What seems partially new, at least to me, is to ask how and why the urban context shifts the ability of an artist to work in non-artistic jobs. And what does this imply about cities and neighborhoods more generally?

Artists are critical: (1) as a deviant extreme case of an occupation that is volatile and linked to jobs that are transitory. They may be distinctly illuminating as a "creative class" but underpaid as workers compared to others like IT engineers; (2) artists often lead gentrifying processes in cities, maybe in part by their combination of low income and high talent—does this sound familiar to us as academics, and grad students?; (3) artists may be distinctly drawn to move to a location by amenities like museums or arts schools or galleries; (4) artists are themselves important urban amenities, in cafes, street life, and giving a neighborhood a bohemian, tolerant, distinctive outlook. Kotler stresses this nationally, Sharon in Greenwich Village, Soho. The symbolism of Loft Living.
I use the term artist loosely; many ideas apply to "creative and individualistic" occupations and persons generally. Whether they are a Kasse Fuer Sich or not.
That is, what characteristics of a city: (1) attract and retain artists or potential artists; (2) of different sorts (painters vs. actors vs. others); (3) permit them to work in non-artistic jobs; (4) that they find appealing because; (5) employers hire artists or at least don't dislike them (Rich Lloyd finds bar owners in at least some neighborhoods LOVE to hire artists since they work seriously, look good, and accept low pay; but I bet in truck drivers' neighborhoods, artists would be less appealing as they might not converse as well with the clients); (6) higher pay—that is what leads to bidding up the price of artists cum bartenders or web designers or some other occupational category where there is an enhancement in attractiveness due to the person also being an artist? (What kinds of degrees have what income impact? Jim Heckman here is working on this. The salary enhancement of a Julliard degree should be more for singing advertisements and less for pothole repair/construction.) The City of Chicago, Dept. of Cultural Affairs, has a study in progress starting from a sample of some 10,000 artists which finds higher pay for those that do art with more commercial applications—graphics design, advertising. Semi-obvious, perhaps, but in need of codification.

Art prices have been studied by some of our economists here. Over the 20th century, one finds an increase in value for younger artists' works, especially after 1945, which David Galenson suggests may be related to adaptability to newer styles of younger artists, and declining relative status of the traditional. The J of Cultural Economics (the entire contents of which are web-accessible) has papers on related points. Co editor Mark Schuster from MIT visited at Chicago last year and talked on these points; (7) Why do cities differ? Population size is obvious but too simple and over aggregated. Detroit is big but who goes there these days? Special groups. (Detroit got its first Starbucks last year.) What else? I analyzed municipal employees' pay differences across cities and found that Detroit and NYC paid almost three times as much as Gary, which had an explicit policy of hiring part time staff to build networks among many different people in the population, to spread the wealth among the many underemployed, and to recruit them to do political work, as well as work at their city jobs. (In City Money) I suggested that the high pay and qualification yet small numbers of staff vs. low pay, larger numbers was an important dimension for classifying city government policy and that it fits with the more general political culture of cities, was consistent with our data. But I did not think about this for artists. Related too: the U.S. in general has an open policy re-immigration and volatile job creation, compared to Western Europe, or even more, Korea or Japan. The average American worker changes jobs in less than four years, temp work is huge, and multiple jobs common. The European artists may be like Americans but just not listed on the official books at all? Or less? Or what? I/we know the situation for young academics in places like Paris, and it is worse than in the U.S., lower pay, more fragmented jobs, etc. And how about East Europe or China? These make even the Parisians look fat and happy. Polish professors used to pick strawberries in Norway in the summer to support their families. Just a little bit of non-American evidence can clarify the narrowness of the range we cover here. (8) City amenity effects—here is where Rich Florida and I would stress the amenities that may attract artists to a location, even if they know they cannot be paid to work as artists, or even if they have no job. They are willing to do multiple, volatile, and transitory jobs since they want to be in NYC or Hollywood, if you are an aspiring actress. Or Houston is a step up if you live in a small Texas town nearby. And Austin is paradise. Even if people choose a job and a city simultaneously, many young, talented persons choose the cool city to be able to shift among jobs without having to leave the city. This is Rich Florida's key point which he documents, but more for high-tech workers. To explore this sort of thing for either artists or creative volatile workers of different job categories would be great. We need to model regional markets more explicitly, too. Some Chicago artists said to Rich Lloyd that they did not go right to NYC since they wanted to start in a less competitive environment. Part of this is higher standards in the top locations, but it is more too. (9) Networks/community—many cultural leaders, artists, foundation people, theater people I see in Chicago say that Chicago is unusual in the degree of "community concern" —that theater people talk to theater people about their ideas and help each other here. Rich Lloyd quotes a screenplay writer who had been in Hollywood and NYC and came back and said that in "other cities" people just talk about money, but in Chicago they share ideas and help create more. How much this exaggerates, or how empirically valid it is, I don't know, but the core idea is the same story emerges in the Silicon Valley and Austin stories compared to Boston that Rich Florida reviews: programmers in bars drive innovation. You need enough density to permit this to happen, but what attracts and enhances communication and networking besides density? Strong ties vs. weak ties is the obvious hypothesis. We have DDB measures of strong and weak ties for every U.S. county, but when I added them to models found they had no impact on migration in the amenities chapter I put up. (10) Hypothesis: If David Brooks is half right, and as tolerance increases as we know from the GSS, we should see many locations being more "artist friendly" and the "location quotient" of Paris and Greenwich Village should decline, and the "density gradient" of artists across the U.S. should flatten. That is there is now an artsy cafe´ in thousands of little U.S. towns, and lofts for painting. Whereas in the 1920s you "had" to go Paris or Greenwich Village. Has anybody mapped this? It would be easier than some things. The same happened to universities in the 1950s and 1960s as the whole system expanded, for a while. (11) How to pursue? Regarding theory, artists may just be the extreme end of a continuum where many others act in similar manner: that is many wannabe artists stop doing any art when they get a time-demanding job. What do we know about workers bridging multiple labor markets simultaneously? And "dropping out" of a field? We worry about "drop out" rates for Ph.D. students, but I put it far higher for bartenders, waitresses, and 20-year old wannabe artists. The term "artist" is hugely open as well. Some studies in Chicago stress that people who take a one-week course in finger painting or the mandolin are at least "participants in art." The numbers skyrocket this way. If we just include BA grads from art schools, is this too narrow? Probably? So what to do? Ideas from labor market sociologists, economists? Others? Re data: Ann Markusen has a paper measuring the numbers of artists of different types by cities across the entire U.S. She shows how to get this from the census and critiques past studies that have generally used the Employment data which hugely undercounts artists (it shows them just as bartenders, for instance, if this is where they fill out pay forms). If instead you ask individuals what their occupations are, you find far more artists. These data are readily available in the U.S. census by cities across the country, and could be combined with other measures to test ideas about how and why cities differ. I would be more cautious about trying to do this by neighborhood (as Andy Beveredge discussed in a recent post) as people can commute within a metro area. (12) Policy implications—there is an emerging field of cultural policy that asks what could a city government do to enhance its attractiveness to artists and culture. What policies could help here? Big and small.

What we can bring to this that complements the individualism of artist/biographers and most economists is explicit attention to context and the institutional underpinnings of what makes different markets and sociopolitical processes work. "Job satisfaction" is too important a concept to leave to strong individualists.

But these are quick reflections from an on-going, lively exchange. How sharpen these ideas or improve them? How much work is there that does parts of this already?

Terry

NOTES

1. Excerpted from some one hundred pages of exchanges.
2. Listserv messages from October 2002 to January 2003
3. To subscribe: All commands must be sent to: LISTSERV@EMAIL.RUTGERS.EDU

Chapter Nine
Amenities Drive Urban Growth:
A New Paradigm and Policy Linkages

Terry Nichols Clark with Richard Lloyd, Kenneth K.
Wong and Pushpam Jain

A PARADIGMATIC REVOLUTION

Our classic urban theories are out of date. Not all need be scrapped, but most
need significant updating. Why? Because of globalization, the most dramatic
force restructuring our cities around the world. The power of the process is no
less if we ignore it; we do so at great risk. Mayors, developers, political party
leaders, and even social scientists need to rethink their paradigms about cities. It
is painful for everyone.

This paper briefly sketches the broader changes with globalization, then
highlights the critical role of amenities and urban political choices about amenities, suggesting where and how they can dramatically shift urban dynamics.

Data come from our Project on Fiscal Austerity and Urban Innovation, an
ongoing study of some thirty-five countries and over seven thousand cities, plus
an in-depth study of one: Chicago. Why Chicago? Because it is an outlier for
many urban processes, in being heavily Catholic and long preserving peasant
traditions like strong neighborhoods and clientelist politics, making it more like
cities globally than most U.S. cities. Its strong hierarchical party tradition distinctly separates it from Tocquevillian democracy in the New England or Northern Italian model of Putnam (1993).

Yet a recent study by Markusen et al (2001) ranks Chicago number one in
the U.S. in the absolute number of high tech jobs, ahead of Silicon Valley. Just a
decade or so earlier, many observers were forecasting that Chicago, as part of

the Rustbelt, was being driven like Detroit into a downward spiral of disinvestment and racial strife with investors and jobs moving to suburbs and the Sunbelt. How could the pessimists have been so wrong? Their paradigms were outmoded. Similar trends are occurring in many older U.S. cities, that demand reconceptualization. Amenities are a key.[1]

THE NEW POLITICAL CULTURE HAS SPREAD WORLDWIDE THROUGH GLOBALIZING PROCESSES

The last two decades of the twentieth century have seen profound transformations of the political systems of the world. What we thought we knew about cities is changing rapidly, due especially to globalization, or in Europe, EUnification, including:

- the end of the Cold War in 1989, and general global peace thereafter;
- the decline of major tariffs and trade barriers, and rise of new regional trading blocks as well as global trade;
- the rapid increase in connectedness via new modes of communication: fax, Internet, fiber-optic cables, digitalization of increasing quantities of information, and the like. First among key elites, but soon thereafter by the broad public as costs of ownership of these devices dropped rapidly;
- drastic expansion of education in much of the world, thus giving more citizens an ability to read, a sense of self-worth;
- decline of agricultural and industrial work, and rise of more professional, service-oriented, and increasingly technically-based jobs, where computers and machines replace people for basic tasks.

GLOBALIZATION: WHAT IS IT AND HOW DOES IT WORK?

Much past work invoked globalization to imply a simple "capitalist" or economic determinism. Globalization is more; it includes culture and amenities which can redefine economic rules. It has three distinct meanings. First is The City as Global Market Participant. This is the fiscal/economic/production meaning, stressing global markets for capital and labor. A key idea is that as global markets rise, national quasi-monopolies and strong-state regulations fall. This is primary a private sector process, but important for local governments as they often seek to encourage local economic development, and production.

Second is globalization where The City is an Entertainment Machine. Here the stress is on consumption, not production: CNN, MTV, Hollywood movies are seen as bringing a standard world fare that may encourage more globally-homogeneous consumption. It can raise and refocus economic aspirations by redefining consumption desiderata. But much of consumption is driven by local specifics: cafes, art galleries, geographic/architectural layout and aesthetic image of a city define its unique attractions (or blandness). Tourism is the world's third largest industry, and attracting visitors has become big business for local officials, who in turn build new stadiums, parks, museums, convention centers, and similar facilities hoping to win visitors from near and far.

Third is The City as Global Democracy. Here the democratizing impacts of global leaders and non-government organizations press cities that lag. Human rights, which grew out of expanding citizens' civil rights, continue to grow in their extent and seriousness of application—to women, children, Indian untouchables, the homeless, illegal immigrants, as well as physical entities that can assume "human" rights: trees, beaches, and endangered species of animals. For instance, a Boston non-profit arranges international trips for physically disabled persons. In Costa Rica, they ask do you have corner cuts in your sidewalks for wheel chairs? If no, is there an organization that presses for the disabled in Costa Rica? If no, let's start one. This spreads Tocquevillian/Putnam civic/voluntary associations globally. Citizen rights expand as organized groups and professionals develop new themes and specialties. This in turn adds new issues to local political agendas, leading political parties to embrace them or be challenged by new parties that champion these new political cultural concerns. Globalization in all three areas illustrates:

- More information about options
- Citizens may redefine their ambitions as they see new options
- More potential and actual contacts
- More persons are incorporated or "empowered," thus illustrating what Adam Smith called an increase in the "extent of the market". It in turn encourages:
- More competition in previous areas that formerly made decisions more by hierarchies or tradition, than by markets.

Caveat: These trends emerged first in Northwest Europe and North America, and should not be over-generalized. They are not a description of most of the world, but they do capture pressures for change operating worldwide.

More important than the technology or the legal framework of constitutions are the actual rules of game by which people live and politics is played. National states with centralized power are being replaced by federalist systems involving shared powers among multiple units of government. Political rules are changing, but not as simply as the technical and legal changes. A new conception of politics is spreading worldwide. We have termed it the New Political

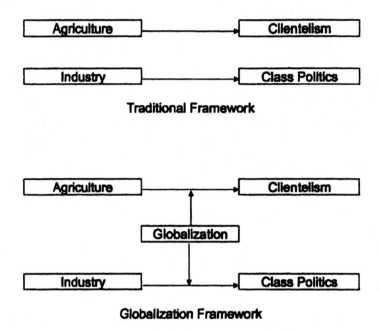

Figure 9.1. Impact of Globalization on Political Processes

Culture, for it is more than democracy; it is a more specific set of rules about politics. It is readily identified by such leaders as President Bill Clinton in the U.S., Prime Minister Anthony Blair in Britain, and Chancellor Gerhard Schroeder in Germany. This *New Political Culture* contrasts with clientelism and class politics. *Clientelism* is common in many less developed countries today, and often seems more natural in an agricultural economy where social relations are intertwined with attachment to the land, and endure over many years. *Class politics* arose with industrialization, led by labor unions and socialist parties, which opposed the hierarchy of industrial management. The traditional patterns are shown first in Figure 9.1.

Globalization is transforming local processes for public officials, and research paradigms for urban analysts. Many global processes can be summarized as a simple box and arrow diagram, which stresses that globalization is not alone or a unique cause, but it "interacts" with other factors like more education and income to *enhance* their effects.

Thus are clientelism and class politics undermined. Global factors, like the internet and travel, complicate the above simple paths, weakening the impact of the local (and national) economic base.

BEYOND THE GROWTH MACHINE

Harvey Molotch's metaphor suggests that the city is a machine geared to creating "growth," with growth loosely defined as the intensification of land use and thus higher rent collections, associated professional fees and locally-based profits (1976). Many urban economists, planners, and political scientists have made similar arguments (e.g. Bradbury, Downs and Small, 1982; Mollenkopf, 1983; Stone, 1989). However, a quarter century later, in the contemporary competition among U.S. cities, the growth machine model has lost much of its power. More research makes it increasingly clear that the simple growth machine model has often been weakly supported.[2] The "new economy" has not spelled the demise of older central city areas, but it has changed the basis for urban economic viability. Traditional forms of capital give way to the primacy of human capital in the form of an educated and mobile workforce (Clark and Gaile, 1998; Florida, 2002). An ideology of growth at any cost, via land use intensification, is not a given. In many locations, "smart" or "managed" growth strategies have replaced the growth machine as the driving civic ideology. Many locations have thus found considerable success in competing for knowledge workers, like Portland, Oregon, which even implemented "a program of financial penalties designed to discourage excessive growth by one of its largest employers, Intel, Inc." (Florida, 2000, p. 24). Such policies run counter to political strategies in which the provision of manufacturing jobs and corresponding patterns of capital intensification are taken as quasi-automatically desirable. These illustrate forcefully the lesson from economics 101, that people maximize utility, not income, and that utility equals income plus amenities. Edward Glaeser (2000b), Harvard urban economist, even suggests that "non-market transactions," essentially amenities, have grown more important than market transactions in explaining urban growth and decline.

What are amenities? The concept comes from economics. Leading observers write: "A pure amenity is a non-produced public good such as weather quality that has no explicit price. In practice, previous empirical studies include some government services such as education and public safety . . ." (Gyourko and Tracy 1991). Chapter 3 elaborates.

Much has changed in the last half century. In prototypical industrial cities like Chicago, we have seen a steady decline in manufacturing employment, and growth in services, followed in turn by more subtle high tech and globalizing processes. This description is well known; but what drives these changes? Which locations attract new high-tech jobs, while others fail? Displacement of manufacturing from central city space changes the class structure of large cities, with political and cultural consequence. Workers whose social location renders them less adaptable to structural change suffer from chronic unemployment or move into subsistence occupations in the service sector (Wilson, 1987); they occupy "spaces of devastation" (Zukin, 1991) within most large cities. Nightmare landscapes of poverty are a feature of former industrial cities in the U.S., and have been studied extensively, ethnographically and demographically.

Yet simultaneously a new elite economy has emerged in these same cities, featuring educated workers in finance, producer services, information technology, and media production. Castells (1989) termed them "informational." They are educated and fluent at manipulating symbols, leading Robert Reich to term them "symbolic analysts" (1991). Similarly, theories of economic innovation from Joseph Schumpeter, Jane Jacobs and Paul Romer stress new ideas as driving jobs and economic growth (see Glaeser, 2000a). Still, this leap of post-industrial production stressed by Castells and Reich, for example, is still not clearly joined to entertainment or consumption by them or by most theorists who have long invoked primarily production-based interpretations to explain general urban processes. We thus stress the critical epistemological implications of our next conceptual step: the "informational city" implies the "city of leisure." Some have described but few interpreted implications of this shift toward consumption. For instance Costas and Bennett (2003) documented the importance of new consumption-oriented strategies for several U.S. cities, but did not locate them in a conceptual framework. Or the fine book by Judd and Fainstein (1999) documents the huge role of tourism in the world economy, yet the authors are still visibly struggling to interpret it. The closest parallel to our approach we have found is Glaeser et al. (2000).

To help systematize these changes in urban growth dynamics, we postulate several new components of change:

(1) There is a rise of the individual citi- zen/consumer in explanatory power, which follows from increases in citizen income, education, and political empowerment. This translates into more individualization and volatility of tastes, creating more numerous and complex "niche markets." The growth of the more affluent as a "new class" however coexists with substantial numbers of "structurally disadvantaged" within the city, and the development of the Entertainment Machine is "structurally uneven" in tilting more toward the more affluent, albeit with important exceptions (see Chapters 2 and 3).

(2) Conversely, we note a decline in large bureaucratic decision-makers in both the public and private sector. In the past they produced large quantities of basic products inexpensively. But as tastes and niche markets differentiate, they are less nimble than small firms and individuals in adapting to rapid change.

(3) There is relative decline in the explanatory power of classical variables affecting the economic base, like distance, transportation costs, local labor costs, and proximity to natural resources and markets—since air travel, fax, the Internet, and associated changes have drastically facilitated contacts among physically distant persons, globally. This shifts the mix of inputs for location of households and firms, increasing the importance of more subtle distinctions in taste, quality of life concerns, and related considerations.

(4) There is a rise of leisure pursuits compared to "work," increasing the relative importance of new or more refined occupations like tour guide or restaurant critic, and creating an increasing differentiation among providers of personal services.

(5) There is a rise of the arts and aesthetic considerations alongside more traditional considerations, in people's lives as well as in modeling the dynamics of cities.

(6) These new tastes create a new role for government and public officials, as they seek to implement these new citizen demands, which are often for "public goods" (clean air, attractive views, pedestrian responsiveness) contrasting with more "private goods" (jobs, contracts, tax breaks to separate persons and firms) in the past. There is a rise of zoning, construction of new public spaces, support for public art in many forms, and the introduction of a host of new considerations into urban political decision-making, since judging the demand for competing public goods is far more complex than private goods. These last elements are elaborated and tested using comparative urban data elsewhere (Clark and Hoffmann-Martinot, 1998); our focus here is on detailing dynamics of urban growth (and decline), and elaborating the profile of the post-industrial city. These changes are more profound for heavily industrial cities, but the fact that they emerge there too shows their pervasiveness and power. Globalization enhances many of these processes, as international criteria and consumer demands via tourists are increasingly added to the local.

DECLINE AND RENEWAL: POSTINDUSTRIAL TRENDS IN U.S. CITIES

Disinvestment and fiscal crises in large U.S. cities during the 1970s led to a bleak prognosis concerning urban fortunes. Many saw the growth of telematics and globalization as undermining the place boundedness of economic activity, which implied that the dense, central investment of capital in urban cores was no longer desirable. New information technologies are an advance with extreme potential impact on spatial organization: "they represent the opportunity to conduct many more economic transactions at a distance—from an employee at home to a central office, from a consumer to a store, from one company to another" (Atkinson, 1998, p. 134). The changes in the technological foundation of economic activity have been consequential for spatial organization. Our theories need corresponding updating. The central place theories that explain the grown and urban morphology of population in cities, as in Loesch and Burgess, was predicated on the centralized locational tendencies of manufacturing; this is no longer adequate given the rise of new information technologies (Gottdiener, 1985). Edge cities and deconcentration are instead the newer catchwords. As unionized manufacturing jobs declined in the old center cities, "structural mismatch" occurred between workers and jobs, and between the built environment and new economic activities, producing patterns of extreme poverty and blight.

But these theories, based on trends for most of the twentieth century, have been disconfirmed by recent change. The most dramatic: empirical results have refuted predictions of the center city's demise. Contrary to most theoretical expectations and widespread policy discussion, the 1980s and 1990s saw a growth in the density of economic activity in many of the world's leading central business districts, even as the importance of globalization and telematics *increased*. This is the opposite of what futurologists of the "wired city" had predicted. While a few urban researchers documented elements of these processes, almost no theorist has seriously sought to address the deeper implications for urban modeling of this major turn-around from decline to growth of central cities. One partial exception is Saskia Sassen who noted "This explosion in the number of firms locating in the downtowns of major cities during that decade goes against what should have been expected according to models emphasizing territorial dispersal; this is especially true given the high cost of locating in a major downtown area" (Sassen, 1994, p. 2). Sassen points out that central cities have enjoyed renewed vitality as postindustrial production sites (1991, 2001). But why? Her main focus is the "world cities" interpretation (more based on production than consumption).

A related view is that cities are important "milieux of innovation" in the information economy. Postindustrial production differs from industrial production in key ways. In particular, it is design intensive and highly flexible vs. the "long run" durable assemblage of traditional industrial production (Lash and Urry, 1994). The proliferation of media provides the content for one such postindustrial activity, since the production of media images is an activity significantly concentrated in urban cores, along with finance and elite producer services.[3] Reich, Castells, Lash and Urry and others highlight the symbolic and expressive content of these activities, and the distinct competencies of their most valuable workers. The question of why some such activities continue to cohere in what were industrially-based city spaces is one of the most crucial puzzles of the contemporary city. The Entertainment Machine provides a key piece of the puzzle not explored by the above theorists.

Contemporary consumption practice extends to the consumption of space. The lifestyle concerns of social participants are increasingly important in defining the overall rationale for, and in turn driving, other urban social processes. Quality of life is not a mere byproduct of production; it defines and drives much of the new processes of production. It has been advanced to explain the population shift from the frost belt into the more (consumption-friendly) climates of the Southern and Western U.S. Castells questions this order of causality, positing the opposite, more traditional view: "so, the 'quality of life' of high technology areas is a result of the industry (its newness, its highly educated labor force) rather than the determinant of its location pattern" (1989, p. 52). His interpretation seems to reflect an earlier reality. It is important that in many urban locales migration patterns of residents, especially elite participants in postindustrial growth sectors, are driven by new quality of life demands. How do we know?

In *City Money* (1983, Chap. 8), Clark and Ferguson in the first statement of this consumption interpretation that we have seen, argued that urban job growth increasingly turned on citizens' consumption patterns and tastes, not on production, and showed that certain past migration and job growth studies could be productively reinterpreted in these terms. Simultaneous equation studies of job and population growth measured the relative impact of each on the other; they were both strong, roughly equal in some estimates. This suggested that migration to a city or to a job was about equal in import for all American migrants. Evidence of such patterns has mounted in the subsequent decade and a half, such as in the suggestive studies of Judd and Fainstein (1999), Glaeser et al. (2000), and Florida (2000). This chapter pushes further in clarifying the analytical logic behind the earlier, mainly statistical results, and illustrates key points with new evidence, mainly ethnographic.

The increasing importance of tourism and convention dollars to central city coffers, both public and private, raises the stakes in the lifestyle game. Talented high tech staff who can locate where they choose drive cities to compete for them with public amenities. This is a reversal of the "smokestack chasing" that was the leading policy of U.S. cities for decades: to offer larger incentives to an individual firm than competing locations. Such private goods competition is far more costly to cities and their tax payers than the public goods of amenities.

Residential patterns since the 1980s have run counter to bleak expectations for some older industrial cities. The concentration of poverty documented by Wilson (e.g. 1987), as a response to de-industrialization coexists with revalorization of some former slums by black, brown and white residents. Gentrification trends indicate that affluent workers, particularly the young, are finding the city not simply a clear destination for work, but also a desirable place to live and play. These changes in the residential profiles of urban neighborhoods are treated by some as indicators of postmodern consumption trends (Harvey, 1990); but many post-modernist interpreters like Harvey still rely heavily on finance or jobs, for instance, Smith (1996, p. 8): "systematic gentrification...is simultaneously a response and a contributor to a series of wider global transformations: global economic expansion in the 1980s: the restructuring of national and urban economies in advanced capitalist countries toward services, recreation and consumption: and the emergence of a global hierarchy of world, national, and regional cities."

Our view is that we should focus more directly on changing preferences of citizens and workers themselves; they are choosing where to live, to change jobs on average every 3.5 years (for the U.S. workforce in 2001 per the BLS, cf. Florida, 2002, p. 104).[4] The gentrified neighborhood as a distinct type of urban community differs considerably from the neighborhoods studied in past classics of urban sociology such as Gans' *The Urban Villagers* (1962) or glorified by Robert Putnam in *Bowling Alone* (2000). The important local amenities are no longer schools and churches and neighborhood associations, as in the urban mosaic of the old Chicago school. A residential population of young professionals with more education and fewer children creates a social profile geared toward recreation and consumption concerns. They value the city over other forms of settlement space because of its responsiveness to a wide array of aesthetic concerns, because it can become a cultural center offering diverse, sophisticated and cosmopolitan entertainment lacking elsewhere.

In the "new economic geography" of Entertainment, cities like Seattle and Portland become central locations for the development of information tech- nologies. A common "explanation" for location of a firm like Microsoft in firm location discussions is often presented with a perhaps disgruntled sigh or laugh: the "personal choice of the top executive," like Bill Gates. The conceptual fallacy here is in implying that the top executives are merely idiosyncratic, simply wrong, or personally selfish—since they did not select a lower-cost or more production-driven location. But this may just be conceptual tunnel vision by the observers. Behind it lies a key to reinterpretation: the top executives may have had in mind not merely themselves in locating in attractive places, but a concern to attract top talent globally to work with them. Provision of lifestyle amenities has become a key feature of urban development that we must recognize conceptually; these two cities are extremes ("deviant cases") in being leaders in "smart growth" strategies, and in their recent dramatic growth.

The absence of children suggests that Yuppies will be less interested in local schools and perhaps churches as relevant amenities. Rather, they are excited by opportunities for recreation, like along Chicago's refurbished north shore lakefront, with its bicycle paths, beaches, and softball fields; and by up-to-the minute consumption opportunities in the hip restaurants, bars, shops and boutiques abundant in restructured urban neighborhoods.

Note a particularly provocative recent finding of four economists and policy analysts (Florida, 2002; Chap. 6 this volume): cities with more gay men have far more amenities than other cities, and amenities and gay men in turn are among the strongest predictors of growth in high tech jobs in multiple regressions controlling about a dozen other variables. What is unclear without more direct evidence is the relative explanatory power of (1) tolerance for diversity as associated with intellectual exploration generally, the sort of favorable production climate that a Bill Gates or Schumpeter might imagine, versus (2) the amenity/consumption rich location which attracts persons whose work may not be the first consideration in selecting the location, or (3) how much are (1) and (2) jointly determined? Our sense that is that many decisions are joint, but then how much weight to assign to different subfactors? So much past work has assumed the dominance of work that we have too limited evidence to date to sort out these competing alternatives. Some of the best are the simultaneous equation studies of job and population growth, discussed above, but their specific results shift with the specific "instruments" or controls introduced (cf. Clark and Ferguson, 1983). Florida (2002) reviews other kinds of studies. How much do growth dynamics vary for different population sectors? Very little work has pursued this; more should.

NPC MAYORS EMERGE
ACROSS THE COUNTRY

Most analysis above is based on private sector dynamics, involving jobs, work, lifestyle, etc. But cities are also driven by public policy, which interpenetrates private decisions. How and where does leadership enter? The key is public leaders who recognize the importance of amenities, and use them to attract new residents. Which do and why?

This is a core question in the Fiscal Austerity and Urban Innovation Project (which Terry Clark coordinates, see the website). We completed a national survey in 1984 and 1996 of mayors in all U.S. cities over twenty-five thousand population. Results suggest the national importance of a pattern of leadership that we have termed the New Political Culture, which is distinctly responsive to consumption rather than just production. It is found in increasing numbers of cities and countries, even if empirically many cities retain elements of clientelism and class politics. The New Political Culture (NPC) includes these points:

(1) The classic Left-Right dimension has been transformed. People still speak of Left and Right, but definitions are changing. Left increasingly means social (primarily consumption) issues, less often traditional class politics (i.e. jobs) issues.

(2) Social and fiscal/economic issues are explicitly distinguished. Positions on social issues like abortion or women's roles or the environment—of citizens, leaders, and parties—cannot be derived from their positions on fiscal issues.

(3) Social issues have risen in salience relative to fiscal/economic issues, and

(4) Market individualism and social individualism grow. The NPC joins "market liberalism" (in the past narrowly identified with parties of the Right), with "social progressiveness" (often identified with parties of the Left). This new *combination of policy preferences* leads NPCs to support new programs, and follow new rules of the game.

(5) Questioning the welfare state. Some NPC citizens, and leaders, conclude that "governing" in the sense of state-central planning is unrealistic for many services. While not seeking to reduce services, NPCs question specifics of service delivery and seek to improve efficiency. National governments decline; local governments grow in importance.

(6) The rise of issue politics and broader citizen participation; the decline of hierarchical political organizations. The NPC counters traditional bureaucracies, parties, and their leaders. "New Social Movements" and "issue-politics" are essential additions to the political process. By contrast, traditional hierarchical parties, government agencies, and unions are seen as antiquated.

(7) These NPC views are more pervasive among younger, more educated and affluent individuals, and societies.

Responsive public leaders respond to citizens with these new views. The NPC emerges more fully and forcefully in cities with less hierarchy, and where citizens have more resources, such as more education, higher income, and more professional and high-technology service occupations. These defining elements and propositions are elaborated in Clark (1996, 1994), Clark and Hoffmann-Martinot (1998).

A second process persists in other cities and neighborhoods: class politics, especially in working class unions and socialist parties. Even if socio-economic changes in cities erode this older working-class base, strong parties may continue these programs and politics, even if citizens change their preferences. How much parties buffer political leaders in this way thus is a critical intervening variable. The U.S. institution of primary elections, where citizens vote on candidates for the party, is but one sharp illustration of the generally weak and citizen-dependent U.S. party system. Thus, where and how urban innovation occurs, and in particular how NPC patterns arise, depends heavily on parties. Traditional class cleavages focus on jobs and deflect concern away from amenities, entertainment, and other new issues to which citizens are increasingly sensitive, fueling demands for more citizen responsiveness worldwide.

To illustrate the NPC patterns in urban development policies, we briefly profile several major U.S. cities whose policies in recent years were shaped by NPC mayors: Michael White in Cleveland, Richard Riordan in Los Angeles, Rudolph Giuliani in New York, Edward Rendell in Philadelphia, and Stephen Goldsmith in Indianapolis. Richard M. Daley of Chicago is pursued further below. Most governed in the 1990s, and set the tone of national urban leadership. These six mayors exemplify efficiently managing city government, especially through contracting-out (Miranda, 1992), focusing on quality of life issues, attempting to attract the middle class and businesses to the city (Wong, 1992), no strong party affiliation, and an interest in the consumption of public education (see Wong et al., 1997). These mayors met regularly and exchanged ideas in "an informal network." Five were reelected with wide margins. What were their management policies?

Michael White, from Cleveland, was a black Democrat and son of a union activist. He contracted out garbage collection, road maintenance, and other city services, making city workers compete against private firms. Mayor White moved the city toward more efficient management, citing an instance when the city's road repair unit outbid a private contractor. He also strongly supported Republican Governor Voinovich in introducing school vouchers in Cleveland to pay for parochial and private schools. White also strongly insisted on holding down taxes.

In Los Angeles, Republican Mayor Richard Riordan contracted out several city services. He required the head of every city department to establish quantifiable goals for the year, strategic priorities for the next three to five years, and tied employee pay to achievement. He distributed a concise budget patterned after private sector corporate reports. He also strongly supported affirmative action, gay rights, and Democratic Senator Dianne Feinstein.

In New York, Republican mayor Rudolph Giuliani cut the budget in most city agencies and contracted out several city services, feuding with the powerful unions over these decisions. He endorsed Democratic Governor Mario Cuomo for reelection, and defended welfare rights of illegal immigrants. Giuliani's community policing efforts (the "broken windows" program) focused on "quality of life" issues such as aggressive panhandling, public drunkenness, vandalism, and disorderly conduct in general. His handling of the post-September 11th, 2001 terrorism earned him global visibility.

All these mayors personify the NPC patterns. They all broke with their cities political pasts of the New Deal left-right, dominated by jobs and work. To add more subtlety, consider the growing dominance of the NPC in Chicago, classically known as a blue collar Democratic city, long incarnated by its mayors named Daley.

HOW DOES CHICAGO ILLUMINATE THESE PROCESSES, AND PROVIDE LESSONS FOR ORGANIZATIONS WORLDWIDE?

Chicago's main industry in the year 2000 was entertainment. The mayor gave speeches about trees, floral landscaping of bare rooftops, and defended gondoliers singing arias on the Chicago River against the barge haulers who claimed the gondolas obstructed traffic. The mayor added that he wanted the Chicago River to become as lively as the Seine in Paris.

Between Mayor Daley I's and Mayor Daley II's eras, Chicago underwent epochal change. Why? The answers are important for Chicago and other governments worldwide, since few governments have changed as deeply and as rapidly as Chicago's—without a visible or violent revolution. Chicago's economic base, culture, and politics have nevertheless been revolutionized in these years, in many respects similar to the revolutions in Eastern Europe, Latin America, and Asia. Governments can learn important lessons from one another about innovations of this magnitude.

Chicago's changes are paradoxically camouflaged by an outdated image that the city, its citizens, and especially its leaders, are conservative. What has changed? Carl Sandburg's "City of the Big Shoulders" continued through the period of Richard J. Daley (Daley I, 1955–1976). Its lifeblood was heavy industry, production, and growth; its citizens were mostly blue-collar. Today, Chicago is a postindustrial city focused on consumption and amenities. Its political life was once dominated by clientelism, patronage, jobs, and contracts—and battles were fought in what game theorists call a "zero-sum" game, where one person's gain is another person's loss. It was zero sum since jobs and contracts are "private goods" that only one participant consumes. If Alderman X got a job, Alderman Y lost it. There is an obvious residue of these concerns in Chicago.

There are always some private goods, but the news is that politics increasingly involves more "public goods" like lakefront aesthetics, which any visitor can enjoy. The view is not "consumed" by just one person as was a job. Other new concerns are multiculturalism and efficient service delivery, which also broadly affect Chicagoans, not just a handful of winners. Coalitions today can accordingly be broader, with more participants and more winners since everyone can consume a "public good," but only a select few get patronage jobs. Instead of zero-sum games we can have more "positive-sum games," with many winners. Politics is no longer necessarily about conflict among subgroups.

The average citizen is no longer conceived of as a mere cog at the bottom of a huge machine, voting as instructed by his precinct captain. Citizens are emerging instead as the ultimate concern, and citizen preferences are key criteria for evaluating policies and promoting or firing leaders, in City Hall and in Chicago businesses. This theme emerges repeatedly in presentations by the mayor and top staff and in policy changes in Chicago. These are deep shifts affecting cities generally, which I trace in a recent book with data for seven thousand cities in twenty-two countries (Clark and Hoffmann-Martinot, 1998). To probe these changes in Chicago, I have interviewed leaders for seventeen years as part of an oral history (book draft: *Trees and Real Violins: Building Postindustrial Chicago*).

Three causes drive this transformation: (1) the transition from industrial to post-industrial society; (2) the shift from local and particularistic social relations to more global and impersonal patterns, heightened by education and electronic communications. These first two support (3) decentralization (even fragmentation) of political leadership and the rise of the citizen/consumer. These dynamics are at the heart of the New Political Culture.

These general transformations come to many cities, but details vary in each. The specific social, cultural, and political context shapes the precise changes. Every city, including Chicago, is unique in its distinct combination of general elements. We can dissect the uniqueness by identifying how and why more general processes work in Chicago.

Just as important as new jobs and new technology for postindustrial society is the diminution of authoritarian social relations in favor of more collegiality and egalitarianism. These follow as people are better educated and perform more professionally. Workers at all levels are increasingly expected to act like "professionals." The postindustrial marketplace is more abstract and cosmopolitan than the old industrial plant. There is more contracting-out of tasks, more provision of services over a distance, and sales to far-off world markets—all made possible by computers, faxes, cheap air travel, the Internet, and so on—the technological sinews of "the wired office." Evidence on transformation of America's 100 largest corporations in this direction is in Clark and Hoffmann-Martinot (1998, p. 147).

Industrial organization once built on such practices as strict seniority, few pay differentials by individual achievement, promotion from within, and the like. Post-industrialism turns all this on its head. Rising national and global competition and precise communication make possible contracting out of tasks and production to small firms worldwide. Local and intense personal relations are often replaced by more abstract and distant relations. This transition is also deeper for most Catholics than for most Protestants; confession, parochial schools, and parish life traditionally taught more social skills and respect for personal authority.

But these are production concerns. The most revolutionary change in the City that Works was that it could do more than "work":

- The city's number one industry has become entertainment, which city officials define as including tourism, conventions, restaurants, hotels, and related economic activities. Tourists rose from 32 million in 1993 to 42.9 million in 1997, with the average business/convention traveler estimated to spend $242/day. This implies that the Chicago economic zone (DMA) took in $16 billion in 1997 and indirectly $29 billion (Shifflet, 1997).
- The most visited park in the entire United States is the Chicago Lakefront; it has far more visitors than the Grand Canyon, although many are from nearby (see boxes). Here the visitor can admire a clear view of the city, since the skyline stands a quarter mile from the waterfront of Lake Michigan—thanks to the Burnham Plan. Much was totally rebuilt in the 1990s: new marinas, walkways, fountains, and beaches surrounding harbors filled with yachts. The lakefront path, which runs the length of the city, has grown swollen with cyclists, joggers, and rollerbladers. Picnickers abound.
- Mayor Richard M. Daley proudly claims to have planted more trees than any mayor in the history of the world, around one million (a City Hall estimate in 2000), as a commitment to environmental and aesthetic sensitivity. Flowers and shrubs, new pavement, street lights, benches, public art, wrought iron fences, and related landscaping were added in thousands of locations around the city in the 1990s (Clark and Foss, 1999).
- The City is a leader among U.S. cities in devising ways to convert polluted land areas (brown fields) into usable property, which new industries and housing can develop productively (Tables 9.1 and 9.2).

Our analysis considers five key components of political culture as these have shifted with leadership patterns. We map Chicago's changes in the last half of the twentieth century by assessing six mayors in these terms. The deepest changes illustrate movement toward the New Political Culture. Figure 9.2 summarizes the key points. These five dimensions define change over time toward five core elements of the New Political Culture.

The more general ideas here draw from four books that chart the rise of the New Political Culture (Clark, 1996; Clark and Hoffmann-Martinot, 1998; Clark and Rempel, 1997; Hoggart and Clark, 2000).

Table 9.1. Popular Chicago Attractions

Attraction	Attendance at Popular Chicago Attractions				
	1999	1998	1997	1996	1995
Navy Pier	7,750,000.00	8,248,000.00	6,081,200.00	4,500,000.00	3,000,000.00
Lincoln Park Zoo	Coming soon	3,000,000.00	3,000,000.00	4,000,000.00	4,000,000.00
John G. Shedd Aquarium	1,851,618.00	1,981,000.00	1,802,385.00	1,775,765.00	1,844,927.00
Museum of Science and Industry	1,656,611.00	1,750,000.00	1,680,234.00	1,760,813.00	2,012,284.00
Art Institute of Chicago	1,358,412.00	1,537,157.00	1,723,549.00	1,669,842.00	2,248,576.00
Field Museum of Natural History	1,501,465.00	1,450,923.00	1,390,481.00	1,212,475.00	1,263,453.00
Sears Tower Skydeck	Coming soon	1,302,307.00	1,380,221.00	N/A	1,441,966.00
Chicago Cultural Center	Coming soon	623,006.00	566,538.00	565,882.00	486,521.00
Museum of Broadcast Comm.	Coming soon	500,000.00	180,000.00	200,000.00	180,000.00
Chicago Children's Museum	Coming soon	471,602.00	554,000.00	600,000.00	N/A
Adler Planetarium	460,815.00	459,626.00	430,000.00	458,357.00	430,502.00
Chicago Symphony Orchestra	Coming soon	272,628.00	N/A	453,059.00	422,790.00
DuSable Museum	147,336.00	171,186.00	168,392.00	247,502.00	220,000.00
Chicago Historical Society	148,284.00	143,201.00	153,634.00	176,015.00	150,000.00

Sources: The Chicago Convention and Tourism Bureau, Mayor's Office of Special Events.
Baseline Comparison: The Grand Canyon National Park hosted 5,000,000 visitors in 1997. *Source:* The Grand Canyon National Park Foundation website.

Table 9.2. Chicago is First in Conventions: Top 10 U.S. Counties for Overnight Meeting Travel

Ranking	County	State	Corresponding City	1998
1	Cook	IL	Chicago	4.53
2	DeKalb	GA	Atlanta	3.52
3	Orange	FL	Orlando	3.3
4	Clark	NV	Las Vegas	2.94
5	Dallas	TX	Dallas	2.86
7	Washington	DC	Washington	2.8
8	Los Angeles	CA	Los Angeles	2.63
9	San Diego	CA	San Diego	2.17
10	San Francisco	CA	San Francisco	2.07
13	New York	NY	New York	1.56

Notes: These are millions of "person-trips" per year. Chicago ranked #1 with 4,530,000 person trips in 1998. It was also first each year back to 1995, the first data point (not shown). These data are collected by D. K. Shifflet and Associates, Ltd. (1998) and made available by the Chicago Convention and Tourism Bureau, Inc. Of course these 4.53 million include overnight meetings near O'Hare airport, but exclude non-overnight conferences at or near the airport, which surely are numerous as well—but obviously generate less revenue for the City of Chicago so were not reported in this study.

It is surprising perhaps to see how low New York ranks, #13, with only about 1/3 of Chicago's person-trips, exacerbated perhaps by city taxes on many aspects of visitor's activities, from hotels to telephone calls, and high labor costs, such as unionized maids in hotels who earn about $30,000/year, etc. This suggests that the costs of consumption are important in a competitive environment, even if New York is nationally unique for some items like Broadway theater.

With Orlando ranked #3 and Anaheim #14, these Disney locations have surged, as has Las Vegas. These three locations specialize in "consumption" but perhaps so much so that they can become "boring" for cosmopolitan adult visitors. At least this is the aesthetic argument which big cities, and architectural/aesthetic/psychological interpreters offer: cities provide richer aesthetic diversity (Judd and Fainstein, 1999; Zukin, 1991).

How about business and civic leaders? In many U.S. cities business leaders have been reportedly powerful in affecting decisions directly or indirectly via a business-oriented "regime" (e.g. Stone, 1989). Common interpretations stress either: (1) the economic or materialist base of politics from Karl Marx onward; or (2) the specific importance of business leaders. Both are increasingly outdated. Concerning No. (1), note that it is quite possible for a mayor or restaurant entrepreneur to seek to use consumption and amenities to maximize the material wealth of the city or individual restaurant. This may be direct and short term, or more indirect and long-term—by seeking to limit density and population growth in hopes that the land value of a less-congested area will grow more valuable due to the amenity value of lower congestion. Regarding No. (2), the specific role of business surely varies by issue area and firm. In some issues, where most

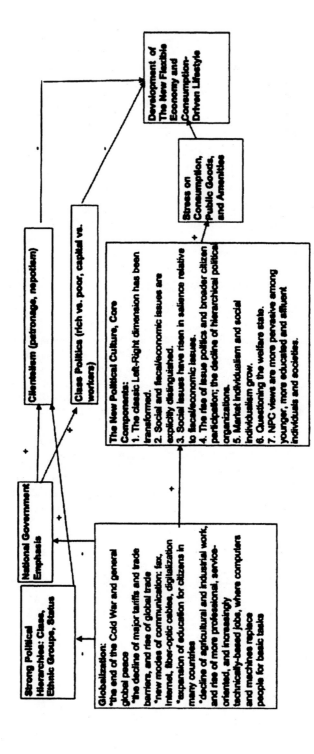

Figure 9.2. Relations among key variables in the amenity framework

Table 9.3. Mayoral Styles Shifted Over Time in Chicago: Key Components of Leadership and New Political Culture

Mayor	Years as Mayor	The Rise of Social and Aesthetic Issues	Fiscal/Economic Issues	The Rise of Independent Organized Groups	Empowerment of Individual Citizens	Policy Focus: Rise of Public Goods, Managed Growth, and Consumption
Richard J. Daley (Daley I)	1955–1976	The "common man" as hero; no clear attention to most later social issues; casual racism; authoritarian/patriarchal governance style	Low taxes; moderate growth in spending after first few years	Classic New Deal in general; the Democratic Party was main electoral tool	De-emphasize citizens compared to neighborhoods and ethnic groups	Reform as official policy for areas like schools; patronage for insiders; City that Works
Michael Bilandic	1977–1979	Sought to be similar to Daley, but lacked the personal loyalty of followers; sought to work with civic and business leaders in many speeches and policies		Classic New Deal in general; the Democratic Party was main electoral tool	De-emphasize citizens compared to neighborhoods and ethnic groups	Reform as official policy for areas like schools; patronage for insiders; City that Works
Jane Byrne	1979–1983	Legitimated women's issues	High spending	First mayoral candidate to defeat machine	Turned her back on reform groups that elected her	Constantly changing policies
Harold Washington	1983–1987	The City that Works Together; multicultural reform	High spending only in last two years	Mobilization of anti-machine groups	CDBG funds spent by neighborhood organizations	Reform as new policy; neighborhood economic development
Eugene Sawyer	1987–1989	Little new policy	Pushed through higher property taxes	Was between machine and reform forces	No empowerment pursued	Little new policy
Richard M. Daley (Daley II)	1989 to present	Continued Multiculturalism; increased tolerance for diverse groups	Moderate spending; more on culture and amenities	Media campaigning; legitimization of groups independent of Democratic party, such as gays	Emphasis on individual citizen	Public goods; managed growth; aesthetic concerns; consumption issues

Caveat: These are trends, but they do not imply that the "new" patterns have eradicated the "old". Compared to other cities, Chicago still has many of the patterns that defined it in the 1950's.

citizens and groups have minimal interest or involvement, active business interests may sway public policy—like which contracting firm gets the contract. In the past, a direct quid pro quo would be openly discussed by aldermen and others in Chicago. But as over twenty-six aldermen have gone to jail since 1971 for accepting bribes and similar offers (Simpson et al., 2002), such directly-targeted contributions have grown more rare. By contrast, firms may legally contribute to a leader's campaign as long they are not given a specific benefit. Some firms thus contribute to many candidates if they are unsure who will win, hoping to have at least more access. This is the "pinstripe patronage" by law and accounting and banking firms and developers that has mushroomed in the 1990s in Chicago.

A third way that business and civic and political leaders are interrelated deserves more consideration, as it grows with the New Political Culture. All sorts of leaders may see the same problems and move toward similar or competing conclusions, either individually or in open discussion, directly or via media coverage and various conferences. This goes on all the time, as cities rethink their policies. The media grow in influence in bringing in perspectives from multiple participants. Editorial page writers would not bother to publish their views if they did not think someone would pay attention to them. Changing the "climate of debate," "framing issues," "adding new items to the public agenda" are labels more consistent with this continuous, pluralistic, and more subtle form of public discourse than "clout" or "exercising power" which imply a command and response imagery increasingly out of date. This more open and pluralistic perspective is especially important when fundamentals are involved, specifically in Chicago's shift toward the New Political Culture in terms of the five dimensions in Table 9.3. Business "interests" can thus become defined very differently across issues. Business interests vary considerably by city. Thus, in locations like Lake Tahoe, business leaders join the consensus in limiting growth; the opposite is true in Lawrence, Kansas, where business leaders and citizens all supported continuous growth (Clark and Goetz, 1994; Logan et al., 1997; Reese and Rosenfeld, 2002 document these points about business interests with considerable U.S. and Canadian urban data).

What of the deeper change—for political, civic, and business leaders—from a commitment to laissez faire business growth and low taxes to support for trees and real violins for Chicago? Listen to a key Chicago business leader:

> The future vibrancy of our city is very dependent upon the arts, says Nuveen Chairman and CEO Timothy Schwerfeger. People can live and work almost anywhere, as communications technology increases the capacity to connect. A place to live is no longer driven by the headquarters of a company. So, quality of life and creating a high-quality environment in which to live, work, and raise a family increasingly is a key competitive issue in attracting people to the city. (Abarabanel, 2000).

NPC SHAPES CITY AGENCIES:
THE CHICAGO STORY

How can amenities and citizen responsiveness replace patronage jobs and clientelist contracts? Attempted worldwide, this normally fails. Chicago is ideal for international consideration, since it was not a smooth, efficient California suburb. Its past patronage makes is more like most governments worldwide.

Two major areas for public amenities and consumption are schools and parks (highly ranked in a summary of past amenity studies by Gottlieb, 1994). Their transformations illustrate patterns that other governments are attempting, globally. With cities growing more visibly important worldwide, Europeans have been visiting and writing about Chicago as an example of what a strong, autonomous mayor can accomplish. Lessons?

Mayor Richard M. Daley broke sharply with Chicago's past. Becoming mayor in 1989, Daley started slowly, but grew increasingly ambitious over more than a decade in office. His reforms in the Park District and Chicago Public Schools were explicitly linked to amenities and quality of life issues, including clean and safe streets.

For decades, schools and parks were handled by separate governments, and mayors followed the dictum of "Don't Make No Waves, Don't Back No Losers" as Rakove (1975) summarized the classic rules of the game. Operationally, this meant that mayors would not speak out publicly on most major policies, but focus narrowly on job and contract implications. Chicago had the worst schools of any major city in the entire U.S., per national test scores.

Daley II sought to reverse this by digging deeply into school policy and management—that is, to change schools to respond to students. He was far more direct and policy-focused than past mayors: "We have a state of emergency in our nation's public schools and chief executives have to take on that challenge. The future of our cities is at stake. All across the nation—families from all racial groups and financial backgrounds are leaving cities because they have lost faith in urban public education. It is true in many American cities, including our nation's capital . . . But it doesn't have to be this way—and I want to offer the mayors, school board officials, businesses and parents around the country a more hopeful vision for the future of our children. I can picture a day when families choose to stay in cities because of the quality public school systems. I can see urban schools that have enough classroom space, modern equipment and safe hallways.

As Mayor of our nation's third largest city, I have to believe in the future of our public schools. Improving schools is the only way to make a lasting change in this country. It is the only way to lift people out of poverty—to cut down on crime—and to create a stronger economy . . . Everything I do as mayor would fail if we gave up on the schools." (Richard M. Daley, June 5th, 1997).

Schools were part of the key to create stable neighborhoods and well-managed city services, to attract middle-class residents and new businesses (Daley, January 8th, 1996; April 25th, 1996).

MANAGEMENT STRUCTURE

Daley gained control over the Park District in 1993 and the Chicago Public Schools in 1995. As they were previously autonomous from the City, Daley asked the state legislature to expand his authority, which they approved. The first major change in both agencies was creating a corporate style management structure, with a board and a chief executive. Daley appointed some of his best managers to head the two agencies. Forrest Claypool, the general superintendent and CEO of the Park District, and Paul Vallas, the CEO at the Chicago Public Schools, were both general managers with no previous field experience in their respective agencies; Claypool was the mayor's former chief of staff and Vallas was City Hall's former budget director. However, they were not recruited from outside Chicago; they had strong, proven track records which won them the trust and close personal understanding of the mayor whose support was critical for them to shoulder their dramatic changes. This made them quite different from the "good manager" who may be hired from outside by private corporations or circulates in smaller city-manager cities. Chicago is more like a Japanese corporation, with its powerful local culture and deep personal commitments. This "particularism" is under girded by a strong Irish Catholic localism and trust that has long colored Chicago leadership (Clark, 1975), even if weakening.

Appointment of the two top officers was followed by 100 percent top management turnover in both agencies. They hired top staff they knew or who were personally loyal to them, in clear contrast to Weberian civil service ideals. The management structure in both agencies is two-tiered, separating the functional from core-agency services. The functional tier covers finance, human resources, communication, and other general operational activities whereas the core-services division addresses education at the Chicago Public Schools and recreation and landscaping at the Park District. This division of management is evident in the pattern of appointment of managers to the school system. The majority of the newly appointed managers under the new administration in non-core services at the Chicago Public Schools (about 91 percent) were recruited from non-CPS agencies. Of these, 55 percent were recruited directly from City of Chicago agencies. In comparison, all new managers (100 percent) in core-services were recruited from within the school system (Wong et al., 1997).

The big management changes were thus implemented by trusted generalists, but service delivery specifics still built on agency experience. Unions and race were also just below the surface, and in the schools, gender: visible black women have been key leaders in the public schools, whose teachers are predominantly black women. Ferman (1996) discussed how Chicago's long tradition of ethnic politics infused ethnicity and race into policy considerations more than in most cities.

Embracing these problem agencies was a major shift from the past, in part sparked by crises at the two agencies. Both Claypool's and Vallas's initial focus was on keeping their agency financially solvent and closing down the deficit. The Park District in 1993 faced an annual deficit of $10 million, and was near its legal debt ceiling. Similarly the Public Schools faced a four-year budget deficit of $1.2 billion in 1995. Claypool and Vallas moved swiftly to balance the budget, and bring fiscal responsibility to the two agencies.

Next was cutting costs through downsizing, efficient management, and contracting out. The Park District reduced its total staff from 4,938 FTE in 1993 to 3,577 for 1997 (−27 percent). The Chicago Public Schools reduced its central office staff from 3,456 in 1995 to 2,740 in 1997 (−21 percent), with barely any reductions in the teaching staff of about twenty-five thousand. The central administration at the Park District and the Public Schools also cut down their operating expenses significantly, 44 percent and 10 percent respectively.

Both agencies contracted out mostly in non-core service areas. Experienced City Hall managers in charge at the two agencies were familiar with contracting-out and the cost differentials, and implemented similar policies swiftly. Contracted out were the print shop, employee health services, workers' compensation, and student records storage (Daley, June 5th, 1997).

Both Vallas and Claypool successfully negotiated with their major unions, and had some skirmishes with other smaller unions. Their success was due to overwhelming support from the mayor, council and active civic groups.

Outcomes-Based Accountability

Vallas and Claypool both defined performance in measurable outcomes. The Park District measures the number of trees planted, amount of green space added, numbers of parks with flower gardens, and overall safety and cleanliness of parks. The schools use scores on standardized tests, attendance rates, conducting school quality reviews, monitoring the school improvement plan, and compliance with the state school code. Vallas's administration targeted improving low-performing schools, based on test scores. In January of 1996, six months in office, Vallas and his administration placed 109 schools on probation, about 20 percent of the district's elementary and high schools. The previous administration had placed only six schools on remediation, a step below probation. Using some of the most draconian measures in the country, the Chicago Public Schools reconstituted seven high schools in 1997, essentially restarting the schools with many new staff.

Effects of Political Control

Vallas and Claypool were both highly charismatic leaders, which motivated agency employees, and also captured great enthusiasm (Chicago Tribune Magazine, February 4th, 1996). Their two successors are young, enthusiastic staff who follow their examples. As one Chicago Public Schools manager summarized the central office mood, "There is a feeling of motion and energy . . ." The mayoral-induced management of the schools and parks led to a clear political mission in the two agencies. The two CEOs outlined long term visions, emphasizing infrastructure investment and major capital improvement projects.

They also stressed aesthetics: parking lots were converted to flowers and trees; wrought iron fences were added around schools across the entire city, giving them stylish new faces.

Another result of mayoral (political) control was increased collaboration between the two agencies, and across different city agencies. A new CPD-CPS program was an after-school program called Park-Kids, where kids went right from schools to the parks for "parking." These highly-acclaimed programs showed concrete commitment to dramatically improved service; children were engaged by them from breakfast to dinner time.

Managing Dramatic Policy Innovation: Lessons from Chicago

The policy preferences of NPC mayors (especially fiscal conservatism combined with social liberalism) led them to pursue productivity improvement seriously. Consumption and amenities replace production and jobs. They see their political constituency as the individual citizen more than the organized group, such as unions and city employees. As governments increasingly embrace such policies, how have leaders fared? Variously. President Jimmy Carter advocated certain NPC themes, but was widely considered a management failure. Chicago in recent years illustrates dramatic innovations in policy, and in management. What lessons emerge?

Contrast two established types of managers with those in Chicago. First is the city manager, the ideal professional of the International City Management Association. For modest innovations, and sound, honest management, the Weberian-Taylor-inspired model of the classic American city manager can work well. High mobility of managers across cities, low-political involvement, weak ties to other staff, superficial knowledge of local civic and neighborhood associations (the professional ethics frown on more)—these conditions discourage "corruption" that might come from personalistic contacts. But they also spell administrative timidity; they discourage big challenges, since they offer a shallow political foundation. Most cities and most people don't want big change very often. Yet some do.

When crises and environmental challenges are more serious and dramatic, the classic administrator will not do. Enter the second model: the administrative entrepreneur as outlined in many Harvard case studies of the Federal government, and some locations like New York under John Lindsay (Lynn, 1981). The archetype is intelligent and ambitious, an aggressive manager, but organizationally rather than politically sensitive; his environment is a more closed than open organization. This assumes weak political leaders who will tolerate such "unchecked" entrepreneurs as staff. In contexts meeting such assumptions, the administrative entrepreneur can accomplish much.

While these two types of managers succeed in some locations, they would have failed in our Chicago cases. Why? Some Chicago elements are unique, but many are shared elsewhere, which suggests that Chicago offers some more general implications for management. Our cases suggest dramatic innovation is plausible when:

- The status quo has lost legitimacy: there is a sense of crisis, or at least "serious mishandling"; this urgency can come from a fiscal or political crisis, or be fueled by a new elected leader seeking change.
- Big policy change can seldom be shielded from elected officials, the press, or general citizenry; hence internal, closed-organizational models, or managers who do not conceive of "external" actors as key, are doomed.
- If political leadership is highly unstable, and divided, competing leaders are likely to challenge each other over each policy step, leak critiques to the press, and make life miserable for creative managers; this was most visibly the case in Chicago under Mayor Harold Washington and Council Wars, when many good ideas were tabled or ignored for years.
- Coherent political leadership can shield managers, and press them further to politically acceptable policies; this was clear in Daley's Chicago in the mid-1990s, where the mayor had no significant opposition, and strong support in the council, civic associations, media, and public.
- The status quo not only was illegitimate, it permitted dramatic cuts in lower- middle-level administration (some 20 percent of total staffs and budget in one or two years). Savings realized from these and other inefficiencies freed up substantial resources for innovative new policies.
- Major layoffs sparked fiery union confrontations; these had stymied initiatives by past mayors Byrne and Washington—weaker mayors who took on unions and lost. Vallas and Claypool followed the Daley tradition of not opening a battle unless you can win.

CONCLUSIONS AND POLICY IMPLICATIONS: TIGHT MANAGEMENT, PUBLIC GOODS, MANAGED GROWTH, AND STRESSING CONSUMPTION

Many mayors and leaders around the world are driven by new concerns, which we have summarized as a New Political Culture. How can it work to deliver amenities and transform service delivery?

The Chicago case study suggests that dramatic policy innovation is more likely from managers who: operate in an environment characterized by high risk and uncertainty, the status quo's legitimacy is low, policy alternatives are actively monitored and criticized by many political participants in an open-system environment, managers are talented and ambitious, but also trusted and personally well-connected to political leaders who support them in good times and bad, political leadership is stable and coherent, general policy direction is clear, and managers have autonomy and encouragement to pursue dramatic change.

The changes in the rules of the political game generate major changes in public policy commitments (outputs). We distinguish three policy output types in the last column of Figure 9.1. First is a *shift from separable to public goods*. This is the core of "reform" in Chicago and many cities. The political "enemy" is clientelism or patronage, which reformers seek to replace. With what? Usually public goods, which are shared widely across a geographic area, ideally the entire city, such as clean air, environmental improvements, and governance procedures open and accessible to all (not just the politically well-connected). By contrast separable goods are consumed by one or a few individuals, such as bread or shoes, or for public policies, a patronage job or contract. Public and separable are analytical distinctions, not always clear by just looking at a city's budget or its downtown—all cities have standard budget categories, public buildings, and roads. What is critical here is how the decisions about them are assessed by the participants. An airport can be interpreted in its implications for public good (it is used by many persons) as well as separable goods (it creates jobs and contracts). Separable goods were once preeminent in Chicago; public goods have risen in salience. Globalization drives public goods generally. Similar procedural reforms are stressed by NPC leaders from Japan to Italy (Clark and Kobayashi, 2000).

What can mayors do if they cannot eliminate poverty with redistributive programs? A major policy alternative is to stress "equity," "due process," "fairness," "incorporation of all groups." These entered Chicago with Harold Washington and continued thereafter. Indeed, institutionalizing open, transparent, universalistic (Protestant-inspired) government programs as the core processes for making decisions and administering them is a major policy to counter inequality, as these procedures are not dependent on personal contacts and favors. No one wants less. But poor people can understand that government budgets are limited, and many accept efficiency measures as legitimate if they feel their leaders are promoting "equality of opportunity" for all, seeking to level the playing field, cutting clientelism, and genuinely concerned about average and poor persons. As a legitimating principle, equality of opportunity can thus replace "equality of results—such as an equal income or housing for all—in a era of national welfare state cutbacks. This transformation has been attempted worldwide; it has worked in Chicago.

The second policy shift is *from pure economic growth to a (slightly) more managed growth*. Consider some examples. A classic (worldwide) policy commitment is economic growth. Chicago was the fastest-growing large city in America in the late nineteenth century. The explicit policy of most Chicago mayors in the twentieth century was similarly growth: developing the economy, creating jobs, building large infrastructure projects (Bradbury, Downs and Small, 1982; Mayfield, 1996; Suttles, 1984, 1990). The "growth machine" was classically illustrated by Mayor Daley I's close ties with leading corporate officials who sought continuous growth.

Some pointed to such unbridled growth, however, as illustrating the rough crassness of the nouveau-riche. Or translated into amenities via zoning policies, Chicago over the years constructed the best and worst architecture in the world, often on the same block. This derives in part from not having a firm commitment to a city or neighborhood plan like some European cities. More specifically, zoning was delegated not to a stringent planning and zoning authority for the entire city, but left to individual aldermen, who could accept or deny building permits, conversions, granting zoning variances, and the like. Preserving clientelism and neighborhood/ethnic autonomy clearly overshadowed the aesthetic concerns of architects and planners. This has changed as part of the third policy development.

Thirdly, *production concerns have been increasingly supplemented by consumption and aesthetic issues*. This overlaps with the first two dimensions in that production involves generating jobs. Post-industrial cities still need an economic base to survive, but Chicago's largest industry has become entertainment (restaurants, hotels, conventions, etc.) Selling it often involves consumption issues (from the standpoint of the conventioneers or tourists). How do mayors and city governments respond to such consumption concerns? By seeking policies that enhance a sense of distinctive urban life style, neighborhood amenities, spending rather than earning of money, and therefore stressing lakefront aesthetics, concerts, restaurants, parks, boulevards, recreation programs in the parks, improving the schools, and reducing crime. That is, doing all those things which make a city a livable and pleasant place. These public-good consumption concerns emerged powerfully in Chicago and other major U.S. cities only in the last years of the twentieth century. They had been enjoyed by European and Asian aristocrats for centuries, but what is new and distinct is the popular diffusion of these concerns.

The more general importance of amenities for urban life, and even as a major cause of urban economic development and population growth, is starting to become recognized by a few economists and urban policy analysts, like Glaeser (2000b) who stresses non-market transactions like education, and beautification. Other research seeks to measure these processes using national urban data and finds substantial impacts of many different amenities from high quality restaurants to bicycle paths on development, population growth, and high tech jobs, for example, Florida (2000, 2002), Glaeser et al. (2000).

Policy conclusions follow from these findings. The most talented members of America's mobile and creative work force are offered jobs by firms in many cities, continuously. Hence they have a wide choice of cities for jobs, such that the decision on where to live and enjoy life can play as large or a larger role than the job offer in the final location decision. Many policymakers follow the New Political Culture emphasis and have moved away from clientelism and patronage, such as seeking to retain individual firms with subsidies and benefits to them, one by one. Instead many invest more in public goods for all citizens (like schools and parks). Many feel these policies are paying off in the new global economy.

NOTES

1. The globalization-changes–paradigms theme is elaborated in Clark (2000) for several specific urban subfields. This chapter explores one: the amenities/growth linkage.

2. Perhaps most convincing are moves in this direction by Logan and Molotch: Logan, Whaley and Crowder (1997) reach this conclusion in reviewing some twenty years of studies on the growth machine, and Molotch et al. (2000) embrace a multicausal approach to explain growth (see Chapter 2 quotations from them). Both stress amenities. Consumption and amenities are different from "use" or "exchange" value, which are broader traditional concepts.

3. As has been well documented (Castells, 1989; Sassen, 1994; Zukin, 1982) routinized administrative tasks, "back office" work, is mostly displaced to "edge city" locales; however, the most intellectually intensive forms of administration and producer services still concentrate in urban cores, suggesting (perhaps?) agglomeration benefits for advanced intellectual production.

4. Florida (2002) reviews evidence in the debate over how much the new economy is driven by workers being forced from stable to flexible jobs, vs. how much they relocate into firms with more flexible work conditions. The more creative workers, he concludes, have considerable autonomy to choose, and often do.

BIBLIOGRAPHY

Abarabanel, J. (2000). Of opera, paradigms, and corporate culture. *Lyric Opera*, 46th Season, 2000–2001.

Atkinson, R. D. (1998). Technological change and cities. *Cityscape*, 3(3), 129–170.

Bradbury, K. L., Downs, A., and Small, K. A. (1982). *Urban decline and the future of American cities*. Washington, DC: Brookings Institution.

Castells, M. (1989). *The informational city*. Oxford: Blackwell.

Chicago Tribune Magazine (1996, February 4th). Tough love: Paul Vallas' job is to teach the Chicago Public Schools a lesson in discipline.

Clark, S., & Gaile, G (1998). *The work of cities*. Minneapolis: University of Minnesota Press.

———(1975). The Irish ethic and the spirit of patronage. *Ethnicity, 2*, 305–359.

———(1994). Clientelism, U.S.A.: The dynamics of change. In: L. Roniger and A. Guns-Ayata (Eds), *Democracy, Clientelism, and Civil Society* (pp. 121–144). Boulder, CO: Lynn Rienner.

———(1996). Structural realignments in American city politics: Less class, more race, and a new political culture, *Urban Affairs Review, 31*(3) (January), 367–403.

———(2000). Old and new paradigms for urban research: Globalization and the fiscal austerity and urban innovation project, featured essay in *Urban Affairs Review, 36*(1) (September), 3–45.

———(Draft). *Trees and real violins: Building post-industrial Chicago*. Book MS.

Clark, T. N., and Ferguson, L. (1983). *City money*. New York, NY: Columbia University Press.

Clark, T. N., and Foss, G. (1999). City ideas that work, special report: Public art project captures international interest, local hearts. *Nation's Cities Weekly, 22*(43) (October 25th), 1–7–9.

Clark, T. N., and Goetz, E. G. (1994). The anti-growth machine. In: T. N. Clark (Ed.), *Urban Innovation: Creative Strategies in Turbulent Times* (pp. 105–145). London—Newbury Park—New Delhi: Sage.

Clark, T. N., and Hoffmann-Martinot, V. (Eds) (1998). *The new political culture.* Boulder, CO: Westview Press.

Clark, T. N., and Kobayashi, Y. (2000). *The new political culture in Japan*. Tokyo: Keio University Press.

Clark, T. N., and Rempel, M. (Eds) (1997). *Citizen politics in post-industrial societies*. Boulder, CO: Westview Press.

Costas, S., and Bennett, L. (2003). *It's hardly sportin': Stadiums, neighborhood development, and the new Chicago*. Northern Illinois University Press (forthcoming).

Daley, R. M. (1996, April 25th). State of the city address. Mayor's Office, City of Chicago.

———(1996, January 8th). State of education address. Mayor's Office, City of Chicago.

———(1997, June 5th). National press club address on Chicago public schools. Mayor's Office, City of Chicago.

Ferman, B. (1996).*Challenging the growth machine*. Lawrence, KS: University Press of Kansas.

Florida, R. (2000). Competing in the age of talent: Quality of place and the new economy. Report Prepared for The R.K. Mellon Foundation, Heinz Endowments, and Sustainable Pittsburgh.

———(2002). *The rise of the creative class*. New York: Basic Books/Perseus.

Gans, H. (1962). *The urban villagers*. New York: Free Press.

Glaeser, E. L. (2000a). Cities and ethics. *Journal of Urban Affairs, 22*(4), 473–494.

———(2000b). The future of urban research: Nonmarket interactions. *Brookings—Wharton Papers on Urban Affairs*, 101–149.

Glaeser, E. L., Kolko, J., and Saiz, A. (2000, July). *Consumer City*. National Bureau of Economic Research, Working Paper 7790.

Gottdiener, M. (1985). *The social production of urban space*. Austin: University of Texas Press.

Gottlieb, P. (1994). Amenities as an economic development tool: Is there enough evidence? *Economic Development Quarterly, 8*(3) (August), 270.

Gyourko, J., and Tracy, J. (1991). The structure of local public finance and the quality of life. *Journal of Political Economy, 99*(4), 774–806.

Harvey, D. (1990). *The condition of postmodernity.* Oxford: Blackwell.

Hoggart, K., and Clark, T. N. (Eds) (2000). *City governments and their citizens, research in urban policy* (Vol. 8). JAI Press/Elsevier.

Judd, D., and Fainstein, S. (Eds) (1999). *The tourist city.* New Haven: Yale University Press.

Lash, S., and Urry, J. (1994). *Economies of signs and space.* New York: Sage.

Logan, J. R., Whaley, B. R., and Crowder, K. (1997, May). The character and consequences of the growth regimes: An assessment of 20 years of research. *Urban Affairs Review, 32*(5), 603–630.

Lynn, L. E. (1981). *Managing the public's business.* New York: Basic Books.

Markusen, A., Chapple, K., Schrock, G., Yamamoto, D., and Yu, P. (2001). *High-tech and i-tech: How metros rank and specialize.* Project on Regional and Industrial Economics Humphrey Institute of Public Affairs, University of Minnesota.

Mayfield, L. (1996). The reorganization of urban politics: The Chicago growth machine after World War II. Ph.D. thesis, University of Pittsburgh.

Miranda, R. (1992). Privatization in Chicago's city government, In: K. Wong (Ed.), *Research in Urban Policy, 4. Politics of Policy Innovation in Chicago.* Greenwich, CT: JAI Press.

Mollenkopf, J. H. (1983). *Contested city.* Princeton: Princeton University Press.

Molotch, H. (1976). The city as a growth machine. *American Journal of Sociology, 82*(2), 309–330.

Molotch, H., Freudenburg, W., and Paulsen, K. E. (2000). History repeats itself, but how? City character, urban tradition, and the accomplishment of place. *American Sociological Review, 65*(December), 791–823.

Putnam, R. (1993). *Making democracy work.* Princeton: Princeton University Press.

———(2000). *Bowling alone.* New York: Simon and Schuster.

Rakove, M. L. (1975). *Don't make no waves, don't back no losers.* Bloomington: Indiana University Press.

Reese, L. A., and Rosenfeld, R. A. (2002, May). Reconsidering private sector power. *Urban Affairs Review, 37*(5), 642–675.

Reich, R. (1991). *The work of nations: Preparing ourselves for 21st century capitalism.* New York: Alfred A. Knopf.

Sassen, S. (1991, 2001). *The global city* (2nd ed.). Princeton: Princeton University Press.

—— (1994). *Cities in a world economy.* Thousand Oaks, CA: Pine Forge Press.

Simpson, D., with Adeoye, O., Feliciano, R., and Howard, R. (2002). Chicago since September 11th (2001), Draft Paper, University of Illinois at Chicago.

Smith, N. (1996). *The new urban frontier: Gentrification and the revanchist city.* Routledge: New York.

Stone, C. (1989). *Regime politics.* Lawrence, KS: University Press of Kansas.

Suttles, G. (1984). The cumulative texture of local urban culture. *American Journal of Sociology, 90,* 283–304.

———(1990). *The man-made city.* Chicago: University of Chicago Press.

Wilson, W. J. (1987). *The truly disadvantaged: The inner city, the underclass, and public policy.* Chicago: University of Chicago Press.

Wong, K. (1992). Policy innovation in the political and fiscal context. In: K. Wong (Ed.), *Research in Urban Policy, 4. Politics of Policy Innovation in Chicago.* Greenwich, CT: JAI Press.

Wong, K. et al. (1997). Integrated governance as a reform strategy in the Chicago public schools. A Report from the Department of Education and Irving B. Harris Graduate School of Public Policy Studies, University of Chicago.

Zukin, S. (1982). *Loft living: Culture and capital in urban change.* Baltimore: Johns Hopkins University Press.

———(1991). *Landscapes of power.* Berkeley: University of California Press.

Chapter Ten
Scenes: Social Context in an Age of Contingency

Daniel Silver, Terry Nichols Clark, and Clemente Jesus Navarro Yanez

THE SALIENCE OF SCENES: CULTURE AND URBAN ATTRACTIVENESS

This chapter proposes a new analytical framework for the study of culture and place, developing the concept of "scenes" as clusters of urban amenities. By stressing how individual amenities cluster, we extend earlier chapters of this volume. In the years to come, scenes may join such traditional concepts as race, class, gender, and national origin. Why scenes, why now, and even more the future? These four past concepts are primordial; scenes are not. As societies grow less tight and closed and hierarchical, the primordial "structures" explain less. This idea extends the propositions of chapters one and two. Scenes grow more important in less industrial, more expressively-oriented and contingent societies where traditional constraints fall and self-motivated action around consumption, leisure and amenities is a more important feature of social cohesiveness and interaction. The world is moving in these directions. Social science concepts of the primordial reflect the past more than the future, although the present combines all these elements in any empirical context.

The scenes framework adds to concepts such as neighborhood and workplace by specifying fifteen dimensions of the urban scenescape. Like neighborhood and workplace, scenes reduce anomie, but because of their focus on consumption and the use of specific amenities, they are more consistent with today's ethos of contingency, moving beyond traditional ideas of the fundamental power of social, family and occupational background. We introduce a new amenities-focused database to measure and analyze scenes and their dimensions for each of 40,000 U.S. zip codes. We illustrate the framework by applying it to one distinct type of scene, bohemia, and analyze its position in the broader social system.

Scenes stress culture, since culture adds meaning. Many social scientists avoided the use of culture from the 1970s to 2000 or so. Although "the cultural turn" brought culture "back in" to sociological research (Smith 1998; Bonnell and Hunt 1999; Steinmetz 1999; Molotch 2003; Mohr 2003; Harding 2007; Alexander 2003; Swidler 1986), it did so usually without locating cultural practices in concrete cities, spaces and places.[1] Ironically, in the years when sociologists stressed economic and other constraints, economists began to study cultural activities systematically. Terming them "amenities," defined broadly as "non-market transactions,"(Glaeser, Kolko and Saiz 2004) economists have built many models of consumption and lifestyle. But they largely assume that individuals act in isolation and that each amenity (e.g., restaurant or museum) can similarly be analyzed atomistically. This research seeks to join the amenities and consumption work from economics and cultural geography with core social and cultural processes. It aims to combine the (renewed) concern for culture in sociology with a more systematic and comparative approach to neighborhoods, cities and regions.

Cities and Culture

This turn to culture as connected with distinct places and spaces dovetails with a shift in urban development research, which in the past decade has increasingly stressed cultural amenities as attracting "high human capital individuals" whose innovations drive economic development (Glaeser, Kolko and Saiz 2004; Florida 2002; Clark 2004; Markusen, Schrock and Cameron 2004). Vibrant artistic communities, thriving music and theater, lively restaurants, beautiful buildings, fine schools, libraries and museums contribute to a better local "quality of life." In increasingly post-industrial societies, it is claimed, where labor-intensive production is giving way to knowledge- and information-intensive production, more individuals have more time to enjoy and define themselves by their engagement with the "amenities of life."(Fogel 2000) Cities are quickly becoming centers of consumption rather than production (Glaeser, Kolko and Saiz 2004). Culture and tourism are gaining momentum, adding intangible value to what is there and restructuring the existing stock of capital (Sacco and Blessi 2006). Residents respond by exercising "symbolic ownership" over the aesthetic and ethical images projected by their local establishments (Deener 2007). But these formulations raise many questions.

Earlier urban development theorists did not explore specifics of culture and amenities. Economists (such as Roback 1982) pioneered by adding culture and amenities to urban research. But typically they used climate-related amenities (i.e., humidity, clean air) and studied their impact on land value (Zelenev 2004 reviews this tradition). Amenities were important to urban economists if they increased land value, but the process of how and why was largely ignored. Some Continental economists (e.g., Santagata 2004) write about cultural districts, extending industrial district ideas, but these, as in some more Marxian studies of consumption (Zukin 1989), frame culture and consumption as largely driven by broad economic changes. So does the "post-modernism" of Inglehart (1990), downplaying specifics of culture and politics. Florida (2002) suggests that street life and bicycling, rather than opera and bowling, attract creative people who favor multi-tasking and autonomy, although differences among "creative" lifestyles are not explored (Florida 2008 begins to remedy this).

There is considerable ferment over conceptual approaches to the sociological study of cultural activities, evidenced in the shift from mass culture criticism to increased questioning about the distinctiveness of broad divisions such as "high" vs. "low" culture, "formal" vs. "informal," "elite" vs. "popular," or "passive" vs. "participatory" as meaningful dimensions to capture cultural experiences (Peterson and Kern 1996; Abbing 2006; Lizardo and Skiles 2008). In both sociology in general and urban studies in particular, translating the "meanings of social life"–theoretically and empirically–into specific analyses of the concrete role of culture in defining the character of places and spaces and in driving social processes has been difficult. "Culture" remains a contested concept with a range of meanings.[2] "Culture" typically includes the traditional high arts of opera, Shakespearean theater and classical symphonies. Does it also include local, authentic items like Chicago blues or Carolina barbecue? How about experimental, innovative avant-garde art galleries, cutting-edge theater and novel architectural forms? Does it extend as far as adding an aesthetic perspective to more standard fare: street-level culture, beachfront entertainment, and arts and crafts fairs? These and other definitional issues invoke distinct paradigms and can shape competing priorities for policymakers, to invest in or ignore. Class, race, gender, neighborhood and political culture, in turn, invoke competing criteria for theoretical, ideological and policy allocation debates by political leaders, foundation officials, public intellectuals and an urban populace increasingly divided along moral in addition to class axes (Sharp 2005).

Empirical issues are complicated not only by these issues of "high" and "low," but also by the fact that cultural activity involves more than the arts. Cultural meanings and codes are expressed in, and define, different styles of life and situations, shaping what it means to frequent restaurants, cafes, sporting events, parks and more. And culture is more than the "cultural industry" or "cultural districts" (Alexander 2003) because cultural amenities are not only, or even mainly, sites of economic activity, and their attraction is not reducible to economic factors; cultural amenities may well generate jobs and economic development, but they do so (at least in part) because they provide places where people can express their lifestyles, generating independent value (Currid 2007). Culture is not disembodied; cultural products and meanings exist in geographic spaces, ecologically distributed across neighborhoods, cities, regions and nations. Distinct urban cultures may emerge spontaneously in response to citizens' lifestyles, but private and public actors also seek to produce them intentionally; they are both top-down and bottom-up. How can we see form and structure amidst such variety? New conceptual and empirical resources are needed.

Enter "scenes." As settings-structuring shared cultural consumption, scenes provide a new conceptual fulcrum for cultural analysis. Scenes include the arts, but also beaches, cafes, restaurants, sporting events, street life and more. Scenes join these together, permitting a range of seemingly diverse activities–from sipping coffee to listing to music to reading poetry–to be analyzed as part of one social process. Scenes provide ways of social belonging attuned to the demands of a culture in which individuals increasingly define themselves less by primordial attachments to home or family background or class or party or confession and more contingently and expressively, in terms of lifestyle and sensibility (Joas 2004). Just as neighborhoods and family contextualize residence and heredity, and occupations contextualize achievement and work, scenes provide specific social contexts for individuals to interact on the basis of their contingently cultivated sensibilities as to how to dress, eat, listen to music, look at art, and more. By articulating the concept of scene, developing techniques for measuring scenes, and showing how the social consequences and correlates of scenes vary across local contexts, we lay out a research program that injects culture into urban studies in a systematic and comparative way.[3]

WHAT IS A SCENE? THE SITUATED CHARACTER OF URBAN CULTURE

Social Consumption, Culture and Territory

The arts, in particular, and consumption, in general, occupy an important place in recent studies of urban development (Markusen, Shrock and Cameron 2003; Markusen and King 2003; Glaeser, Kolko and Saiz 2004; Clark 2004; Molotch 2003; Currid 2007; Florida 2002; Lloyd 2006; Scott 2000). Yet these rarely specify how distinct types of arts and amenities differentially affect urban change. Nor do they identify contexts within which arts and amenities are embedded–not to mention the effects of geographically (and temporally) varying combinations and densities of amenities, as well as differences in their aesthetic and ethical symbolisms.

What they lack is a conception of cultural consumption as a structured, embodied and emplaced social activity that can come in varying forms and degrees. To fill this gap, we draw on recent work in cultural and youth studies that has begun to develop the notion of scene as just such a form of activity. Irwin (1977) links expressive and leisure groups and their resulting social connections, identifying certain grand scenes such as surfing and hippiedom. Straw (1991, 2002) defines music scenes as "geographically specific spaces for the articulation of multiple musical practices,"(Straw 2002:8) stressing the useful flexibility of the concept (compared to the more rigid counter-culture, class, art world or movement),[4] and (Straw 2002, 2004) reviews many meanings of the term in discussions of popular music. Blum (2003) seeks to ground scenes in "urban theatricality," with a "grammar" of scenes that includes mortality, transgressiveness, exhibitionism, extensiveness, regularity and more. Bennett and Peterson (2004) compile descriptions of various music scenes, dividing them into groups of local, translocal and virtual scenes; Lena and Peterson (2008) treat scenes as one stage in the life course of music genres. Hitzler et al. (2005) link scenes to the "rise of youth" as a specific phase of the life course. Leach and Haunss (2009) build on this approach to explore the connections between scenes and social movements. Lizardo and Skiles (2008) summarize the emerging "scene perspective" in popular culture studies. They highlight how sub-cultural codes (e.g., Goth unconventionality or Club glam or Salsa authenticity) can determine membership and status within a scene.

In these discourses, the concept of scene has turned attention to the specific locales and places, the constellations of establishments and activities, in which cultural practices are articulated. Some urban development scholars have drawn from this work (cf., Currid 2007 on Hebdige's 1979 discussion of punk cultural places), stressing that scenes are less starkly demarcated and demanding than oppositional counter-cultures. Here, scenes are primarily indicated by "diverse, open and amenity-rich places,"(Currid 2007:107) constituting nodes in which the cultural and social generate the economic (Florida 2008).

Our approach to scenes extends these past efforts. We join key insights from cultural, youth, music and urban studies to build a more flexible and differentiated notion of scenes suitable for comparative studies of how scenes vary in specific locales and how those variations impact key urban development variables. Generally, these diverse approaches to the phenomenon suggest to us that scenes should be conceived as *places devoted to practices of meaning making through the pleasures of sociable consumption.* The possibilities for, and practices of, sociable consumption available in a place (its restaurants, cafes, galleries, clubs, stores, theaters) articulates a range of experiences and values, and these are what define that place as the scene it is. Thus, a scene is more than (1). neighborhood (2). physical structures (3). persons labeled by race, class, gender, and education. We include these but stress (4). specific combinations of these and activities (like attending a concert). These four components are in turn defined by (5). the values and experiences scenes enable people to actualize. We stress three general and fifteen specific dimensions of scenes. The three general dimensions are legitimacy, a right or wrong way to live; theatricality, a way of seeing and being seen by others; and authenticity, as a meaningful sense of identity. Scenes enable participants to share in a certain mood–listening to a certain style of music, dressing in a certain manner, eating in a certain ambiance. Such moods embody distinctive feelings as to what is right, genuine and beautiful. These, in turn, are transformed when combined in different ways: a tattoo parlor, water pipe store and modernist art gallery make a different scene than do a tattoo parlor, motorcycle shop, gun shop and biker bar. Each involves an affirmation of transgression, but that transgression is fused with different dimensions of meanings, like self-expression and tradition, in which the meaning of the whole scene changes–from Avant-garde to Don't Tread on Me. Thus, such dimensions can join in ideal-typical combinations such as Bohemia.

Scenes generate meaningful social spaces of consumption rather than of work or residence. What matters are the CDs one listens to (jazz or indie pop or country, say), the types of foods and restaurants one enjoys (barbecue or fusion, for example), the clothes one buys and wears (leather or African print), and more. These are not necessarily determined by how creative one's job is: we prefer to disaggregate occupations Florida calls creative. His creative class is not a homogenous consumption block–teachers, engineers, lawyers, programmers may not listen to the same music or go to the same restaurants. Jobs weakly predict how people play. Consumption groups and occupation groups need not align (Markusen 2006). That one values a colleague's drive at work does not straightaway mean that one welcomes him to the barber shop scene or country line dance. Nor is one's consumption and leisure activity in scenes straightaway determined by ascriptive, particularistic ties of kinship and neighborhood; a younger brother deep into the vegan punk scene need not share this interest with his older brother, and within the scene their shared blood or heritage may not bring status to the older brother. More important for the scene is sharing and expressing its sensibilities.

These are analytical distinctions, and it is possible to stress one perspective over the other: depending on the types of practices and relationships it promotes, a place can be more or less a scene, more or less a neighborhood, more or less an industrial cluster. Overlaps may generate considerable strains and productive tensions,[5] and advocates of one perspective often reduce the others to their own.[6]

A full study of the place of the scene in the broader social system would need to map out the potential interactions between scenes, neighborhoods, and work–not to mention politics, families, and religion. Nevertheless, what is clear is that scenes mark arenas in which consumption can become a shareable and m-

Table 10.1. Contrasting Scenes, Neighborhoods and Industrial Clusters

Space	Scene	Neighborhood	Industrial Clusters
Goals	Experiences, Sociability	Necessities, basic services, housing	Works, products
Agent	Consumer	Resident	Producer
Physical Units	Amenities	Homes/Apartments	Firms
Basis of social bond	Lifestyles/ Sensibilities	Being born and raised nearby, long local residence, heritage	Work/ production relations

eaningful activity, and that the dynamics of this general process merit study in their own terms so that we can develop more systematic theories for a spatial sociology of consumption.

The Internal Dimensions of Scenes: Theatricality, Legitimacy, and Authenticity

Our conception of scene seeks to capture a range of key symbolic dimensions of consumption, going beyond identifying amenity-rich places to the specific values and experiences different constellations of amenities promote. Building on past work that highlights the performative character of social interaction in general (e.g., Goffman 1959, 1974; Alexander 2003), we include *theatricality* as one of our three general dimensions of scenes. Yet we treat theatricality as multi-dimensional; it is not only raw *exhibitionism*, bodies on display. We thus include four additional sub-dimensions of theatricality, all relevant in past discussions about scenes: deviance (*transgression*) and conformity (the *formal* theatricality of manners and etiquette) as well as outward shine (*glamour*) and inner intimacy (the *neighborliness* of a pub or folk scene).

Still, we deny that theatricality is the Ur-scene of Every Scene, and so add two other broad dimensions: first, *legitimacy*. We build on authors (like Weber 1978; Bellah 1996; Elazar 1975; and Habermas 1981) who stress the moral values implicit in everyday practices and in scenes (as in the Haenfler 2006 discussion of the strong moralism in straight-edge punk scenes). But again we include five sub-dimensions. These highlight temporal aspects of legitimacy: *tradition*, in stressing the authority of the past (as in classicism), *charisma*, the auratic presence of a star performer, *utility*, the value of future outcomes (as in, say, benefit concerts); they also highlight spatial aspects of legitimacy: *egalitarian-*

ism, the value of universal ideals (as in the global moralism of fair trade coffee) and *individual self-expression*, the value of personal adaptiveness to particular situations (the non-repeatable uniqueness of an improvised solo or encounter).

Our third general dimension builds on authors (like Taylor 1992, 2007; Heidegger 1996; as well as Grazian 2003 and Urquia 2004 in the scenes literature) who highlight *authenticity*. Authenticity in discussions of scenes often focuses on ethnicity, but the category has broader significance in that the artifice associated with scenes' theatricality raises questions about what it means to be genuine rather than phony. Thus, following Taylor (1989) we suggest that there are many ways of getting in touch with "the real" rather than the fake that have been central to the cultural traditions out of which scenes grow and thrive. We identify five, starting at the particular (the authenticity of the *local* contra the foreign), and moving outward to the most general, through notions of the authentic self rooted in *state* citizenship (rather than class or religious community, famously articulated by Rousseau), *ethnicity* (as in Herder), *corporation* (Nike vs. knockoffs, cf. Taylor 2007) and *reason* (from Kant to Hegel).

Time and space preclude a more thorough discussion of our model's theoretical logic and limits. Table 10.2 simply catalogs the fifteen dimensions of scenes and provides illustrative examples of some of their indicators from our national database of urban amenities. Note, however, that our measures were constructed using the procedures outlined below and in the appendix from not just these but some 650 amenities.

RECOGNIZING SCENES: TOWARDS SYSTEMATIC AND COMPARATIVE ANALYSIS OF URBAN CULTURAL LIFE

Others have noted that assessing urban attractiveness requires studying the mix of amenities, built environment and people. This has typically turned researchers toward ethnography (Lloyd 2006) or anecdote (e.g., the tattooed programmer invoked by Florida 2002).[7] We seek to retain some of the conceptual holism and subtlety of ethnography, and do ethnographic work ourselves. But codifying scenes dimensions and measuring them helps place individual cases in broader context.

The concept of scene, consistent with the phenomenological character of ethnographic approaches, permits theorizing meanings internal to urban cultural spaces in terms of the qualities they manifest as *valuable* and the *holistic networks* within which any single amenity is located. How, then, do we know what

Table 10.2. The Symbolic Dimensions of Scenes

Theatricality

Scenes generate a chance to see and be seen, shaping the bearing and manners of their members. Participants can enjoy the essentially social pleasure of beautifully performing a role or a part, or of watching others do so. This is the pleasure of appearances, the way we display ourselves to others and see their images in turn.

Sub-Dimension	Example	Sample Amenity Indicators
Glamour	Standing on the red carpet at Cannes gazing at the stars going by	Fashion Shows & Designers; Designer Clothes & Accessories; Beauty Salons; Nail Salons; Motion Picture & Video Exhibition; Motion Picture & Sound Recording Studios; Agents, Managers for artists & other public figures; Film Festivals; Night Clubs; Jewelry Stores; Casinos
Formality	Going to the opera in a gown or white tie and tails	Formal wear & costume rental; Opera Companies; Fine Dining; Private Clubs; Dance Companies; Night Clubs; Golf courses & country clubs; Theater Companies & Dinner Theater; Religious Organizations; Offices of Lawyers; Professional Organizations
Transgression	Watching a performance artist pierce his skin	Body Piercing Studios; Tattoo Parlors; Adult Entertainment: Nightclubs; Adult Entertainment: Comedy and Dance Clubs; Leather Clothing Stores; Skateboard Parks; Casinos; Beer, Wine, & Liquor Stores; Gambling Industries
Neighborliness	Attending a performance by the community orchestra	Bed & Breakfast Inns; Civic & Social Organizations; Religious Organizations; Golf Courses & Country Clubs; Sports Teams & Clubs; Playgrounds; Elementary & Secondary Schools; Fruit & Vegetable Markets; Coffee Houses; Pubs; Baked Goods Stores;
Exhibitionism	Watching weightlifters at Muscle Beach	Adult Entertainment: Night Clubs; Fashion Shows & Designers; Body Piercing; Tattoo Studios; Health Clubs; Fashion Shows & Designers; Beauty Salons; Nail Salons; Discotheques

Table 10.2. (Continued)

Authenticity

The human possibility to be realized in a scene, even where it is highly theatrical, may also be defined by the extent to which a scene affirms a sense of rootedness, confirming or reshaping a sense of primordial identity. Participants may share in the pleasure of having a common sense of what makes for a real or genuine experience. This is the pleasure of identity, the affirmation of who we are at bottom and what it means to be genuine and real rather than fake and phony.

Sub-Dimension	Example	Sample Amenity Indicators
Local	Listening to the blues in the Checkerboard Lounge, landmark of the Chicago blues	Bed & Breakfast Inns; Historical Sites; Fishing Lakes & Ponds; Marinas; Book Dealers: Used & Rare; Antique Dealers; Scenic & Sightseeing Services; Nature Parks & Other Similar Institutions; Spectator Sports; Sports Teams and Clubs; Microbreweries; Fruit & Vegetable Markets
Ethnic	Recognizing the twang of Appalachia in the Stanley Bros.' Voices	Ethnic Restaurants (approximately 40 cuisines); Ethnic Music; Ethnic Dance; Folk Arts; Cultural and Ethnic Awareness Programs; Language Schools; Gospel Singing Groups; Martial Arts Instruction
Corporate	Reviling a Britney Spears show because she is a corporate creation	Marketing Research; Management Consulting Services; Warehouse Clubs & Superstores; Designer Clothes & Accessories; Fast Food Restaurants; Business & Secretarial Schools; Department Stores Convention & Trade Shows; Public Relations Agencies; Spectator Sports; Amusement & Theme Parks; Advertising & Related
State	Visiting the Gettysburg Battlefield	Political Organizations; Embassies and Delegations; Historical Sites; American Restaurants
Rational	Reveling in the cosmic scope of human reason at a planetarium	R & D in Physical, Engineering, and Life Sciences; Scientific R & D Services; Colleges, Universities, and Professional Schools; Planeteria; Aquariums; Human Rights Organizations; Management, Scientific, & Technical Consulting; Exam Preparation and Tutoring; Libraries & Archives; Computer Training; Offices of Lawyer

Table 10.2. (Continued)

Legitimacy

In addition to their theatricality and authenticity, scenes may be defined by a sense of what is the right and wrong way to behave. Participants can share in the pleasure of a common sense of being in the right or rejecting those in the wrong. This is the pleasure of a good will, acting on the basis of an authority one takes to be valid.

Sub-Dimension	Example	Sample Amenity Indicator
Traditional	Sharing in the stability and assurance of hearing Mozart performed in the Vienna State Opera as you believe it was earlier	Genealogy Societies; Historical Sites; Opera Companies; Antique Dealers; Fine Arts Schools; Libraries & Archives; Family Restaurants; Family Clothing Stores; Religious Organizations; Dance Companies; Museums
Utilitarian	Attending a benefit concert because it contributes to positive outcomes or savoring the value of efficient production at a museum of industry	Fast Food Restaurants; Technical & Trade Schools; Warehouse Clubs & Superstores; Business & Secretarial Schools; Management Consulting Services; Convenience Stories; Business Associations; Junior Colleges; Computer Systems Design; Database & Directory Publishers; Exam Preparation & Tutoring; Educational Exhibits
Egalitarian	Enjoying the democratic implications of a crafts fair	Human Rights Organizations; Salvation Army; Public Libraries: Elementary & Secondary Schools (Public); Environment & Wildlife Organizations; Junior Colleges; Services for Elderly & Disabled Persons; Social Advocacy Organizations; Individual & Family Services; Religious Organizations
Self Expressive	Enjoying hearing a jazz musician play something that could only be improvised spontaneously at that particular moment	Dance Companies; Fashion Shows/Designers; Yoga Studios; Art Dealers; Comedy Clubs; Body Piercing; Tattoo Parlors; Recorded Music Stores; Vintage & Used Clothing; Custom Printed T-Shirts; Music Festivals; Fine Arts Schools; Graphic Design Services; Independent Artists, Writers & Performers; Musical Groups & Artists; Performing Arts Companies; Sound Recording Industries; Hobby, Toy, & Game Stores; Interior Design Services; Karaoke Clubs

Table 10.2. (Continued)

Sub-Dimension	Example	Sample Amenity Indicator
Charismatic	Watching a Chicago Bulls game because of the charismatic aura of Michael Jordan rather than because one is a Chicagoan	Designer Clothes & Accessories; Fashion Shows/Designers; Motion Picture & Video Exhibition; Art Dealers; Dance Companies; Historical Sites; Motion Picture & Sound Recording Industries; Musical Groups & Artists; Performing Arts Companies; Promoters of Entertainment Events; Spectator2 Sports; Fine Arts Schools; Sports Bars; Sound Recording Studios

sort of scene exists in a given place? Our proposal is to measure the dimensions of scenes empirically as they are indicated by clusters of urban amenities, allowing us to undertake what Baudelaire called a "botany of the sidewalk." For example, the combination of amenities composing a given scene may promote a sense of self-expressive legitimacy, transgressive theatricality, local authenticity, anti-rational authenticity and anti-corporate authenticity—this combination we call a "bohemian scene." Another cluster of amenities might promote neighborly theatricality, traditional legitimacy and local authenticity—a more "communitarian scene." Our conceptual apparatus focuses on the meaning of these distinct sets of values created by different combinations of the core fifteen. One can then analyze and interpret combinations with far more richness than by simply counting individual amenities or actors or producing case studies in splendid isolation.

Our analytical framework thus grounds systematic and comparative analysis of embedded urban culture. Research may proceed from inductive and deductive standpoints, and pursue intensive and extensive research strategies (of individual cases or large Ns). Inductively, the empirical distribution and levels of the fifteen dimensions can generate a *scene profile* for neighborhoods, cities or metropolitan areas. Deductively, the framework helps specify *theoretical ideal-typical scenes* by *ex-ante*-defined combinations of sub-dimensions, against which empirical scenes can be measured.[8]

MEASURING SCENES: CLUSTERING INDIVIDUAL AMENITIES INTO MEANINGFUL SCENES

Combining our conceptualization of scenes with our amenities database allows us to begin to formulate and test hypotheses about the relations between (varieties of) cultural attractiveness and more traditional developmental factors (income, cost of living, etc.). How to do so empirically? By systematically scoring the meanings of distinct physical spaces of consumption. Operationally a scene is *a specific cluster of amenities* constituted by the ensemble of meanings or value orientations offered to the potential consumer. By scoring the value orientations of individual amenities, coding individual amenities in our database on each of the fifteen sub-dimensions with a five-point scale,[9] analyzing how they combine in distinct territories (neighborhood, city, MSA, region...), we capture distinct cultural experiences of separate territories.[10] In our framework, the *analytical units* are the fifteen sub-dimensions measured for every amenity in a territory; these dimensions are the minimal analytical components of the scenes approach. By contrast, the amenity (like a restaurant or museum) is the *observational unit*. We do not count amenities, but analyze their implicit substantive meanings. The cultural life of cities is the focus, not the components or size of the cultural, leisure or tourist industry.[11]

Ideally, the specific amenities should meet at least two criteria. First, the analysis should highlight consumption-oriented rather than production-oriented establishments (factories are not included, while cafes are). Second, the amenity should be potentially present across all territories under analysis in approximately similar form; local users should be able to reveal their preferences by patronizing a shoe store or Thai restaurant if they choose. But in other localities if citizens prefer catfish restaurants, the local market should not prohibit a catfish restaurant from emerging. The amenities, such as these types of restaurants, should be linked with similar meanings among potential cultural consumers; they should be "functionally equivalent."(Van Deth 1998) Standardized amenities such as Starbucks and McDonalds meet this criterion relatively straightforwardly; less standardized amenities are more difficult, for example, cultural centers (which offer diverse activities) or restaurants (which differ by cuisine and price) (Kaple et al. 1996).

Because there is no systematic database of all possible amenities across U.S. cities that could guarantee these two conditions, we assembled a national database of amenities from sources where the agency constructing each variable has ideally been sensitive to these criteria, such as the Yellow Pages or U.S. Census Bureau. This maximizes coverage of potential amenities (varieties of types) and territories (minimal units, as zip codes), and limits definitional ambiguity.[12] Our database includes hundreds of amenities such as theaters, restaurants, bookstores, dance companies, jazz clubs, museums, gospel choirs, and liberal arts colleges. It covers all U.S. metro areas and rural areas, some forty thousand zip codes. Levels and changes in more traditional factors such as education, crime, housing prices, and ethnic and class demographics can be analyzed to measure their relative contributions to various scenes. No such massive and comprehensive database has previously been generated. It took us five years with some dozen assistants, and is still growing.

We coded roughly 650 amenities from high to low on each of the fifteen scene dimensions. Hence the analysis can "travel empirically" from the observational unit–individual amenities–to the minimal analytical unit–the fifteen scenes dimensions. To compare scenes, we created a performance index for each territory by (1) multiplying the number of amenities of a given type in a zip code by that amenity type's score on each sub-dimension, and then summing the products for each of the fifteen sub-dimensions. We then (2) divide this product by the total number of amenities in the zip code. These provide a scene profile for each U.S. zip code based on the fifteen dimensions of legitimacy, theatricality and authenticity. The whole scene emerges in the combination of amenities, distinguishing for example, places with cafes and lawyers offices from others with cafes adjacent to nightclubs and bars. To be sure, scenes and zip codes are not neatly aligned, and the limits of this measure are legion. Other measures are no doubt possible and necessary, as is on-the-ground ethnographic work that can capture subtle variations of amenity usage and meanings. Nevertheless, this analytical profile permits analysis of consumption activity as a situated social phenomenon using the criteria above: (1) meanings and value orientations (2) interconnected in a holistic way and (3) situated in space and time. The appendix discusses index construction.

ANALYZING SCENES: VALIDATION BY SCENESCAPE ANALYSIS

What picture of the American scenescape emerges from these profiles? Do our measures provide a valid proxy of the cultural life of cities? Because there are no similar measures to contrast our proposal against using "construct-validity" (convergent or divergent) (Webber 1990:18-19), we initially pursue validation by "face validity" (are theoretical concepts and measures adequate to the judgements of researchers or to previous knowledge, do the scenes measures discriminate among different cultural contexts that are well documented by previous literature?) and "hypothesis validity" (can the measure illuminate theoretical relationships (Webber 1990:18-22), are the scenes measurements confirmed by the "culture and cities" literature?).

BASIC DESCRIPTIVE INSIGHTS: CONFIRMING EXPECTATIONS OF REGIONAL AND URBAN CULTURAL LIFE BY CROSS-TERRITORIAL COMPARISONS

Simple statistical analysis of our measures of scenes helps to document the cultural variations among different regions, cities and local contexts.

We have pursued many descriptive analyses for face validity and more. Some brief examples: Scenes in the Northeast and West have amenities that rely more on individual self-expression for their legitimacy, while those in the South and Midwest express more traditionalistic legitimacy. Scenes in the South and Midwest contain amenities that offer neighborly theatricality, while northeastern and especially western scenes manifest more transgression. These fit common views. As an example: we tabulated glamour for each Los Angles zip code, and found Hollywood close to the top and Watts scores near the bottom. These regional differences are striking, as they confirm that our methods yield results consistent with broad expectations from other sources, and identify cultural contexts varying within an emerging more expressively-oriented consumer society.

Equally striking are variations between New York City, Chicago and Los Angeles as widely discussed global centers identified with the new economy, where rents, education, arts and culture, technology jobs, and young people are rapidly increasing (Gyourko, Meyer and Sinai 2006; Cortright 2001; Currid 2007). Yet these three cities reveal strikingly different patterns: from the clustering of finance in downtown New York (Sassen 2001), to Mayor Richard Daley's enthusiastic embrace of culture and aesthetics as central to urban policy (Clark forthcoming), to the individualism, fragmentation and image-building that lead some to name Los Angeles as ground zero of the post-modern age (Dear 1981). Critical differences appear in Figure 10.2a and Figure 10.2b.

Compared to all U.S. zip codes (scored 0), scenes in these three cities are legitimated more by individual self-expression and utility than by tradition and egalitarianism; they encourage transgression, glamour and formal codes more than neighborliness; and they root identities in rational calculation, the state and corporation more than in local culture. Broadly, "urbanism as a way of life" (Wirth 1938; Simmel 1971) continues in the late modern city, as more abstract, formal, distanced social relations are linked with heightened individualism and weaker primordial ties.

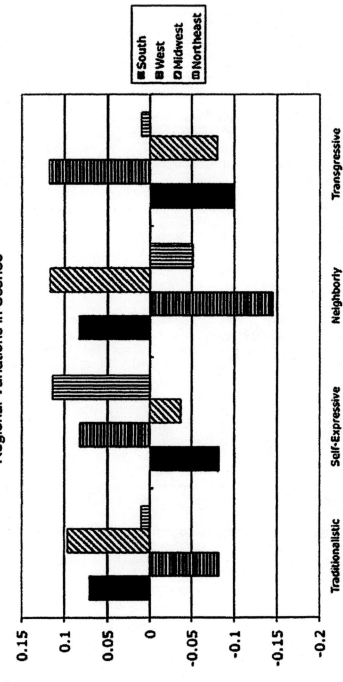

Regional Variations in Scenes

Traditionalistic · Self-Expressive · Neighborly · Transgressive

Legend: South · West · Midwest · Northeast

Figure 10.1. Regional Variations in Scenes. These are simple correlations, Pearson r's, of dummy variables of the four major U.S. regions with some of the sub-dimensions of scenes. Each zip code is assigned 1 if it is within the region, and 0 if it is not.

Urban Variations in Scenes

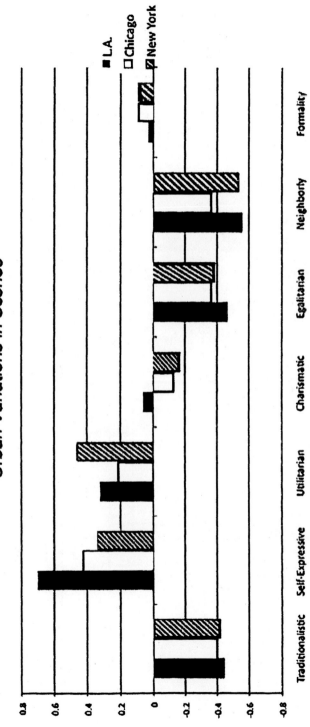

Figure 10.2a. Urban Variation in Scenes. These are z-scores of the mean performance scores (like Traditionalistic) of all zip codes within each of the county areas overlapping these three cities: Los Angeles County, Cook County, and the five county boroughs of New York. They show the strength of these scenes-dimensions in these cities relative to the national average.

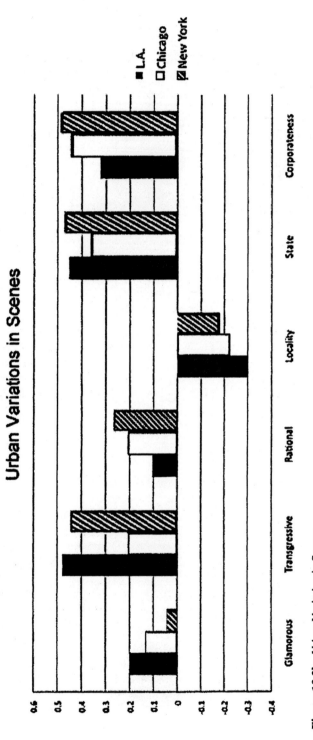

Urban Variations in Scenes

Legend: L.A. ■ Chicago □ New York ▨

Figure 10.2b. Urban Variation in Scenes.

The three cities also show striking differences. Los Angeles scenes are defined much more by individual self-expression and glamour, highlighting more amenities such as art schools, arts organizations and information, movie theaters, dance companies, yoga studios, exercise and fitness classes, and infant and children's clothing accessories.

New York scenes more strongly affirm that identity is based in the power of reason and the stamp of the corporate brand; they legitimate themselves by appeals to efficiency, activity and material success, and promote the formal theatricality of the business suit and the dress code, featuring, relative to Chicago and Los Angeles, more amenities such as night clubs, book stores and book publishers, art dealers, designer clothing and accessories, convenience stores and delicatessens, advertising agencies and newsstands. In Chicago, scenes are the most neighborly, traditionalistic and egalitarian of the three, stressing more amenities such as pizza restaurants, bowling alleys, churches, parks and playgrounds, cemeteries and public libraries. Similar demographic patterns are here mediated by different cultural settings, which in turn might well account for divergent economic and political outcomes that would be otherwise difficult to capture. This all has much face validity and is consistent with recent urban scholarship. These data are simply the first to document these patterns so systematically.

Perhaps even more striking than these differences in levels are different *relations* among the sub-dimensions of scenes. Figure 10.3 shows correlations *within* New York City, Chicago and Los Angeles of charismatic legitimacy by zip code, and Figure 10.4 shows correlates of self-expressive individualism scores with selected sub-dimensions.

THEORETICAL ELABORATIONS: HOW SCENE ANALYSIS REFRAMES BOHEMIA

The New York Times columnist David Brooks (2000) is credited with identifying a "Bobo" orientation which joins 1960s bohemian values with 1980s bourgeois budgets, as illustrated by President Bill Clinton. Brooks subtly describes several cases, especially Bobo cities such as Burlington, Vermont and Bethesda, Maryland. Richard Florida (2002) used Brooks' Bobos as his core concept, but retitled it the "Creative Class" at the publisher's suggestion; the book relies less on "class" and more on Bobo-like tolerance, which Florida holds is a key driver of urban innovation. Richard Lloyd's "neo-bohemia" (2006) builds on these but makes the strongest case for a more literal bohemia as an urban dynamic, closer to nineteenth and early twentieth century classic bohemias: contra Brooks and Florida, Lloyd claims that creativity requires breaking eggs, challenging authority. Brooks' work is self-identified "comic sociology," and offers only subtle anecdotes as evidence. Lloyd's evidence is an ethnography of Chicago's Wicker

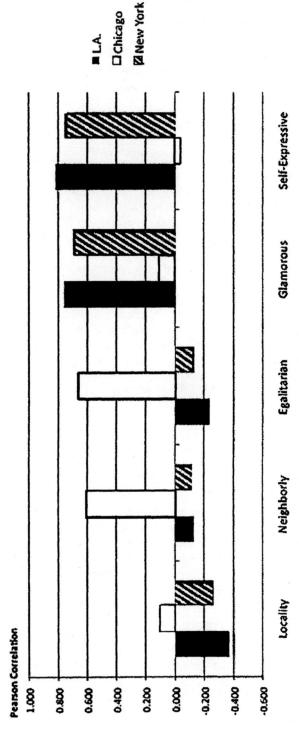

Figure 10.3. Correlations with Charismatic Legitimacy in New York, Chicago and Los Angeles

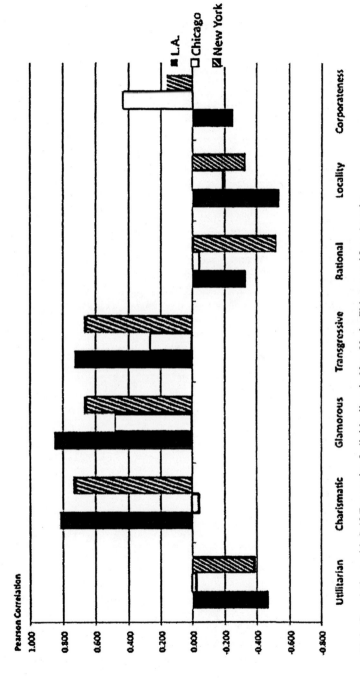

Figure 10.4. Correlations with Self-Expressive Individualism in New York, Chicago and Los Angeles

Park neighborhood that provides sensitive insight but does not locate this case in comparison with others. Florida's prime systematic measures of bohemian tolerance are the percent of gays and artists in a metro area. He correlates these with patents and other innovation measures, but Clark's (2004) reanalysis suggests that gays were largely spurious, and education was a more important indicator of creativity.

The classic statements of Murger, Balzac and Baudelaire focused on Paris but (neo)bohemia is increasingly woven into the post-industrial political economy, as a testing ground for new styles and patterns of consumption, analogous to that of scientific and technological research on the side of production (Campbell 1989), and a defining half of the modern spirit (Grãna 1964). Our scenes approach provides more precise tools to capture and analyze these ideas. As Murger, Balzac and Baudelaire suggested, an ideal-typical Bohemian scene has a distinct shape (see also Grãna and Grãna 1990). Our coding of Bohemia draws on such past and recent discussions to determine how a Bohemian scene combines the fifteen sub-dimensions of scenes, as shown in Table 10.3.

Defined thusly, a scene is more Bohemian if it exhibits resistance to traditional legitimacy, affirms individual self-expression, eschews utilitarianism, values charisma, promotes a form of elitism (Baudelaire's "aristocracy of dandies"), encourages members to keep their distance, promotes transforming oneself into an exhibition, values fighting the mainstream, affirms attending to the local (Balzac's intense interest in Parisian neighborhoods), promotes ethnicity as a source of authenticity (cf., Lloyd 2006:76),[13] attacks the distant, abstract state, discourages corporate culture and attacks the authenticity of reason (Rimbaud's "systematic derangement of all the senses").

Table 10.3. Ideal-Typical Bohemia

Traditionalistic	Self-Expressive	Utilitarian	Charismatic	Egalitarian	Neighborly	Formal	Glamorous	Exhibitionistic	Transgressive	Local	Ethnic	State	Corporate	Rational
2	5	1	4	2	2	3	3	4	5	4	4	2	1	2

Notes: 1 is negative, 3 is neutral, and 5 is positive.

Scenes whose amenities generate profiles that are closer to this ideal type receive a higher score on our Bohemian Index (measured as the value distance from the "bliss point" defined by Table 10.4).[14] This measurement from a bliss point is analogous to policy distance analyses in voting (e.g., Riker and Ordeshook 1973). While we continue to investigate alternative measures of Bohemia, in practice the index identifies many neighborhoods which others cite as distinctly Bohemian: in Chicago, the highest scoring neighborhoods in 2000 include Bucktown, Wicker Park, Humboldt Park and Logan Square, all commonly perceived as Bohemian at the time (Lloyd 2006), even if they have since changed.

Analyzing our Bohemian Score as dependent variable in a regression including all U.S. zip codes and a number of standard urban development variables (summarized in Clark 2004) provides insight into where the most bohemian American scenes are.

Bohemian clusters of amenities are stronger in locations with larger populations, increasing populations, more retirees, higher income, fewer residents with graduate and professional degrees, increasing numbers of college graduates, more crime, and fewer non-whites. Baby boomers, youth and Democratic voting (in both simple correlations and regression coefficients) are not significant, nor are change in income, retirees, youth population and baby boomers.[15]

Comment on these results: First, bohemian scenes are stronger in areas with higher crime rates. The "established" or "bourgeois" theory that crime indicates social disorganization and "would repel most residents" does not hold in a Bohemian scene, which inverts this anti-crime value. Our finding confirms the River Styx theme from Baudelaire to Lloyd. While Baudelaire noted "the magic" in "murky corners of old cities,"[16] Lloyd (2006:78) stresses that "the manifest dangers of the neighborhood coincide with the bohemian disposition to value the drama of living on the edge

A second set of important findings concerns age. Florida and Lloyd both stress the youthful nature of their neo-bohemias, but we find that retirees are *more* numerous in bohemias than youth. "Youth" does not *necessarily* translate into edgy creativity–there are "square" and "establishment" and many other types of youth. What seems to matter more is how various contexts channel and transform the energy of youth. Bohemias may include "old-timers" that lend a form of authenticity to the neighborhood (Brown-Saracino 2007), and the denizens of "rural bohemias" such as Carmel, CA may be older (Austin 1990). Moreover, there may be a particularly strong connection between bohemias and what we have elsewhere termed the "grey creative class."[17]

Third, the finding that voting patterns are not significantly connected with Bohemian neighborhoods suggests that whatever sense of political legitimacy and activism Bohemias create often operates outside of standard notions of parties. The Red and Blue map is too simple. To understand how scenes generate political identification—in cafes, poetry groups, punk clubs and galleries—it is necessary to move past models building heavily on party voting.

We find more when we repeat the same basic analysis of zip codes within the three largest cities. The main finding in Figure 10.5 is that in Chicago the percent of college graduates increases in more Bohemian zip codes; this same effect is insignificant in Los Angeles and New York. The common explanation

Table 10.4. A continuous scale of "bohemianness" as dependant variable: national regression results

Independent Variables	Standardized Regression Coefficients
% 18–24 year old (1990)	-.003
	(-0.292)
Change in % 18-24 (2000/90)	-.018*
	(-2.155)
% 25-34 year old (1990)	-.035*
	(-2.307)
Change in % 25-34 year old (2000/90)	-.027**
	(-2.647)
% Non-White (1990)	-0.086***
	-(10.139)
Change in % Non-White (2000/90)	-.001
	(-.155)
% Baby Boomers (1990)	.021
	(1.212)
Change in % Baby Boomers (2000/90)	0
	(.001)
% Retiree (1990)	.046***
	(3.766)
Change in % retiree (2000/90)	.016
	(1.594)
Total Population in 1990	.209***
	(24.982)
Population change 2000/1990, logged	.061***
	(8.571)
Vote cast for president, % democratic 1992	-.006
	(-.717)
Crime rate (1998)	.027***
	(3.422)
	(.597)
Change in % college graduate (2000/1990)	.036***
	(4.397)
% graduate/profession degree (1990)	-.061**
	(-2.826)

Table 10.4. (Continued)

Independent Variables	Standardized Regression Coefficients
Difference in % Prof/Grad degree 2000/1990	.023
	(1.467)
Per capita income (1990)	.064***
	4.636
Change in per capita income (2000/90)	-.022**
	(-2.738)

Notes: t-ratios are reported in parentheses
Dependent Variable: Bohemian Index
Adjustd R-squared: .053
*p < .05 (two-tailed)
**p < .01 (two-tailed)
***p < .001 (two-tailed)

for such dynamics is cost or income, but these Bohemian results hold strong after we control income and the other variables in the model.

Interpretation? Bohemia is no silver bullet for urban development. In Chicago, the Neo-Bohemian thesis that artist neighborhoods fuse with educated young people to meet the needs of the new culture-driven economy is empirically supported. However, the thesis demands contextualization, as such Bohemian neighborhoods are *not* significant attractors of the college educated in New York and Los Angeles. In New York, zip codes with 25-34 year olds seem sharply distinct from bohemian neighborhoods. Moreover, in New York, both college graduates and 25-34 year olds reside in zip code scenes that feature corporate authenticity ($r = .326$ and $.238$, respectively), while both groups are declining over the 1990-2000 decade in more corporate-authenticated scenes in Chicago and Los Angeles. Los Angeles contrasts most with the "neo-Bohemia leads to growth thesis" because college grads in Los Angeles increase more in higher income zip codes and with more young persons. Related: glamorous scenes in Los Angeles attract the young and educated more strongly than in the other cites ($r = .493$ vs. .32 in Chicago and .17 in New York).[18] Perhaps the unique ways that Chicago (as shown in figures 10.3 and 10.4) combines individual self-expression with utilitarian legitimacy and corporate authenticity increase the likelihood that its Bohemians may become "useful labor" (Lloyd 2006); or perhaps timing matters, as Chicago's bohemian scene has bloomed only recently in comparison to New York's. Still, these strong results document the power of local scenes in transforming simpler national patterns. By pointing to specific differences in both levels and dynamics of scenes across three major cities, scene analysis helps cultural analysts become more conscious of the multiple institutional and other mechanisms that join to create specific types of scenes.

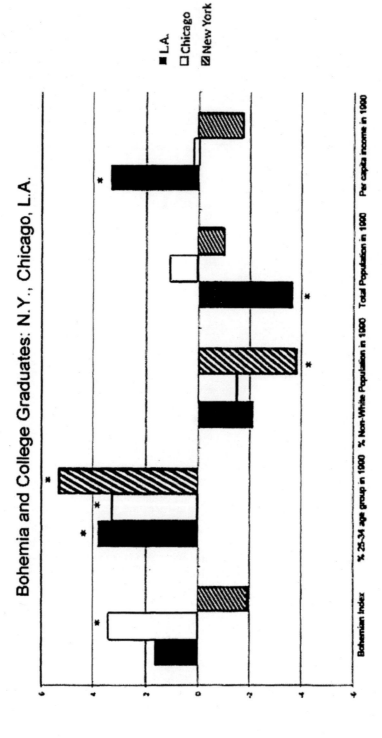

Figure 10.5. College Grads Increasing in Chicago Bohemias more than in Los Angeles, Decreasing in New York

Notes: Figure 10.5 summarizes regression results within New York, Chicago, and Los Angeles. Change in college graduate share of the population is the dependent variable and the Bohemian Index, 25 through 34-year-old population, non-white population, total population, and per capita income are independent variables. The standardized regression coefficient appears as the height of each bar; starred variables are significant at the .05 level. Because the N of zip codes is much smaller in these city-level regressions, we reduced the number of independent variables from the model in Table 10.7. Despite stronger intercorrelations among the city-level independent variables than in the national model, results stay generally similar. Namely, bohemia is significant within Chicago but not in L.A. and N.Y. It is also important to note that the adjusted R-squared's are higher in the L.A. (.27) and N.Y (.24) models than in the Chicago model (.07), again illustrating Chicago's distinctive urban dynamics.

A SCENES-BASED PROGRAM FOR CULTURAL POLICY AND URBAN STUDIES

Leisure and consumption as vehicles of personal expression have increased in the past century. This brings, as Nobel economist Robert Fogel (2000) suggests, a need to engage in questions about quality of life that cuts across class divisions. If Fogel is right that, in a society where leisure time has massively risen, "non-material" or "spiritual" goods and inequalities are increasingly becoming key drivers of social change (as Inglehart 1990 and others stress), then differences about *which* spiritual goods and how to *arrange* them will become increasingly central social and policy questions. Scenes-based research suggests one way to address this more precisely.

There is little use in speaking of *the* coming of the creative class or *the* rise of Neo-Bohemia in flexible capitalism or *the* advent of omnivorous cultural consumption among the new elite or *the* transformation to a knowledge economy or *the* transition to post-industrialism. Accepting these as important general trends, the more critical and sensitive question then becomes the *concrete* one about *which* creativity (and where), *which* Bohemianism (and where). The scene within which any of these processes occurs not only shapes the direction toward which they move, it helps to define what it means to be creative or Bohemian or omnivorous or knowledgeable or beyond industry, and so to pursue the goals associated with those terms. These are not clear uncontested concepts, as was illustrated by the positive and negative takes on crime in Bohemian and non-Bohemian scenes. As leisure and consumption increase in salience, disputes over how to answer questions of the sort captured in our fifteen scenes dimensions are likely to heighten, sometimes as new points of conflict.

These observations suggest eight axial points of a scenes-based agenda for urban and cultural policy studies:

(1) *Conceptualize the city as pluralistic, diverse, and filled with competing subcultures.* Government typically acts in distinct policy arenas such as hous-

ing or culture, which differ just like neighborhoods. We see the world more as an ecology of games and scenes than as a monolithic unity.

(2) *Identify growth dynamics of distinct scenes.* Identify scenes with neighborhoods (via zip codes etc.). Invest in key amenities to make each scene more vital, relying on its impact on the specific, local scenescape.

(3) *No city represents the nation or the world.* There is no Middletown. Disputing Michael Dear's claim that L.A. is "the city of the future," our more culturally relativistic perspective suggests instead: No one city is The Future.

(4) In addition to production, *feature consumption.*

(5) *Culturally strong neighborhoods remain separate from the workplace.* Chicago's remarkably rich neighborhoods differ from the European social democratic tradition, where workers would reside in homes built near their factories, and social life was more driven by production. Explore the implications of such work/home contexts as they transform scene dynamics.

(6) *Multiple research methods.* Use in-depth cases, oral history, ethnography, content analysis, archival history, voting, interviews of leaders, qualitative, quantitative and more.

(7) *Include the metro area.* Think not solely of a single metropolitan government, but look for cooperative, voluntary civic and intergovernmental patterns, some built from specific agreements among local governments and private contracting groups, others involving citizen values that lead them to prefer one location over another.

(8) Connect *global* changes in many urban dynamics with *local* interpretations of those changes. Theorizing more precisely about multiple levels of socioeconomic processes–from global to metro to zip code–can lead to more precise operational models which methods such as Hierarchical Linear Modeling can help assess and calibrate.

All of these require elaboration. The effort of this research has been to show how the concept and reality of scenes provide a new, powerful tool to help do so.

Our concepts and our data can be fruitfully expanded and merged with other approaches to enhance the power of each. We are working with teams from Finland, France, Spain, Portugal and Korea to specify cross-national scenes patterns. Our ongoing work seeks to expand and refine our concepts and methods to distinguish globally-shared and nation-specific patterns, and then to generalize the nation-specific results. For example "Korean scenes" often feature extended families–in weddings, funerals and college preparatory schools. We analyze the impact of these variables on others, such as rent. Indeed rent differences across Korean scenes are strongly influenced by college prep schools, not so in the United States (Lee, Clark and Anderson 2007). These analyses need to be combined with more narrow economic variables or individualistic/socialization-oriented discussions of identity or self-realization. Studies of race, ethnicity, religion, class as well as civic groups and neighborhoods can be enhanced and sharpened by adding these scenes components, highlighting the specific cultural setting within which any of these operates, and allowing for systematic comparisons of the relative impact of each.

ACKNOWLEDGMENTS

We thank Lawrence Rothfield and Timothy Hotze for helpful comments on earlier versions of this article. We gratefully acknowledge the support of the Cultural Policy Center at the University of Chicago, Urban Innovation Analysis and National Research Framework, Government of Spain (the Cultural Dynamic of Cities project, grant CSO2008-04288).

APPENDIX: BUILDING MEASURES OF SCENES

Table 10.2 provides illustrative samples of our amenities indicators for the fifteen dimensions. In producing our indexes, 140 amenities were used, drawing from the U.S. Census of Business, and over five hundred more from online yellow pages services and the Urban Institute's Unified Database of Arts Organizations. A team of coders scored each amenity 1-5 for each of the fifteen scene dimensions, with 5 positive, 3 neutral, and 1 negative. Our approach to systemizing the coding was to try to lay out highly detailed criteria, then to structure them via simple decision-trees that would automate the process. Whenever we found intercoder reliability fell below $r = .8$ we would add more detail to the criteria and decision-trees. Our operational definitions are thus highly detailed. We generated dozens of pages of definitional criteria for the fifteen scenes sub dimensions, available to others with complete scoring and amenity lists at http://public.me.com/tnclark1/Scenes Project Data and Syntax.

The performance score measures all of a scene's amenities. A few stylized, extreme examples illustrate how it works. Let us imagine an absolutely pure transgressive scene–Berkeley's Telegraph Avenue to the max. And let us say that this scene contains five amenities, and that, in this example, all of these are body piercing studios and tattoo parlors. All would receive a score of 5 on the sub-dimension of transgressive theatricality. If we then multiply each of the 5 amenities by its transgression score of 5, we find that each one is putting out 5 units of transgressiveness (5 "transgressies," we could say). The sum total of transgressiveness in the scene would thus be twenty-five transgressies. If we then divide this total by the total number of amenities in the scene (5), we find that the average experience of transgression in this scene is...5!

Now, let's consider what the performance score on transgressive-theatricality would be for a stylized version of Chicago's Wrigleyville. Let us assume that this scene has two body piercing salons, four bars, two Chinese restaurants, and one Starbucks. In this case, the body-piercing salon would receive a 5 for transgression, the bars might receive 4's, the Chinese restaurants 3's (neither promoting nor denying resistant behavior), and the Starbucks a 2 (their standardization and ubiquity, let us say, may be viewed as impediments to instituting transgressive practices). So, by multiplying the number of each type of amenity by its transgressive-theatricality score, we see that the body piercing salons would be generating ten transgressies, the bars sixteen, the Chinese restaurants six, and the Starbucks two. If we sum those, we find that the whole scene provides thirty-four units of transgression to its consumers. Divide that total by the number of amenities in the scene (nine), and we see that the average experience of transgression per amenity in this scene is…3.8. Still more than a neutral experience (3), but not as intense as Telegraph's 5.

NOTES

1. To be sure, some geographers and sociologists have recently discussed the concept of place or space (much of which is summarized in Gieryn 2000 and Relph 2006).

2. See, e.g., Parsons 1951; Alexander 2003; Griswold 2004; Swidler 1986; Sewell 1999.

3. Even if we frequently use the term "urban," most comments and data cover all local contexts.

4. By contrast, Tanner et al. (2010) stress that the concept of scene should not be over-extended, and that its applicability in particular to oppositional sub-cultures, such as some types of rap music, is limited.

5. There is no doubt that the emergence of scenes as an increasingly important social formation generates new social strains, just as the differentiation of production and residence continues to do. Analysis of the interchanges and interpenetrations among scene, family, work, politics and religion is an important subject of our further work, as is how scenes change in and organize experience of time. Likewise, analysis of virtual scenes is an important field of research, although, following Gieryn 2000 and because of the distinct role of theatricality and hence visibility in scenes, we consider only non-virtual scenes here.

6. From the perspective of work and class, the experiences in scenes are commonly interpreted as promoting or opposing the interests of different classes—elite art for the elite class, mass art for the non-elite, both judged by how they block or support the dominating or emancipatory interests of classes, depending on where one stands (Bourdieu 1984; Dimaggio 1982). From the perspective of the traditional residential neighborhood, the looser, more transient glue that holds a scene together can seem to offer short-term commitment, shallow friendships and anomie, unlike the deep ties of classic neighborhoods (Wirth 1938; Sennett 1998). From the scene perspective, the job one holds and the place one lives are driven by the scenes of which they are a part. For instance, Lloyd (2006) shows that in Chicago's Wicker Park scene, "coolness" drives hiring decisions rather than the other way around. Clark (2004) shows that amenities drive location decisions (see also Florida 2002 and Brooks 2000).

7. This move is understandable, as the data to study such questions have often been unavailable or difficult to acquire. This is hardly surprising, given that the cultural sector has traditionally been subdivided: those interested in opera or ballet have not considered restaurants or bookstores, while others exploring football or country music have ignored museums and jazz clubs. Omitting these associated key elements of a scene, however, has meant that past estimates of how amenities have an impact on urban development have been misspecified, statistically biased by omission of key variables.

8. We have elsewhere identified twelve ideal-typical scenes such as Disney Heaven, Bobo's Paradise, Black is Beautiful, that variously combine the fifteen sub-dimensions. See Clark (2007).

9. The coding process required many details and fine judgments and tests for validity and reliability reported elsewhere. Our general strategy was to use the coding process to add operational detail about each dimension. We computed intercorrelations among coders' results almost weekly, and if they fell below .8, we would meet, discuss and add more conceptual consistency in writing with more detail about how and what to code, to make the criteria as explicit and consistent as possible for any future coder/analysts to use or recode differently. See scenes.uchicago.edu for the complete database and scores.

10. This operational option does not preclude the possibility of applying the same framework to non-physical amenities such as cultural events: regular annual celebrations, festival, fairs, bike rallies and the like

11. In comparative analysis it is critical to define the "theoretical unit" to be compared, because the result should make reference to this unit, not to the unit used to observe and/or measure the analytical properties intended to be studied (cf., Przeworski and Teune on "levels of analysis" vs. "level of observation" (1970:49-50)). In cross-national or cross-city analysis, the analyst has to transcend names of the city or country and interpret the analytical meaning they represent (Przeworksi 1987). Our approach to scenes follows a similar logic.

12. Our database combines information from the surveys of individual attitudes and behavior from the DDB Lifestyle Survey, amenities from The Urban Institute, online Yellow Pages, the Census of Economic Activity, and various socio-economic variables as causes and correlates of scenes (scenes.uchicago.edu). Considerations of feasibility and cost-efficiency also guided our selections (Kaple et al. 1996).

13. For neo-bohemians, "sharing the streets with... nonwhite residents... is part of their image of an authentic urban experience."(Lloyd 2006:78)

14. Operationally, we subtract the distance of each zip code on each of the fifteen dimensions from the Bohemian "bliss point" defined in Table 10.6. We then aggregate these fifteen distances and take the reciprocal score.

15. Although changes in income and changes in 25-34 year olds are significant at the .01 level, and changes in 18-24 year olds are significant at the .05 level (all negative).

16. Lloyd cites the complete verse: "In murky corners of old cities where/everything–horror too–is magical./ I study, servile to my moods, the odd/and charming refuse of humanity."

17. A paper called "The Grey Creative Class: Why it is Critical for Cities and Culture," is in draft, and is available from the authors on request.

18. It also may be worth noting that, while in N.Y. and L.A., youth and education tend to point in the same direction (both groups tend to rise in relation to the same dimensions), in Chicago the two often point in different directions (the educated are rising in Chicago's glamorous scenes, but youth are declining).

18. This chapter overlaps with Daniel Silver, Terry Nichols Clark and Clemente J. Navarro. Scenes: Social Context in an Age of Contingency. *Social Forces*, July 2010, Vol. 88, No. 5, pp. 2293-2324.

BIBLIOGRAPHY

Abbing, Hans. 2006. *From High to New Art.* Amsterdam University Press.

Alexander, Jeffrey C. 2003. *The Meanings of Social Life: A Cultural Sociology.* Oxford University Press.

Austin, Marry. 1990. "Rural Bohemia: Carmel, 1900s." Pp. 497-504. *On Bohemia: The Code of the Self-Exiled.* César Grāna and Marigay Grāna, editors. Transaction Publishers.

Bellah, Robert, et al. 1996. *Habits of the Heart.* University of California Press.

Bennett, Andy, and Richard Peterson. Editors. 2004. *Scenes: Local, Translocal, and Virtual.* Vanderbilt University Press.

Blum, Alan. 2003. *The Imaginative Structure of the City.* Montreal & Kingston: McGill-Queen's University Press.

Bourdieu, Pierre. 1984. *Distinction.* Harvard University Press.

Bonnell, Victoria E., and Lynn Hunt. Editors. 1999. *Beyond the Cultural Turn. New Directions in the Study of Society and Culture.* University of California Press

Brooks, David. 2000. *Bobos in Paradise: The New Upper Class and How They Got There.* Simon & Schuster.

Brown-Saracino, Japonica. 2007. "Virtuous Marginality: Social Preservationists and the Selection of the Old-timer." *Theory and Society* 36(5):437-68.

Campbell, Colin. 1989. *The Romantic Ethic and the Spirit of Modern Consumerism.* Blackwell.

Clark, Terry Nichols, and Seymour Martin Lipset. 2001. *The Breakdown of Class Politics: A Debate on Post-Industrial Stratification.* Johns Hopkins University Press.

Clark, Terry Nichols, and Vincent Hoffmann-Martinot. Editors. 1998. *The New Political Culture.* Westview Press.

Clark, Terry Nichols. 2004. *The City as an Entertainment Machine.* Research in Urban Policy 9. Elsevier.

————2007. "Making Culture Into Magic: How Can It Bring Tourists and Residents?" *International Review of Public Administration* 12(1):13-25.

————Forthcoming. *Trees and Real Violins: Building Post-Industrial Chicago.* Available at: www.faui.org.

Cortright, Joseph, and Heike Mayer. 2001. *High Tech Specialization: A Comparison of High Technology Centers.* Washington DC: The Brookings Institution.

Currid, Elizabeth. 2007. *The Warhol Economy: How Fashion, Art and Music Drive New York City.* Princeton University Press.

Dear, Michael. 2005. "The Los Angeles School of Urbanism." *Geographische Rundschau* 57(1):30-36.

Deener, Andrew. 2007. "Commerce as the Structure and Symbol of Neighborhood Life: Reshaping Community in Venice, California." *City and Community* 6(4):291-314.

DiMaggio, Paul. 1982. "Cultural Entrepreneurship in Nineteenth-Century Boston, I: The Creation of an Organizational Base for High Culture in America." *Media, Culture and Society* 4(1):33-50.

Elazar, Daniel. 1975. "The American Cultural Matrix." Pp. 13-42. *The Ecology of American Political Culture.* Daniel J. Elazar and Joseph Zikmund II, editors. Thomas Y. Crowell.

Florida, Richard. 2002. *The Rise of the Creative Class.* Basic Books/Perseus.

———2008. *Who's Your City?* Basic Books.

Fogel, Robert William. 2000. *The Fourth Great Awakening & the Future of Egalitarianism.* University of Chicago Press.

Glaeser, Edward. 2000. "The Future of Urban Research: Non-market Interactions." Pp. 101-49. *Brookings-Wharton Papers on Urban Affairs.* Washington, DC: The Brookings Institution.

Glaeser, Edward, Jed Kolko and Albert Saiz.. 2004. "Consumers and Cities." *The City as an Entertainment Machine. Research in Urban Policy 9.* Elsevier.

Gieryn, Thomas. 2000. "A Space for Place in Sociology." *Annual Review of Sociology* 26:463-96.

Goffman, Erving. 1959. *The Presentation of Self in Everyday Life.* Doubleday.

———1974. *Frame Analysis: An Essay on the Organization of Experience.* Harper & Row.

Grāna, César. 1964. *Bohemian Versus Bourgeois; French Society and the French Man of Letters in the Nineteenth Century.* Basic Books.

Grāna, César, and Marigay Grāna. 1990. *On Bohemia: The Code of the Self-exiled.* Transaction Publishers.

Grazian, David. 2003. *Blue Chicago: The Search for Authenticity in Urban Blues Clubs.* University of Chicago Press.

Griswold, Wendy. 2004. *Cultures and Societies in a Changing World, Second Edition.* Sage.

Gyourko, Joseph, Christopher Mayer and Todd Sinai. 2006. *Superstar Cities.* Available at: http://www.nber.org/papers/w12355.

Habermas, Jürgen. 1981. *The Theory of Communicative Action.* Beacon Press.

Haenfler, Ross. 2004. "Rethinking Subcultural Resistance: Core Values of the Straight Edge Movement." *Journal of Contemporary Ethnography* 33(1):406-36.

Harding, David J. 2007. "Cultural Context, Sexual Behavior, and Romantic Relationships in Disadvantaged Neighborhoods." American Sociological Review 72(3): 341-64.

Heidegger, Martin. 1996. *Being and Time: A Translation of Sein und Zeit.* SUNY Press.

Hitzler Ronald, Thomas Bucher and Arne Niederbacher. 2005. *Leben in Szenen. Formen jugendlicher Vergemeinschaftung heute..* VS Verlag für Sozialwissenschaften.

Inglehart, Ronald. 1990 *Culture Shift in Advanced Industrial Society.* Princeton University Press.

Irwin, John. 1977. *Scenes.* Sage Publications.

Joas, Hans. 2004. "Morality in an Age of Contingency." *Acta Sociologica* 47(4): 392-99.

Kaple, Deborah A., Lori Morris, Ziggy Rivkin-Fisch and Paul DiMaggio. 1996: *Data on Arts Organizations; A Review and Needs Assessment, with Design Implications.* Princeton University, Centre for Cultural Arts and Cultural Policies.

Leach, Darcy K., and Sebastian Haunss. 2009. "Scenes and Social Movements." *Culture, Social Movements, and Protest.* Hank Johnston, editor. Ashgate Publishing: 255-276.

Lee, Jong Youl, Terry Nichols Clark and Chad Anderson. 2007. "The Effect of Cultural Amenity Factors in Driving Urban Growth." Paper presented at the Midwest Sociological Society Annual Meeting, April 12-17, Chicago.

Lena, Jennifer, and Richard Peterson. 2008. "Classification as Culture: Types and Trajectories of Music Genres." *American Sociological Review* 73(5):697-718.

Lizardo, Omar, and Sara Skiles. 2008. "Cultural Consumption in the Fine and Popular Arts Realms." *Sociology Compass* 2(2):485-502.

Lloyd, Richard. 2006. *Neo-bohemia: Art and Commerce in the Postindustrial City.* Routledge.

Markusen, Ann. 2006. "Urban Development and the Politics of a Creative Class: Evidence from the Study of Artists." *Environment and Planning A* 38(10):1921-40.

Markusen, Ann, and David King. 2003. *The Artistic Dividend: The Arts' Hidden Contributions to Regional Development.* Minneapolis, MN: University of Minnesota's Project on Regional and Industrial Economics, Humphrey Institute of Public Affairs.

Markusen, Ann, Greg Schrock and Martina Cameron. 2004. *The Artistic Dividend Revisited.* Minneapolis, MN: Project on Regional and Industrial Economics, Humphrey Institute of Public Affairs, University of Minnesota.

Molotch, Harvey. 2003. *Where Stuff Comes From: How Toasters, Toilets, Cars, Computers and Many Other Things Come to be as They Are.* Routledge.

Mohr, John W. 2003. "The Cultural Turn in American Sociology–A Report from the Field." *Culture* 17(2-3):1-5.

Parsons, Talcott. 1951. *The Social System.* The Free Press.

Peterson, Richard A. and Roger M. Kern. 1996. "Changing Highbrow Taste: From Snob to Omnivore." *American Sociological Review* 61(5):900-7.

Przeworski, Adam, and Henry Teune. 1970. *The Logic of Comparative Inquiry.* John Wiley & Sons.

Przeworski, Adam. 1987. "Methods of Cross-national Research, 1970-83: An Overview." Pp. 31-40. *Comparative Policy Research.* Meinolf Dierkes, Hans N. Weiler and Ariane Antal., editors. WZB-Publications.

Relph,   Edward.   2006.   "Aspects   of   Place."   Available   at: http://ted.relph.googlepages.com/pldplace

Riker, William, and Peter Ordeshook. 1973. *An Introduction to Positive Political Theory.* Prentice-Hall.

Roback, Jennifer. 1982. "Wages, Rents and the Quality of Life" *The Journal of Political Economy* 90(6):1257-78.

Sacco, Pier Luigi, and Giorgio Blessi. 2006. "European Culture Capitals and Local Development Strategies: Comparing the Genoa and Lille 2004 Cases." *Homo Oeconomicus* 233(4):1-31.

Santagata, Walter. 2004. "Cultural Districts and Economic Development." Pp. 1101-18. *Handbooks in Economics General.* Victor Ginsburgh and David Throsby, editors. Elsevier Science.

Sassen, Saskia. 2001. *The Global City: New York, London, Tokyo.* Princeton University Press.

Scott, Allen John, 2000. *The Cultural Economy of Cities.* London.

Sennett, Richard. 1998. *The Corrosion of Character: The Personal Consequences of Work in the New Capitalism.* Norton.

Sewell, William. "The Concept(s) of Culture." Pp. 35-61. *Beyond the Cultural Turn: New Directions in the Study of Society and Culture.* Victoria E. Bonnell and Lynn Hunt, editors. University of California Press.

Sharp, Elaine B. 2005. *Moral Politics in American Cities.* Kansas University Press.

Simmel, Georg. 1971. "The Metropolis and Mental Life." Pp. 324-39. *On Individuality and Social Forms: Selected Writings.* Donald N. Levine, editor. University of Chicago Press.

Smith, Philip. Editor. 1998. *The New American Cultural Sociology.* Cambridge University Press.

Straw, Will. 1991. "Systems of Articulation, Logics of Change: Scenes and Communities in Popular Music." *Cultural Studies* 5(3):361-75.

——2002. "Scenes and Sensibilities." *Public* 22(23):245-57.

——2004. "Cultural Scenes." *Society and Leisure* 27(2):411-22.

Swidler, Ann. 1986. "Culture in Action: Symbols and Strategies," *American Sociological Review* 51(2):273-86.

George Steinmetz. Editor. 1999. *State/Culture: State-Formation after the Cultural Turn.* Cornell University Press.

Tanner, Julian, Mark Asbridge and Scott Worthy. Forthcoming. "Listening to Rap: Culture or Crime and Cultures of Resistance." *Social Forces.*

Taylor, Charles. 1992. *The Ethics of Authenticity.* Harvard University Press.

——1989. *Sources of the Self.* Cambridge University Press.

Taylor, Charles. 2007. *A Secular Age.* Harvard University Press.

Urquia, Norman. 2004. "'Doin' it Right': Contested Authenticity in London's Salsa Scene." Pp. 96-112. *Music Scenes: Local, Translocal and Virtual.* Andrew Bennett and Richard Peterson, editors. Vanderbilt University Press.

Van Deth, Jan W. 1998. "Equivalence in Comparative Political Research." Pp. 1-19 *Comparative Politics: The Problem of Equivalence.* J.W. van Deth, editor. Routledge.

Weber, Max. 1978. *Economy and Society: An Outline of Interpretive Sociology.* Guenther Roth and Claus Wittich, editors. University of California Press.

Webber, Robert P. 1990. *Basic Content Analysis.* Sage.

Wirth, Louis. 1938. "Urbanism as a Way of Life." *American Journal of Sociology* 44(1):1-24. .

Zelenev, Alexei. 2004. "Amenities: Recent Economic Studies." Pp. 235-52. *The City as an Entertainment Machine. Research in Urban Policy 9.* Terry Nichols Clark, editor. Elsevier.

Zukin, Sharon 1989. *Loft Living: Culture and Capital in Urban Change.* Rutgers University Press.

Index

About the Authors

Anne Bartlett is a Ph.D. candidate in the Department of Sociology at the University of Chicago. She holds a degree in Sociology and Social Policy from the University of the West of England and Masters degree in Sociology from the University of Chicago. Prior to this, she worked in various capacities in the British government for over fifteen years. Her Ph.D. research centers on the changing nature of political subjectivity in London, particularly as it pertains to the lives of refugees and migrants. Her other areas of interest include sociological theory, globalization, human rights and evolving forms of political culture.

Terry Nichols Clark is Professor of Sociology at the University of Chicago. He holds MA and Ph.D. degrees from Columbia University, and has taught at Columbia, Harvard, Yale, the Sorbonne, University of Florence, and UCLA. He has worked at the Brookings Institution, The Urban Institute, Department of Housing and Urban Development, and US Conference of Mayors. His books include *Citizen Politics in Post-Industrial Society, City Money, The New Political Culture, and Urban Innovation*. Since 1982 he has been Coordinator of the Fiscal Austerity and Urban Innovation (FAUI) Project, which includes a data base of over ten thousand municipalities in up to thirty-five countries. It is the most extensive study to date of local government in the world, including data, some seven hundred participants, a budget exceeding $20 million, and fifty published books, much available on the website http://www.src.uchicago.edu/depts/faui/archive.html

Richard Florida is the author of the groundbreaking book, *The Rise of the Creative Class: And How It's Transforming Work, Leisure Community and Everyday Life* Basic Books 2002, stressing the rise of creativity as an economic force. He is the H. John Heinz III Professor of Economic Development at Carnegie Mellon University, where he is founder and co-director of the Software Industry Center. He has been a visiting professor at MIT and Harvard University's John F. Kennedy School of Government. He is co-author of five

281

other books, including Industrializing Knowledge; Beyond Mass Production and The Breakthrough Illusion, and more than a hundred articles in academic journals. He earned his Bachelor's degree from Rutgers College and Ph.D. from Columbia University.

Gary Gates works in the Population Studies Center of The Urban Institute in Washington DC 20037. He completed his Ph.D. at Carnegie Mellon University, and is a leading researcher on gays in the U.S.

Edward Glaeser is a Professor of Economics at Harvard University. He teaches urban and social economics and microeconomic theory. He has published dozens of papers on cities, economic growth, and law and economics. In particular, his work has focused on the determinants of city growth and the role of cities as centers of idea transmission. He also edits the Quarterly Journal of Economics. He received his Ph.D. from the University of Chicago in 1992.

Pushpam Jain completed a Ph.D. at the University of Chicago.

Jed Kolko is at the Department of Economics, Harvard University.

Richard Lloyd teaches at Vanderbilt University, he completed his Ph.D. at the University of Chicago. His research interests include urban culture. Postindustrial economy, and labor force participation.

Dennis Merritt completed a BA at the University of Chicago and MA at DePaul University. He was Analysis Manager of the Fiscal Austerity and Urban Innovation Project for four years.

Albert Saiz is in the Research Department, Federal Reserve Bank of Philadelphia. He completed a Ph.D. in Economics at Harvard.

Daniel Silver is a doctoral candidate in Social Thought at the University of Chicago, where he also received his M.A. His research focuses on the social organization and meaning of unproductivity, both in classical social thought and in contemporary society. He has published in the *European Journal of Sociology*, has been a Mellon Fellow for Humanistic Studies, a Junior Fellow at the Olin Center for Inquiry into the Theory and Practice of Democracy, and a Researcher at the University of Chicago Cultural Policy Center.

Kenneth Wong is Professor of Public Policy and Education and Professor of Political Science at Vanderbilt University. He also serves as Associate Director of the Peabody Center for Education Policy at Vanderbilt University. He was Associate Professor in the Department of Education and the Social Sciences Division at the University of Chicago, where he earned his doctorate in political science. He has conducted research in American government, urban school reform, state finance and educational policies, intergovernmental relations, and federal educational policies (Title I). He is author of Funding Public Schools:Politics and Policy (1999), and City Choices: Education and Housing (1990), and a co-author of When Federalism Works (1986). He is currently the President of the Politics of Education Association.

Clemente Jesus Navarro Yanez is Senior Lecturer of Sociology, head of the Urban Political Sociology Centre and in charge of the Local World Observatory (Pablo de Olavide University, Spain). His research focuses on urban political sociology. He is currently coordinating the Fiscal Austerity and Urban Innovation project in Latin America. He also participates in the European Project Political Leadership in European Cities. He has published in scientific journals such as *Revista Internacional de Sociología, Analise Sociale, Sociologia Ruralis and Internacional Journal of Regional and Urban Research* and received the 'Best published book award' (Spanish Political Science Association, 2007).